A Research Agenda for Knowledge Management and Analytics

Elgar Research Agendas outline the future of research in a given area. Leading scholars are given the space to explore their subject in provocative ways, and map out the potential directions of travel. They are relevant but also visionary.

Forward-looking and innovative, Elgar Research Agendas are an essential resource for PhD students, scholars and anybody who wants to be at the forefront of research.

Titles in the series include:

A Research Agenda for Knowledge Management and Analytics
Edited by Jay Liebowitz

A Research Agenda for Heritage Tourism
Edited by Maria Gravari-Barbas

A Research Agenda for Border Studies
James W. Scott

A Research Agenda for Sales
Edited by Fernando Jaramillo and Jay Prakash Mulki

A Research Agenda for Employee Engagement in a Changing World of Work
John P. Meyer and Benjamin Schneider

A Research Agenda for the Entrepreneurial University
Edited by Ulla Hytti

A Research Agenda for Place Branding
Edited by Dominic Medway, Gary Warnaby and John Byrom

A Research Agenda for Social Finance
Edited by Othmar M. Lehner

A Research Agenda for Knowledge Management and Analytics

Edited by

JAY LIEBOWITZ

Visiting Professor at Seton Hall University and the former Distinguished Chair of Applied Business and Finance, Harrisburg University of Science and Technology, USA

Elgar Research Agendas

 Edward Elgar
PUBLISHING

Cheltenham, UK • Northampton, MA, USA

Published by
Edward Elgar Publishing Limited
The Lypiatts
15 Lansdown Road
Cheltenham
Glos GL50 2JA
UK

Edward Elgar Publishing, Inc.
William Pratt House
9 Dewey Court
Northampton
Massachusetts 01060
USA

A catalogue record for this book
is available from the British Library

Library of Congress Control Number: 2020950861

This book is available electronically in the **Elgar**online
Business subject collection
http://dx.doi.org/10.4337/9781800370623

ISBN 978 1 80037 061 6 (cased)
ISBN 978 1 80037 062 3 (eBook)
Printed and bound by CPI Group (UK) Ltd, Croydon, CR0 4YY

Contents

Contributors

Ramin Assa has established four knowledge management (KM) strategies since the early 2000s, from the ground-up, in several distinct organizations. His focus is on the people side of KM and Business Intelligence where he employs change management, behavioral science and community management principles to promote and establish a culture of knowledge sharing and collaboration. He has also pioneered use of innovative technologies such as Artificial Intelligence (AI), Machine Learning, Knowledge Portals and Search Engines to optimize information exchange experiences. In 2019, he was selected to explore KM's role in clinical innovations and proposed an enterprise-wide federated program to meet the needs of large organizations with multiple, critical and complex lines of business. He has also served as a senior adviser in building and deploying expert finder solutions.

Francisco J. Cantu-Ortiz is Professor of Computer Science and Artificial Intelligence. He was Associate Vice-Provost for Research, leader of the world university rankings at Tecnologico de Monterrey (2002–17), head of the Center for Artificial Intelligence (1989–2002), and head of the Center for Informatics Research (1985–89). He is member of the QS Advisory Board for University Rankings, member of the Steering Committee of EduData Summit, and consultant for Enago-Academy in strategic alliances for research planning of higher education institutions. His research interests include data science, knowledge systems, AI and research analytics, research strategy, and science and technology management. He has published scientific articles in research journals, conferences and edited books, has been an invited speaker at various international conferences, and is a certified National Researcher by the National Council for Science and Technology, Mexico. He has an interest in epistemology and philosophy of science and religion. He holds a Ph.D. in Artificial Intelligence from the University of Edinburgh, UK, an M.Sc. in Computer Science from North Dakota State University, U.S.A., and a B.Sc. in Computer Systems Engineering from Tecnologico de Monterrey (ITESM), Mexico.

Kenneth Carling is a professor in Microdata Analysis at the School of Technology and Business Studies, Dalarna University, Sweden. He earned his Ph.D. in Statistics in 1995 at Uppsala University. Before arriving at Dalarna University in 2001, he worked with hospital productivity at the Swedish Research Institute SPRI, labor market policy at the research agency IFAU, financial stability at the Central Bank of Sweden, and served as Senior Lecturer at Yale University. Over the years he has been a member of, inter alia, INFORMS, the American Statistical Association, and served as President of the Swedish Statistical Society (The Cramér Society). He has taught and published some 50 articles in academic journals, foremost in Economics, Operations Research, and Statistics. In recent years his research interest has mostly focused on the transportation, mobility of goods and humans, and environmental challenges that constitute important work programs in the European Commission's Horizon 2020.

Kimiz Dalkir is an Associate Professor and Director of the School of Information Studies at McGill University with a Ph.D. in Educational Technology, and an MBA and B.Sc. in Human Genetics. Dr. Dalkir wrote *Knowledge Management in Theory and Practice* (MIT Press, 3rd edition published 2017), which has had an international impact on KM education and on KM practice. She has also published *Intelligent Learner Modeling in Real-Time* (LAP, 2014), co-edited (with S. McIntyre, P. Paul and C. Kitimbo) *Utilizing Evidence-Based Lessons Learned for Enhanced Organizational Innovation and Change* (ICI Global, 2015), and co-edited (with R. Katz) the more recent *Navigating Fake News: Alternative Facts and Misinformation in a Post-Truth World* (ICI Global, 2020). Dr. Dalkir's research focuses on tacit knowledge sharing and organizational learning. Prior to joining McGill, Dr. Dalkir was Global Practice Leader KM for Fujitsu Consulting, and she has worked in the field of knowledge transfer and retention for 17 years with clients in Europe, Japan and North America.

Cheng Gong is a Ph.D. student in Knowledge and Innovation Management at the Institute for Knowledge and Innovation Southeast Asia (IKI-SEA), Bangkok University, Thailand, and a former project director of Sino-Russian Education Cooperation in Yunnan Communications Vocational and Technical College, China. She was inducted into BGS (Beta Gamma Sigma) for academic excellence. Her educational background and working practices in South Korea and Russia have given her a base from which to approach many topics. Her research interest is in digital transformation, knowledge management, innovation management and change management.

Johan Håkansson is a professor in Microdata Analysis at the School of Technology and Business Studies, Dalarna University, Sweden. He earned his Ph.D. in Human Geography in 2000 at Umeå University. He has taught and published some 30 articles in academic journals, foremost in Geography, Management, and Operations Research. His research interest has mostly focused on retail management, spatial planning, logistics, mobility management and environmental challenges. He is currently principal investigator for a project focusing on last mile deliveries, recognized by The Royal Science Academy as one of the top 50 Swedish innovation projects. He presently teaches Ph.D. and Master students in Business Intelligence, Data Science, and Microdata Analysis on Data Collection and Data Quality.

Michael E. D. Koenig is Professor Emeritus at Long Island University, and former and founding dean of the College of Information and Computer Science at LIU. His career has included both academic positions (dean and professor at Dominican University and associate professor at Columbia University), and senior management positions in industry (Manager of Information Services for Pfizer Research, and Vice President at The Institute for Scientific Information and at Tradenet). He received his Ph.D. from Drexel University, an MBA in mathematical methods and computers and an MA in library and information science from the University of Chicago, and a BA in psychology from Yale University. He is the author of more than one hundred peer-reviewed scholarly publications, including more than a dozen on the topic of KM. He has co-edited three monographs on the subject of KM published for the American Society for Information Science and Technology, including "Knowledge Management: What Works and What Doesn't," and is the co-author (with Claire R. McInerny) of *Knowledge Management (KM) Processes in Organizations: Theoretical Foundations and Practice* (Morgan & Claypool, 2011). Koenig is a past President of The International Society for Scientometrics and Informetrics, and was a Fulbright Scholar in Argentina. He is the recipient of the Jason Farradane award for "outstanding work in the information field" from CILIP, the Chartered Institute of Library and Information Professionals (formerly the Library Association of the UK). He was honored with the Award of Merit, their highest award, from the Association for Information Science and Technology.

Jim Lee's experience as a consultant is focused on knowledge management, using an approach to KM solutions by applying proven process improvement and quality management principles for his clients. Most recently he was the KM leader at the world leader in financial services, and also formerly the practice leader of APQC's KM advisory services. Prior to joining APQC, Jim began his KM career as a global knowledge manager at Cap Gemini Ernst &

Young. His clients have included some of the largest organizations in the world in geographies such as the Americas, Africa, Europe, the Middle East and Asia. Jim is a board member of a non-profit education organization and a past adjunct professor at two universities. He has spoken at more than 50 national and international conferences on knowledge management and project management since 1997.

Simon Li earned the degrees of Doctor of Engineering and Master of Science in Knowledge Management from the Department of Industrial and System Engineering of the Hong Kong Polytechnic University in 2020 and 2010, respectively. His research interests include knowledge and innovation management, big data analytics, data science, business intelligence and data mining. Dr. Li is serving several local universities in the areas of teaching and researching on business intelligence, data mining, data science, information systems, and computer science. Prior to joining academia, Dr. Li had spent more than 25 years serving the information technology areas of both private and public sectors of Hong Kong.

Jay Liebowitz is a Visiting Professor in the Department of Computing and Decision Sciences in the Stillman School of Business at Seton Hall University. He previously served for 6 years as Distinguished Chair of Applied Business and Finance at Harrisburg University of Science and Technology. Previously, he was the Orkand Endowed Chair of Management and Technology in the Graduate School at the University of Maryland University College (UMUC). He served as a professor in the Carey Business School at Johns Hopkins University. He was ranked one of the top ten knowledge management researchers/practitioners out of 11,000 worldwide, and was ranked #2 in KM Strategy worldwide according to the January 2010 *Journal of Knowledge Management*. At Johns Hopkins University, he was the founding Program Director for the Graduate Certificate in Competitive Intelligence and the Capstone Director of the MS-Information and Telecommunications Systems for Business Program, where he engaged over 30 organizations in industry, government and not-for-profits in capstone projects. Prior to joining Johns Hopkins University, Dr. Liebowitz was the first Knowledge Management Officer at NASA Goddard Space Flight Center. Before NASA, Dr. Liebowitz was the Robert W. Deutsch Distinguished Professor of Information Systems at the University of Maryland-Baltimore County, Professor of Management Science at George Washington University, and Chair of Artificial Intelligence at the U.S. Army War College.

Dr. Liebowitz is the founding Editor-in-Chief of *Expert Systems with Applications: An International Journal* (published by Elsevier), which was ranked #1 worldwide for AI journals according to the h5 index of

Google Scholar journal rankings (March 2017). ESWA was ranked third worldwide for OR/MS journals (out of 83 journals), according to the 2016 Thomson impact factors. He is a Fulbright Scholar, IEEE-USA Federal Communications Commission Executive Fellow, and Computer Educator of the Year (International Association for Computer Information Systems). He has published over 40 books and a myriad of journal articles on knowledge management, analytics, intelligent systems and IT management.

Dr. Liebowitz served as the Editor-in-Chief of *Procedia Computer Science* (Elsevier). He is also the editor of the new Data Analytics Applications book series (Taylor & Francis). In October 2011, the International Association for Computer Information Systems named the "Jay Liebowitz Outstanding Student Research Award" for the best student research paper at the IACIS Annual Conference. Dr. Liebowitz was the Fulbright Visiting Research Chair in Business. He has lectured and consulted worldwide.

Joanna Paliszkiewicz is a Full Professor at Warsaw University of Life Sciences – SGGW. She is the director of the Management Institute. She is also an Adjunct Professor at the University of Vaasa in Finland. She is well-recognized in Poland and abroad for her expertise in management issues: knowledge management and trust management. She has published over 200 papers/manuscripts. She is also the author/co-author/editor of ten books. Dr. Paliszkiewicz serves as the deputy editor-in-chief of the *Management and Production Engineering Review*. She is an associate editor for the *Journal of Computer Information Systems*. Dr. Paliszkiewicz is the vice president of two associations: the Polish Association for Production Engineering and the International Association for Computer Information Systems.

Anthony J. Rhem is a recognized thought leader in AI, KM, Big Data, Information Architecture and Innovation. Since 1990, Dr. Rhem has served as CEO/Principal Consultant of A.J. Rhem & Associates (AJRA). AJRA is a consulting, training and research firm focusing on knowledge management, AI and system integration. As a consultant, strategist and advisor, Dr. Rhem has worked with U.S. Fortune 500 corporations in retail, communications, finance, insurance, legal, logistics, education, healthcare, U.S. government and the military. Dr. Rhem is an active presenter at KM and AI conferences both domestic and international, and is an established technology author and continues to write articles and books in KM and AI.

Vincent Ribiere is an enthusiastic and creative international consultant and professor with a passion for helping organizations solving their organizational knowledge and innovation management challenges. He is the founder and managing director of the Institute for Knowledge and Innovation Southeast Asia (IKI-SEA), a center of Excellence at Bangkok University, as well as the Program

Director of the PhD program in KM and Innovation Management. He delivers keynote speeches and workshops at various international professional and academic conferences, and is the author of more than 80 publications.

Vida Skudienė is a professor in management, head of the MSc programme Innovation and Technology Management at ISM University of Management and Economics, and serves as a visiting professor at Nagoya University of Commerce and Business, Japan. She conducted her Ph.D. research at the University of South Carolina, U.S.A. Her research concentrates on organizational behavior, innovation management and relationship markering. Professor Skudiene has presented her research at international conferences in France, Japan, Israel, the U.S.A. (Hawaii, Chicago), Greece, Croatia, France, Spain, Norway, Jamaica, Sweden, Portugal and Italy (Boccioni), and has published over 60 articles and contributed to several books. She is the chief editor of and a contributor to *Innovation Management: Perspectives from Strategy, Product, Process and Human Resources Research* (Edward Elgar Publishing, 2020). Vida Skudiene has been teaching and doing reserach at EDHEC university in France, IPAM Instituto Portugues de Administracao de Marketing and Catholica University in Portugal, Zagreb School of Economics and Management in Kroatia, Reykjavik University in Island, Aarhus University in Denmark, Salento University in Italy, and the University of Northern Colorado, U.S.A. She is a member of editorial review boards of *Baltic Journal of Management*, *Business and Economics Journal*, and *Organizations and Markets in Emerging Economies*, and is a recepient of several research awards such as ISM Distinguished Scholar Award; Best Paper Award from Clute Institute, France; The International Academy of Business and Public Administration Disciples; and Marketing Management Association Awards, U.S.A.

Eric Tsui joined the Computer Sciences Corporation (CSC) in 1989 after years of academic research in automated knowledge acquisition, natural language processing, case-based reasoning and knowledge engineering tools. He has designed and delivered numerous public and custom-designed knowledge management and technologies workshops. His research strengths include cloud-based business innovation and knowledge services. He joined Hong Kong Polytechnic University in 2005 and, until 2018, was the leader of the M.Sc. program in Knowledge Management. He has also consulted for many government departments and private organizations in Australia, Hong Kong, Japan, Singapore, Malaysia, Thailand and Brunei. Professor Tsui is an honorary advisor of KM to three HKSARG departments. He has received many Knowledge Management and E-Learning awards and was twice listed as an Outstanding/Exemplary Academic in the 2015/16 and 2016/17 Hong Kong Polytechnic University Annual Reports.

Jan Vanthienen is full professor of information systems at KU Leuven (Belgium), Department of Decision Sciences and Information Management. He has done extensive research on business rules, processes and decisions, decision analytics, and business analysis, and has published numerous papers in well-known international journals and top conference proceedings. He is a member of Leuven.AI (KU Leuven Institute for Artificial Intelligence) and received an IBM Faculty Award in 2011 on smart decisions. Jan is actively involved as an initiator and task force member in the Decision Model & Notation (DMN) standard at OMG. He is also member of the IEEE task force on process mining, and co-author of the Business Process Mining Manifesto. Currently, Jan is head of the Department of Decision Sciences and Information Management of KU Leuven.

Douglas Weidner is a U.S. Air Force Academy graduate and past combat pilot. He has an MBA in Business Economics, and an M.Sc. in Operations Research. His work experiences were as both internal and external consultant in many diverse, analytical fields and industries: Operations Research, Financial Analysis, Strategic Planning, Total Quality Management (TQM), and Business Process Re-engineering (BPR), plus transformational change management. He has been totally involved in KM since its beginnings. As a U.S. Department of Defense (DoD) think tank consultant, he designed a process-oriented "Knowledge Base Tool" (KBase) in 1994. It originally housed DoD's BPR Methodology. In 1995, he became Chief Knowledge Engineer for what evolved into a $30 billion defence contractor. Subsequently, he founded the KM Institute to educate and certify KM practitioners, which now exceed 10,000 individuals. His courses and resources provide a robust KM Body of Knowledge (KMBOK)™ and recent research work has been on maturity models (MATURE™).

Kaiyu Yang is a Ph.D. student in Knowledge Management and Innovation Management at the Institute for Knowledge and Innovation Southeast Asia (IKI-SEA), Bangkok University, Thailand. She is a faculty member of the School of Foreign Languages at Baise University, China. Her research interest is in knowledge management.

Qiping Zhang is an Associate Professor in the Palmer School of Library and Information Science and the director of the Usability Lab. Dr. Zhang holds a Ph.D. and an M.Sc. in Information and Library Studies from the University of Michigan and an M.Sc. and B.Sc. in cognitive psychology from Peking University in Beijing, China. Dr. Zhang's general research areas are human–computer interaction, social informatics and distance learning. Her primary interests lie in the areas of computer-supported cooperative work (CSCW) and computer-mediated communication.

Foreword

Jim Lee

In the three decades since knowledge management has been identified, defined, acknowledged as a discipline, researched, and practiced worldwide, numerous books on the subject have emerged from both researchers and practitioners alike. In many cases, these books review the field of knowledge management through the lens of case studies, as a compilation of "tools," or intended for a specific audience such as business practitioners. These types of targeted texts are useful when seeking a concise view on the topic of knowledge management. In the case of *A Research Agenda for Knowledge Management and Analytics*, however, a more holistic approach is taken to advance the state of understanding and application of knowledge management.

Edited by Jay Liebowitz, this book is truly an example of both collaboration as well as breadth and depth of topics. I've been fortunate to know Dr. Liebowitz since 2005 when we met where he spoke at a conference I attended. Regarding collaboration, Dr. Liebowitz has not only sought subject matter experts in their respective fields, but also he has brought together a global view of knowledge management with contributors from North and Latin America, Europe and Asia. While other books often provide only a single cultural perspective on the topic of knowledge management, *A Research Agenda for Knowledge Management and Analytics* is a compilation of both researcher and practitioner global perspectives to ensure the readers of the book will gain a wide range of insights from leading institutes, universities, and practicing thought leaders.

In my own work over 20 years as a knowledge management consultant and researcher, the topics in this book represent issues faced in the past as well as emerging topics that haven't yet been fully fleshed out simply because they're still evolving—all topics for which I and many others certainly could have used effectively had we the expertise provided in this book. Some key themes addressed by the book: measuring the value of knowledge management via analytics; innovation; lessons learned; and views of knowledge management from information science, organizational, and technology perspectives, would have given me additional insights during my consulting engagements and research studies to business, public sector, and NGO clients around the world.

Readers should be aware, however, that this is not simply a book of retrospectives on topics that have in the past and continue to be of interest to knowledge management professionals. The drive to incorporate artificial intelligence and analytics solutions with knowledge management strategies and applications is clearly the next frontier for the domain. The intricateness of sense-making from human thought and explicit exposition of knowledge to proper interpretation by AI is not a trivial exercise. On this topic, the chapters devoted to AI represent critical research and understanding of the potential benefits and caveats of the intersection of machine learning and human interaction.

Anyone who wishes to elevate their knowledge—and application of knowledge management and analytics—would easily recognize many, if not all, of the names of the subject matter expert contributors. I can't emphasize enough the combination of diversity and expertise that makes this book stand out among the others in a knowledge management library. I look forward to adding it to mine!

Jim Lee
Former APQC Practice Leader of Knowledge Management Advisory Services

Preface

Over the years, a number of books have been written that examine the issues, trends, challenges, and opportunities for knowledge management. Some of these leading sources include, in chronological order:

- Liebowitz, J. (ed.) (1999), *The Handbook on Knowledge Management*, CRC Press.
- Holsapple, C. (ed.) (2003), *Handbook on Knowledge Management*, Volumes 1 and 2, Springer.
- Leidner, D. and I. Becerra-Fernandez (eds.) (2008), *Knowledge Management: An Evolutionary View*, M.E. Sharpe Publishers.
- Liebowitz, J. (ed.) (2012), *The Handbook on Knowledge Management: Collaboration and Social Networking*, 2nd edition, CRC Press.
- Liebowitz, J. (ed.) (2016), *Successes and Failures of Knowledge Management*, Morgan Kaufmann.
- Jennex, M. (ed.) (2020), *Current Issues and Trends in Knowledge Management, Discovery, and Transfer*, IGI Global.

In addition, as of January 2020 on Google Scholar, 105,000 publications appear with "knowledge management" in the title, 21,700 publications with "knowledge sharing" in the title, and 90,200 publications with "analytics" in the title. In terms of theses and dissertations, hundreds have already been published on knowledge management, knowledge sharing, and analytics. Also, there are over ten international journals that specialize in knowledge management alone.

So, the question is: Why do we need another book or publication that examines the current state-of-the-art and future research issues of knowledge management (and analytics)?

My personal view in answering this question lies in the very nature of what knowledge management is supposed to offer as a basic underlying principle—that is, to help integrate knowledge across disciplinary or functional lines. In other words, knowledge management should leverage knowledge both internally and externally, and serve as the integrative mechanism for building bridges across isolated islands (or silos) of knowledge.

The challenge has been that KM, in today's world, really needs to leverage the key attributes offered by other fields, like analytics, AI (artificial intelligence), intuition-based decision making, blockchain, IoT (Internet of Things), etc., to provide a "synergistic" effect to improve decision making. Over the past 40 years since "knowledge management" was first coined, the field has advanced in applying additional rigor and science behind the art. However, by now, I would have expected almost every organization to be doing "knowledge management" without having to call it as such. That is, KM should already be part of the fabric of an organization. In many organizations worldwide, this still isn't the case and perhaps KM needs more of a symbiotic relationship with other important emerging fields, like analytics and AI as examples.

Thus, the focus of this book is to take a step back and look at the KM field in terms of how best to advance the current state-of-the-art which includes leveraging the knowledge gained from such fields as analytics and AI. In looking ahead over the next 3–5 years, we can carve out a research agenda for knowledge management and analytics to help new doctoral students, junior faculty, and young practitioners in the field further what we have now, in order to build a better tomorrow.

As we look towards the future, how can we improve the KM field? The chapters in this book highlight the various research gaps, issues, applications, challenges, and opportunities as related to KM. Certainly, we must continue to provide the necessary rigor to further support the KM discipline. In the spirit of KM and knowledge sharing, we must continue to borrow, adapt and leverage from other disciplines. And, as KM educators, we must continue to enhance our KM curricula to take advantage of the emerging technologies and methodologies today and tomorrow.

I am indebted to the leading worldwide contributors of this book who provide their keen insights in helping to shape this applied research agenda. I am especially grateful to Jim Lee who wrote the Foreword based on his many years of KM experience at APQC and beyond. I also express my deep gratitude to Rachel Downie, Sabrina Zaher, Claire Annals, and her other colleagues at colleagues at Edward Elgar Publishing for their Research Agenda series and reaching out to me for this particular volume. Of course, my students and colleagues have also been extremely helpful in allowing me to share, apply and leverage knowledge over my almost 40 years in academia. Finally, to answer my family's question, I believe this will be my last book!

Jay Liebowitz, D.Sc.
Washington, D.C.

Introduction to *A Research Agenda for Knowledge Management and Analytics*

Introduction

Knowledge management (KM) has evolved over the years from the early 1980s coining of its name. By now (in 2020), organizations shouldn't even be talking about "knowledge management"—they should already be doing it! Unfortunately, this hasn't been the case for a number of reasons, including KM envisioned as mostly a long-term versus short-term payoff, misunderstanding the benefits of knowledge sharing, not recognizing those who exhibit learning and knowledge sharing behaviors, and a host of other reasons.

Even though a number of journals focus on knowledge management, many organizations still use ad hoc processes to develop and implement KM into their organizations. To help standardize some of these KM processes, the International Organization for Standardization (ISO) knowledge management systems standard was developed in 2018.

Specifically, the ISO 30401 indicates that top management shall establish a knowledge management policy that:

(a) is appropriate to the purpose of the organization;
(b) provides a framework and guiding principles for setting, reviewing and achieving knowledge management objectives;
(c) includes a commitment to satisfy applicable regulatory and other requirements;
(d) sets expectations for all workers with regard to use of the knowledge management system and the cultivation of a culture that values knowledge;
(e) includes a commitment to continual improvement of the knowledge management system;
(f) manages the balance between knowledge sharing and knowledge protection. (https://www.iso.org/standard/68683.html)

In addition to process considerations, the people and cultural components of KM are often overlooked in favor of the technology piece. The adage that "80 percent of KM is people/culture/process and 20% is technology" should ring true to many successful organizations who have implemented knowledge management.

As KM has evolved over the years, what needs to be considered for the next generation of KM? The key word is "synergy". Unfortunately, KM is fading a bit and needs to be strengthened by aligning KM with other emerging areas, such as:

- Analytics
- Intuition-based decision making
- Entrepreneurship and Innovation
- Organizational strategy
- Artificial intelligence (AI)/machine learning
- Augmented reality
- IoT (Internet of Things)
- Intelligence amplification (IA).

In particular, as big data and analytics continue to grow, there are some natural synergies with KM and analytics. For example, KM could play a key role in the management and governance of the use of big data/analytics in organizational settings.

As cognitive computing, AI and machine learning continue to develop, KM can also play a role. For example, DARPA (Defense Advanced Research Projects Agency in the US) has the Lifelong Learning Machines Program that seeks to develop learning systems that continuously improve with additional experience, and rapidly adapt to new conditions and dynamic environments. Here KM plays a key part. In some of the author's recent research on intuition-based decision making, we see that experiential learning is critical in developing intuitive awareness (Liebowitz, 2019; Liebowitz et al., 2019). Again, many of the principles of KM apply here too.

Some other possible synergies for KM and analytics include business process mining. In fact, there is a Business Rules Conference (mainly for industry) held in late Fall each year in the U.S.A. In addition, KM should be part of the strategic intelligence of an organization—that is, strategic intelligence being the intersection of KM, Business Intelligence (Analytics), and Competitive Intelligence) (Liebowitz, 2006).

In looking ahead, the KM educators and practitioners need to do the following:

- Promote greater dialogue between KM and the various communities;
- KM educators/practitioners must be somewhat adept in applying analytics tools, techniques and methodologies, and the Data Analytics educators/practitioners must also develop appropriate KM skills;
- Further investigate areas for collaboration (cognitive computing, executive decision making, IoT, Scientometrics, etc.).

KM Lessons Learned

Have a senior champion and align your KM strategy with your organizational strategies, goals and objectives

Similar to any organizational initiative, it is critical that a senior champion exists to provide the financial and moral support for the KM program to be successful. Not only is senior champion support essential but also aligning the KM strategy with the organizational strategies, goals and objectives is crucial. Without this proper alignment, it would be difficult to assess and evaluate how well the KM initiative (or program) is performing relative to the organization's KPIs (Key Performance Indicators).

Develop a well-designed KM implementation plan (people, process and technology)

A solid KM strategy and resulting KM implementation plan/roadmap should consist of People/Culture, Process, and Technology components. As previously mentioned, the 80–20 rule applies where 80% deals with people/culture and process issues, and 20% is technology. Many organizations will build out a three-year KM implementation plan based on the KM projects proposed as part of the KM strategy.

Develop a formal knowledge retention strategy—start from day one of the employee's life with the organization

Organizational amnesia often occurs, especially as the tenure of employees in the organization increases over the years. With the "graying workforce," due to the demographics in society, knowledge retention should be an important part of the organization's human capital strategy. In fact, a knowledge retention formal process (perhaps an SOP—Standard Operating Procedure) should be created and used from day one of the employee's life with the organization. As the years go by, employees may forget some valuable knowledge and being able to capture this knowledge at the point of "knowledge existence" would reduce the risk of losing it. In addition, the knowledge–engineering paradox exists which states that the more experienced the expert, the more compiled the knowledge, and the harder it is to extract or elicit this knowledge. Thus, doing knowledge retention capture early on will alleviate this issue.

Incorporate KM as part of human capital strategy, succession planning, workforce development, strategic planning, and/or quality management

Many organizations don't need to have a separate KM Program per se. KM can be part of some of the existing programs in the organization. For example, NASA applies KM as part of their project management and risk management efforts. The FDA (Food and Drug Administration in the U.S.A.) has applied knowledge management as part of their quality management efforts. The Annie E. Casey Foundation in Baltimore has incorporated KM as part of their strategic planning efforts. Many other organizations apply KM as part of their human capital strategy, succession planning and workforce development.

Be thoughtful in your approach (knowledge audit, social network analysis, etc.)

In the spirit of knowledge sharing, the KM community can apply some existing techniques to baseline an organization in terms of its knowledge sharing practices and collaboration networks. A knowledge audit is often used to determine the KM practices, gaps and issues for developing a KM strategy. This approach is modeled after the information audit from the Information Systems community. In addition, the use of Social Network Analysis, borrowed from the sociology and education disciplines, can be adeptly used to map knowledge flows and gaps in organizations. Various knowledge management instruments have already been validated over the years which could provide value to the organization under study, so that the wheel isn't reinvented unnecessarily.

Align your KM approaches to fit your organizational culture

Typically, KM approaches are classified under codification ("collection") and personalization ("connection") techniques. Codification techniques could be lessons learned systems, yellow pages of expertise (although, "connection" applies here as well), online multimedia asset repositories, and the like. Personalization/connection techniques include mentoring programs, job shadowing, job rotation and others. Most of the time, organizations will apply both types of approaches but one type will be dominant. To help determine the dominant set of approaches (i.e., codification vs. personalization), organizations should determine if their employees are more systems-oriented or people-focused. The Myers–Briggs Type Indicator, for example, can be used to determine various dimensions of individuals, ranging from introvert/extrovert, sensing/intuitive, thinking/feeling and judging/perceiving. For example, NASA probably has more ISTJ types of individuals where a systems-orientation is preferred. In this case, NASA probably errs more on applying the codification approaches (such as the NASA Engineering Network/Lessons Learned Information System) versus personalization approaches (although, in NASA's case, both approaches are used; see APPEL—https://appel.nasa.gov).

Celebrate the successes, then bring in the bittersweet stories

Showing success through quick-win KM pilots is critical to further convince the naysayers. Celebrate the successes first and then bring in the failures or stories of things that didn't go right. Lessons learned are based on experience, whether positive or negative. Typically, people may learn more from failures than from successes; thus, both experiences are important to capture (Liebowitz, 2016).

Develop KM metrics (especially outcome measures)

Many organizations get caught up on system and output measures. For example, seeing how many times a website is accessed may not necessarily translate to innovations or other outcome measures. In academia, professors and administrators should be more interested in "learning outcomes" than "teaching outcomes." In the same way, KM initiatives should contribute towards outcome measures relating to the organization's KPIs and strategic goals.

Don't force-fit technology (people/culture/process are where the rubber hits the road)

An old adage is, "if all you know is a hammer, then every problem looks like a nail." Thus, KM professionals shouldn't force-fit technology to the KM-related problem. Look first at the problem requirements, then decide if there is an appropriate technology that could be used to address the issue. Again, the key elements are usually the people/culture/process in terms of gaining the most value from a KM initiative.

KM is just one part of your "strategic intelligence"

Knowledge management should be one of the skill sets in one's decision making kit. It should be part of one's "strategic intelligence" (Liebowitz, 2006), whereby business intelligence/analytics, Artificial Intelligence (AI), competitive intelligence (CI), and other key disciplines play a major role.

Knowledge Sharing Tenets for Success

In order to be successful for KM programs, here are some knowledge sharing tenets that should be followed (Liebowitz, 2012):

- Enhance reward and recognition system to include learning and knowledge sharing competencies;
- Acquaint people with knowledge sharing and its benefits;
- Share the message that with creativity comes failure and we all benefit from talking about our successes and our failures;
- Integrate knowledge sharing into everyone's job;
- Educate people about what types of knowledge are valuable and how they can be used;
- Make sure the technology works for people, not vice versa.

References

Liebowitz, J. (ed.) (2006), *Strategic Intelligence: Business Intelligence, Competitive Intelligence, and Knowledge Management*, CRC Press.

Liebowitz, J. (ed.) (2012), *The Knowledge Management Handbook: Collaboration and Social Networking*, 2nd edition, CRC Press.

Liebowitz, J. (ed.) (2016), *Successes and Failures of Knowledge Management*, Morgan Kaufmann/Elsevier.

Liebowitz, J. (ed.) (2019), *Developing Informed Intuition for Decision Making*, Taylor & Francis.

Liebowitz, J., Y. Chan, T. Jenkins, D. Spicker, J. Paliszkiewicz and F. Babiloni (eds.) (2019), *How Well Do Executives Trust Their Intuition?*, Taylor & Francis.

1. Knowledge management: library and information science writ large

Qiping Zhang and Michael E. D. Koenig

1. The LIS Origin of KM

The origin of Knowledge Management, KM, is conventionally traced to the realization on the part of the major consulting firms that the Internet, particularly intranets specific to a particular organization, were marvelously useful tools with which to share information within that organization. From that came the realization that in applying intranets for their own organization, and in the process creating lessons learned databases, expertise locators, communities of practice, and so on, they had developed tools that constituted an expertise that could be very successfully marketed to other organizations. In short, they realized that they had an important new product. An important new product of course deserves a crisp and compelling new term, a new name, a compelling new descriptor in LIS terminology. The name that arose was Knowledge Management.

1.1 First Users of the Term "Knowledge Management"

The first users of the term "Knowledge Management" appear to have been at consulting firms like Arthur D. Little, McKinsey and Company, and Ernst and Young (EY). The first KM event was a conference at the Four Seasons Hotel in Boston, organized by the Center for Business Strategy at Ernst and Young in the spring of 1993 (Prusak, 1999). The term KM began appearing in the management literature in the early 1990s. There were, however, articles about what we would now recognize as KM well before that. A classic such article is Don Marchand's "Information Management" (Marchand, 1985), which any observer now would call KM. The development of KM is well treated by Prusak

1

(1999), Koenig (2000), Koenig and Neveroski (2008), and McInerney and Koenig (2011), the latter including a rather detailed description of the stages of KM development.

The origin of KM also owes a great deal to the attention paid to intellectual capital (IC), the recognition that the knowledge and information possessed by an organization is a very important part of its capital and assets (not just the traditional components described as capital, such as financial capital or tangible and physical assets), and that IC needs to be preserved, created, used, and measured. The development of intellectual capital can be traced back to Peter Drucker (Hibbard, 1997). The key promoters of IC were Sveiby, author of *The Invisible Balance Sheet* (Sveiby, 1989); Stewart, whose article in Fortune magazine, "Your Company's Most Valuable Asset: Intellectual Capital" (Stewart, 1994) was widely read and quoted; and Edvinsson who illustrated the large-scale implementation of IC at a large organization, Skandia (Edvinsson, 1994, 1997). While enthusiasm for attempting to measure IC receded dramatically, simply due to the recalcitrant and intractable nature of measuring information and knowledge (McInerney and Koenig, 2011), the focus played an important role in propelling the development of KM. As a consequence, KM has been described, using equestrian terminology, as a creation "by the Internet out of intellectual capital" (Koenig, 2000). But, the IC movement also served to confirm that knowledge, the domain of librarianship, is the substrate of KM.

1.2   Different Focus of KM and LIS

KM is not only logically, but also realistically, a straightforward extension of library and information science (LIS). The difference is that LIS is primarily about locating, organizing and deploying information external to the organization, while KM is primarily about the organization's own knowledge and information, as well as the organizational culture and strategy. The classic expression, in the early days of KM, illustrates the focus on the organization's own knowledge and information: "If only Texas Instruments knew what Texas Instruments knew" (Davenport and Prusak, 1998; O'Dell and Jackson, 1998). Liebowitz and Paliszkiewicz (2019) make the point that Borko's (1968) classic definition of "information science," probably not bettered to this date, is so inclusive that there is no functional part of KM that is not included within it.

KM's extension of library and information science is, however, an extension that has substantially grown in breadth, and has become much more central to management decision making. The extension is not about the functional components of KM work; rather, it is about how to set the scene for KM to function. Another way to make the distinction is that the fundamental difference that emerges between LIS and KM is that KM involves issues that need to be addressed at a much higher level in the organization than LIS issues historically have been treated. Perhaps the most compelling illustration of that point is that KM involves how to design the organization's very structure, and how to design and implement the organization's compensation and reward system so as to facilitate information and knowledge sharing. LIS historically never concerned itself at any really substantive level with such issues. The closest it came were some attempts at embedding LIS professionals within research teams, a topic frequently discussed and advocated in the LIS literature, but seldom implemented in practice. KM practice, however, has greatly expanded upon that idea, and in many cases takes it for granted. It is common now to assign KM members to divisions, departments, teams and projects.

1.3   Three Stages of KM

The essential commonality of KM and LIS was not initially realized by the KM community. As Koenig (1992, 2000) has pointed out, KM emerged in three clear stages. The first stage was about deploying the technology and setting up the intranets. The second stage was about appreciating the human factor aspects of KM – the recognition that it is pointless to set up the systems, no matter how capable and elegant, if people don't use them. The hallmark phrase for stage 2 was "communities of practice." Stage 3 was about content and content description. It's no use getting people onto the system if they can't find what they want or need. Stage 3 was the knowledge organization stage; the hallmark phrase was "content management." It was not until stage 3, approximately in the late 1990s, that what might be called the traditional IT-driven KM community realized that what they were calling taxonomies, a term borrowed from the natural sciences, were fundamentally the same as what the LIS community had been developing for years as syndetic structures and knowledge classification schemes. The fact that this realization occurred rather late in the development of KM applications continues to obscure the fact that KM is logically an extension of LIS, and not a separate domain.

1.4   Development of a Semantic Web

What has recently reinforced the recognition of the overlap between the IT and the LIS components of KM is the desire to build a truly functional "semantic web." These developments are coalescing around the recognition that the structure of the semantic web at the granular level will be based on "triples": subject, predicate, and object combinations. Both the LIS and the IT communities arrived at the same conclusion simultaneously, and had the good sense to realize that they were attempting to create the same thing. Some developments in the semantic web community, particularly the areas of taxonomy and ontology, concerning data description and structuring (e.g., RDF, Resource Definition Framework, and SPARQ, the RDF query language) can be traced to the LIS tradition. Others (such as the web ontology language, OWL) can be traced to the Internet/IT tradition. Increasingly, new developments are simply jointly related. A good example of overlap is the two major players within this taxonomy/ontology area. One, Data Harmony (accessinn.com), descends directly from the LIS side, while the other, Synaptica (synaptica.com), clearly descends from the IT side. This area is increasingly coalescing into one community. These are the tools that KM managers increasingly need to be familiar with. They are rooted in and will be developing from and within the LIS tradition.

1.5   Push Technology and SDI

One KM practice that derived directly from the LIS realm is so called "push methodology"; that is, sending information out to users, rather than waiting for them to ask for it. This is a straightforward extension of *selective dissemination of information* (SDI). SDI developed concurrently with "machine readable databases" in the1960s. It was simply the notion that a standing query could be run whenever a batch of new update tapes arrived. (Yes, computer searches were run in batch mode against computer tapes, before online capability appeared on the scene.) When online search capability arrived, the obvious thought was to store the retrospective search as a search profile that could be run to update and add to the search when new material was added to the database. The next logical extension was to ask users to describe their topical interests, particularly research interests, and then write a profile to reflect those interests and run it periodically and routinely. Thus, SDI was born. It was a particularly compelling idea at the time before effective online capability when a retrospective literature search could require 12 hours of the company's mainframe computer (the author's personal experience at Pfizer in the early 1970s), while a weekly or fortnightly search of just the new tapes could relatively easily be shoehorned in. A historical note is that in corporate libraries ("special libraries") it was common practice, well before computers arrived, for librarians to scan newly arrived journal issues, and alert researchers and executives to relevant articles, a "manual" SDI service.

A good example of the unawareness within the IT and KM communities of KM's LIS antecedents is Marcia Bates' (2002) description of being contacted by an information broker who had been retained to resolve a friendly argument among two dot-com companies as to which company had invented push technology. Their goal, as Bates explains, was to confirm that no third party had invented it earlier, that there was no "prior art." The companies were stunned to be informed that push technology originated in pre-DASD (*direct access storage device*) tape-based bibliographic databases in the LIS and documentation world in the early 1960s (Luhn, 1961).

1.6   The Networked Information Age

An aside, but a relevant one that makes an important point about the very early LIS basis of KM in the LIS community in the digital age, is the phenomenon of LIS professionals bemoaning the frequent popular press item about the modern networked information age. The offending article traces a bit of history and points out that the networked information age goes back well before the Internet, and typically mentions the origin of the Arpanet at MIT in the early 1970s. The librarian immediately wonders "OK, where is the follow-on paragraph about librarians and remote database searching over Tymnet and Telenet even before the Arpanet?" – that is, where the networked information age began.

1.7   Taxonomy Boot Camp

A telling token of KM's fundamental debt to LIS is the two-day Taxonomy Boot Camp provided at the annual KMWorld Conference. Commencing in 2006, it has now been running for fifteen years. It is aimed not at experienced KM practitioners, but at those entering the KM domain. A close look at the syllabus for Taxonomy Boot Camp reveals that it is basically composed of the concepts of LIS 101, classification and cataloging. There is a new crop of KM neophytes every now and then. A major contribution of LIS to KM will continue to be in the area of education and training. As pointed out, KM is a continuation and elaboration of LIS. The chain of continuity is that of organizing information and information resources in a fashion that makes them locatable and retrievable. LIS has historically referred to this area as classification and cataloging, while KM has adopted the term taxonomy for essentially the same thing. The salient point is that the Taxonomy Boot Camp is the closest equivalent that the field of KM has to a Knowledge Management Boot Camp.

2.   Training for KM

There is a marked need for training in the area of KM practice. KM operations are expanding and new recruits are needed. Most practitioners enter the KM realm not from academic programs focusing on KM, or even featuring KM, but rather they transfer over and into KM from line operational jobs within their organization, not from outside the organization. The reason for that is precisely the lack of potential job applicants with KM training. The ideal candidate would be someone with KM training as part of their academic qualifications and enough experience within the organization to have a good sense of its context. There are very few such people. Senior KM people, however, are, not uncommonly, brought in from outside, based on their experience in other organizations. The rationale for this state of affairs is that for bench level or front line KM positions, supporting a particular division or project, it is probably most important that the candidate know a great deal about the context of that division or project, than it is that they have KM experience or training. The assumption is that they can pick up KM techniques or skills on the job. On the other hand, for senior KM positions overseeing a broad range of operations, the assumption is usually that the qualifications needed are successful KM management experience and particularly good interpersonal and communication skills.

For those KM newbies moving into or transferring over to front line or bench level positions, the obvious question is whether on the job learning is sufficient or adequate. Would it not be preferable to have some sort of crash course in KM available to them, a course that could bring them quickly up to speed in KM techniques and tactics? How are those programs to be organized and who runs them? For such persons, typically already employed, the programs need to be easily accessible and relatively brief. Given now the world's COVID-19 constraints, the obvious choice would seem to be online delivery. The question is who is best suited to organize and deliver such programs? Who is in a position to provide such training? As Cervone (2017) makes clear in his study of KM curricula, KM education is scattered, and inconstant; KM programs have come and gone and been restructured with surprising frequency. It is clear that no consistent pattern of KM education has emerged, nor do developments to date (KM has been around long enough to reasonably expect that a pattern should have appeared) suggest that a clear pattern is likely to emerge.

The obvious candidates, then, for KM training and education are:

- LIS programs
- Business schools
- Professional KM organizations and associations
- Independent for-profit KM organizations.

2.1   LIS Programs

The two most obvious providers for KM education and training at present are LIS programs and KM organizations; LIS programs because they have always seen data and information organization as central to their role and have substantial on-board expertise. KM organizations are also a reasonable candidate because presumably they are all about KM.

However, the LIS academic community appears to be making only slow and modest efforts to move in this direction. A recent article reporting on the "Diffusion of KM Education in LIS Schools" (Katuščáková and Jasečková, 2019) illuminates that conclusion. Their study, very international in coverage, found that only one-third of LIS programs had incorporated KM in an aggressive way. Among those schools with a focus on information science as well as LIS, the proportion was close to half. This is still somewhat surprising given that there is an extensive literature calling for (Koenig, 2005) and reporting about the incorporation of KM into LIS programs (Hazari et al., 2009; Roknuzzaman and Katsuhiro, 2010).

2.2   Business Schools

Business Schools (B-Schools), have not aggressively incorporated KM training and education into their curriculums. They have so far been even more passive than LIS programs. The literature about KM in business school curricula is conspicuous by its relative absence, in marked contrast to the LIS literature. Their literature is related to very specific programs, rather than to the field at large (Olszak and Ziemba, 2010). However, as business schools adapt to the consequences of COVID-19, it is quite likely that they will be placing more emphasis upon the online delivery of courses, and upon the creation of programs that can be directed to those already employed and those for whom on-campus programs are simply not practical, including those who already have an MBA. In that context, KM programs would seem to be an obvious opportunity for B-Schools attempting to maintain or recover, or even expand enrollment and revenue. The authors expect that there will be motion on this front.

2.3   Professional KM Organizations and Associations

Professional KM Associations, and there are, or have been, a number of them, are indeed making some efforts. Overall activity among these players seems to be receding a bit.

2.3.1   KMI (kminstitute.org)

The Knowledge Management Institute has an active program of conferences and workshops, and a successful (10,000 graduates in 20 years) program of certification.

2.3.2   NetIKX (netikx.org)

The Network for Information and Knowledge Exchange was founded in 2006, but descends from the 1990s enthusiasm for information resource management (IRM), and the proselytization of Woody Horton. The NetIKX group was created in 1992. Its role remains that of hosting numerous seminars, primarily in London, most of which focus on KM. It also has a relationship with Taxonomy Boot Camp.

2.3.3   KMPro (KMPro.org)

The Knowledge Management Professional Society, founded in 2001, was, for some years, probably the most active professional society, but after internal political difficulties, it has become moribund and its website is no longer active.

2.3.4   IAKM (http://iakm.weebly.com/)

The International Association for Knowledge Management organizes conferences, IFKAD (International Forum on Knowledge Asset Dynamics) and ICKMAP (International Conference on Knowledge Application and Practice), which of course include sessions relating to KM training and education. IAKM, however, plays little role in education and training outside its conference venues.

2.3.5   KMCI (kmci.org)

The Knowledge Management Consortium International, which originated in 1997, was an attempt to link KM with the then new enthusiasm for complexity theory. KMCI discontinued membership in 2002. Its website still describes an extensive array of KM certifications, but the phone number listed on the website is disconnected.

2.3.6   AOK & KMedu Hub (kmeducationhub.de)

The Association of Knowledge Work is no longer active per se. It was discontinued in 2010. The organization, however, maintains KMedu Hub (kmeducationhub.de) that is an extensive list, quite international, of those organizations which provide KM training. Indeed, there is also a list of other organizations which provide similar KM education and training information, in many cases at a more specific national or regional level.

A striking phenomenon is the high morbidity rate for KM associations. Another subtle phenomenon that can be noticed by any long-term KM observer is the very low level of overlap between those persons active with any one of these professional groups and those active with any other. A bibliometric display based on professional association membership and social media would reveal a very dispersed and scattered KM field.

2.4   Broader Scale Professional Organizations

A number of broader scale professional organizations, typically in the library domain, venture into the KM field and offer some KM training and education.

2.4.1   IFLA (https://ifla.org/)

The International Federation of Library Associations has a long history of interest in KM. Its general conferences frequently have sessions to bring librarians up to speed about KM. Its first session focusing on KM was in 1998. In 2003, IFLA created a section on KM, and in 2005, the all-hands opening session at the annual conference was devoted to KM. However, IFLA's audience is librarians who by default are to a degree already in the KM fold. It is not expanding the field.

2.4.2   SLA (https://www.sla.org/)

The Special Libraries Association has a carefully worded and well thought out statement of "Competencies for Information Professionals," a document that could almost equally well be a statement of core competencies for KM. Like IFLA, however, its audience is librarians who are usually already KM-aware and functionally already in the field.

2.4.3   ASIS&T (https://www.asist.org/)

The Association for Information Science and Technology has a special interest group (SIG), devoted to KM. The SIG's archives go back to 2002, but sessions on KM in ASIS&T's annual conferences go back well before that.

2.4.4   ISKO (https://www.isko.org/)

Founded in 1989, the International Society for Knowledge Organization is also interested in the KM field. ISKO has become the parent to the European Knowledge Acquisition Workshop (EKAW) which commenced in 1987. Rather surprisingly, however, the phrase "Knowledge Management" is nowhere to be found in their carefully compiled ISKO Encyclopedia of Knowledge Organization. Despite that, ISKO is an affiliated sponsor of the Washington and London Taxonomy Boot Camps mentioned above.

2.4.5   APQC (https://www.apqc.org/)

The American Productivity and Quality Center was founded in 1977, before KM was a buzzword. It was founded to make American industry more competitive, particularly with Japanese industry. APQC's primary focus was on publicizing, incorporating, and learning from Japanese techniques, particularly the concepts of benchmarking and best practices, and undertaking research about how to improve productivity. Very rapidly, however, APQC came to see KM and the promotion of KM as central to its mission. Consequently, the subject of much of APQC's well-attended conferences, and the focus of much of its research and the subject of many of its publications is KM. In fact, APQC's tag line is now "APQC, the world's foremost authority in benchmarking, best practices, process and performance improvement, and knowledge management." Consequently, APQC runs workshops and webinars specifically about KM issues. APQC is a major resource for the field.

2.5   Independent For-Profit KM Organizations

Some independent for-profit organizations have entered the field – they sense opportunity and have established an expertise.

2.5.1   Information Today (informatintodayinc.com)

A major player in this area is Information Today, organizers of the annual KMWorld Conference, whose origins come from the library database world. Information Today is a long-time player in the area of trade shows and conferences centered on the library and information domain. Well before there was a Google or an Amazon, they were the organizers of the National Online Conference (New York) and co-sponsors of the International Online Conference (London). It is sobering to realize that barely more than 20 years ago it was quite reasonable and appropriate to label a combined conference and trade show devoted almost entirely to library systems and services and to bibliographic databases, the *"National Online" meeting*. It was still a world in which Google and Amazon and Facebook did not yet exist, and in which the most active group of online system users were librarians. Rather seamlessly, the National Online Conference morphed into the KMWorld Conference. The conference, as much a trade show as a conference, features how-to and lessons learned sessions, many aimed at newbies to the field. It has become, at least in North America, the major route of KM education for those entering the field. A major component of the KMWorld Conference, as mentioned above, is the Taxonomy Boot Camp, which has become successful enough to be offered as a stand-alone event, and which is given in London as well. One can expect this model to continue successfully, but to transition to a more online-enabled delivery model.

2.6   Future Directions for Training and Education

The activity related to KM training and education seems to be primarily in the hands of LIS programs and other organizations such as the Knowledge Management Institute (KMI) and Information Today (KMWorld). What is clear is that KM training and education very much descended from the LIS/ database domains, either LIS academic programs or for profit organizations targeting the LIS community.

3.   Future Directions for LIS-related KM

There are many future directions for LIS to pursue related to KM because of the potential benefits of KM for the LIS profession (Liebowitz and Paliszkiewicz, 2019). In the following, two such directions are identified and will be discussed: the semantic web, and concept identification and retrieval.

3.1   The Semantic Web

The semantic web (also called Web 3.0) deals with annotating information based on underlying common use of knowledge representation so that such semantics can be reused by computer systems/artificial intelligence or machine learning for users to find, organize, access and maintain the information they seek (Davies et al., 2007). While the World Wide Web uses HTML, a markup language to describe format, XML provides a markup language for semantics (Warren, 2006). In addition, the underlying principles and technologies of the semantic web are built based on LIS areas of taxonomy and ontology. The new development of the semantic web provides opportunities to improve knowledge management. By integrating human involvement in information/ knowledge management activities and integrating knowledge creation and use, it provides a flexible reference mechanism to knowledge objects and knowledge contributors.

Semantic technologies have been widely researched and applied in many areas. For the area of data quality management, some have focused on the development of the semantic data quality management (SDQM) framework (Fürber, 2015; Fürber and Hepp, 2013). Others use ontologies to develop new semantic applications for different sectors such as life sciences, healthcare, government, or technology-intensive sectors (Sheth and Stephens, 2007).

As semantic-based knowledge management becomes a critical enabler for improving organizational performance, more organizations will use the power of semantics in their business strategies (Eine et al., 2017). Compliance issues such as financial compliance (particularly money laundering, anti-terrorism), environmental concerns and non-discrimination are increasingly important. Consider money laundering and the thousands of corporations chartered in the Cayman Islands, many if not most with overlapping ownership, in many cases deliberately created to foster obscurity. Who ultimately is the beneficiary of any particular financial transaction? This is an issue designed to be elucidated by the concepts of the semantic web. Another area of semantic web application is ontology-based big data management (Eine et al., 2017; Fensel, 2002). No matter whether a large enterprise or a small or middle-sized organization, an ontology-based big data management system will acquire, maintain and access weakly structured data sources in order to reduce the complexity of business data and processes. Finally, semantic wikis are another example of application of semantic technology (Schaffert, 2006). By annotating existing wiki links based on their content, semantic technologies (RDF, OWL, Topic Map, or Conceptual Graphs) make the inherent structure of a wiki accessible to machines (agents, services) beyond mere navigation. The semantic wiki development will provide support not only to collaborative knowledge engineering through linguistic processing techniques, identification of similar concepts, but also to collaborative learning through automated structure analysis and guided questions based on underlying ontological knowledge.

While the semantic web has been applied in the area of LIS/KM applications, we expect to see substantial development work in this area.

3.2   Concept Identification and Retrieval

Information retrieval systems traditionally rely on textual keywords to index documents and queries. Documents are retrieved based on the number of keywords shared with the query. Such lexical-focused retrieval leads to inaccurate and incomplete results when different keywords are used to describe the same concept in the documents and in the queries. In addition, the relationship between these related keywords may be semantic rather than syntactic, and capturing it thus requires access to comprehensive human knowledge.

Concept-based retrieval approaches attempt to overcome this problem by relying on concepts rather than on keywords to indexing and retrieval. The key is to retrieve documents that are semantically relevant to a given user query. To successfully retrieve relevant information, indexing should be achieved using the concepts of the document that an author intends to highlight. Thus, concept-based retrieval is achieved by using manually built thesauri, by relying on term co-occurrence data, or by extracting latent word relationships and concepts from a corpus.

Different concept identification indexing methods have been developed for information retrieval. First, a fuzzy ranking model calculates the relevance ranking based on the user preference. It is indexed by concept identification (Kang et al., 2005). Second, lexical databases such as WordNet and WordNet domains are used for concept identification. The identified concept is then weighted based on the definition of concept centrality. The resulting semantic-based retrieval approach is shown to be more effective than traditional IR approaches (Boubekeur and Azzoug, 2013; Boubekeu et al., 2010). Third, several techniques address the issue of textual variation in the documents and queries in IR systems (Aronson, 1996; Riloff, 1995). By normalizing both document text and queries, text words are replaced with concepts discovered by a program mapping texts to the concepts in the meta thesaurus. Actual retrieval is accomplished by processing the normalized text using a traditional statistical IR system.

Concept identification indexing approaches have been used for information retrieval in different domains. Zheng and Yu (2015) developed a system for medical information retrieval. The medical terms in electronic health records (EHRs) are often hard for patients to understand. By exploring topic model and key concept identification methods to construct queries from the EHR notes, they provided tailored online consumer-oriented health education materials. Lin et. al. (2012) implemented a concept-based IR system for engineering domain-specific technical documents. While technical documents often have complicated structures, their partitioning approach separates each document into several passages, and treats each passage as an independent document. Passages are generated according to domain knowledge, which is represented by base domain ontology.

Concept-based video retrieval is a promising area. Traditional video retrieval is based on the textual description of the video, which is manually indexed by library experts using controlled vocabularies. While social tagging by general users is easy and fast, their labels are ambiguous, limited, and overly personalized. Furthermore, unlabeled video segments remain notoriously difficult to find. The emergence of the new field of content-based image retrieval from the 1990s facilitates searching in video at a segment-level by means of large sets of automatically detected (visual) concepts. Machine-driven labeling derives meaningful descriptors from video data. Central to the issue is the notion of a semantic concept: an objective linguistic description of an observable video entity. The challenge is the semantic gap, the lack of correspondence between the low-level features that machines extract from video content and the high-level conceptual interpretation of video segments by an interacting user (Smeulders et al., 2000). Snoek and Worring (2008), after reviewing over 300 references, pointed out that concept-based video retrieval can be achieved by empowering a video search engine with its automated detection, selection under uncertainty, and interactive usage. Its success is due to the interdisciplinary influences from information retrieval, computer vision, machine learning, and human–computer interaction.

There are a variety of concept-based IR software tools (Haav and Lubi, 2001). Concept-based IR embed "intelligence" to search tools to manage effectively search, retrieval, filtering, and presenting relevant information. Rahman and Roy (2017) developed two IR techniques TextRank and POSRank to determine a term's importance based on not only its co-occurrences with other important terms but also its syntactic relationships with them. It leads to identification of better quality search terms than baseline terms. Poshyvanyk et al. (2013) proposed a concept location tool using formal concept analysis and latent semantic indexing, an advanced IR approach. By mapping textual descriptions of software features or bug reports to relevant parts of the source code, it presented a ranked list of source code elements. For the given ranked list, the approach selects the most relevant attributes from the best ranked documents, clusters the results, and presents them as a concept lattice. This approach was shown to be effective in organizing different concepts and their relationships present in the subset of the search results. Egozi et al. (2011) provided a concept-based information retrieval system using explicit semantic analysis (ESA). The system extracted new text features automatically from massive human knowledge repositories, thus augmenting keyword-based text representation with concept-based features. The high-quality feature selection becomes crucial in this setting to make the retrieval more focused. In summary, the research on concept identification retrieval will continue to grow in the future.

References

Aronson, A. R. (1996). The effect of textual variation on concept based information retrieval. In *Proceedings of the AMIA Annual Fall Symposium* (p. 373). American Medical Informatics Association.

Bates, M. (2002). After the dot-bomb: getting web information retrieval right this time. *First Monday* 7(7), July. https://firstmonday.org/ojs/index.php/fm/article/view/971/892.

Borko, H. (1968). Information Science, What is it? *American Documentation* 19(1), 3–5.

Boubekeur, F. & Azzoug, W. (2013). Concept-based indexing in text information retrieval. *arXiv preprint arXiv*. DOI: 10.5121/ijcsit.2013.5110.

Boubekeur, F., Boughanem, M., Tamine, L. & Daoud, M. (2010, October). Using WordNet for concept-based document indexing in information retrieval. In *Fourth International Conference on Semantic Processing (SEMAPRO), Florence, Italy*.

Cervone, F. (2017). What does the evolution of curriculum in knowledge management programs tell us about the future of the field?, *VINE Journal of Information and Knowledge Management Systems* 47(4): 454–66.

Davenport, T. & Prusak, L. (1998). *Working Knowledge: How Organizations Manage What They Know*. Boston, MA: Harvard Business School Press.

Davies, J., Lytras, M. & Sheth, A. P. (2007). Guest editors' introduction: semantic-web-based knowledge management. *IEEE Internet Computing* 11(5), 14–16.

Edvinsson, L. (1994). *Visualizing Intellectual Capital at Skandia*, Skandia's 1997 Annual Report. Stockholm: Skandia AFS.

Edvinsson, L. (1997). Developing intellectual capital at Skandia. *Long Range Planning* 30(3), 366–73.

Egozi, O., Markovitch, S. & Gabrilovich, E. (2011). Concept-based information retrieval using explicit semantic analysis. *ACM Transactions on Information Systems (TOIS)* 29(2), 1–34.

Eine, B., Jurisch, M. & Quint, W. (2017). Ontology-based big data management. *Systems* 5(3), 45.

Fensel, D. (2002). Ontology-based knowledge management. *Computer* 35(11), 56–9.

Fürber, C. (2015). *Data Quality Management with Semantic Technologies*. Dordrecht: Springer.

Fürber, C. & Hepp, M. (2013). Using semantic web technologies for data quality management. In *Handbook of Data Quality*, ed. Shazia Sadiq (pp. 141–61). Berlin/Heidelberg: Springer.

Haav, H. M. & Lubi, T. L. (2001). A survey of concept-based information retrieval tools on the web. In *Proceedings of the 5th East-European Conference ADBIS* (Vol. 2, pp. 29–41).

Hazari, A., Martin, B. & Sarrafzadeh, M. (2009). Integration of Knowledge Management with the Library and Information Science Curriculum: some professional perspectives. *Journal of Education for Library and Information Science* 50(3), 152–63.

Hibbard, J. (1997). Knowing what we know. *Information Week*, 653 (October 20), 46–64.

Kang, B. Y., Kim, D. W. & Kim, H. J. (2005). Fuzzy information retrieval indexed by concept identification. In *International Conference on Text, Speech and Dialogue* (pp. 179–86). Berlin/Heidelberg: Springer.

Katuščáková, M. & Jasečková, G. (2019. Diffusion of KM education in LIS schools, *Journal of Education for Library and Information Science* 60(1), 83–100.

Koenig, M. E. D. (1992). Entering Stage III – the convergence of the stage hypotheses. *Journal of the American Society for Information Science* 43(3), 204–7.

Koenig, M. E. D. (2000). The evolution of knowledge management. In T. K. Srikantaiah and M. E. D. Koenig, *Knowledge Management for the Information Professional* (pp. 23–36). Medford, NJ: Information Today for the American Society for Information Science.

Koenig, M. E. D. (2005). KM moves beyond the organization: the opportunity for librarians. *Information Services and Use* 25(2), 87–93.

Koenig, M. E. D. and Neveroski, K. (2008). The origins and development of knowledge management. *Journal of Information and Knowledge Management* 7(4), 243–54.

Liebowitz, J. & Paliszkiewicz, J. (2019). The next generation of knowledge management: implications for LIS educators and professionals. *Online Journal of Applied Knowledge Management* 7(2), 16–28.

Lin, H. T., Chi, N. W. & Hsieh, S. H. (2012). A concept-based information retrieval approach for engineering domain-specific technical documents. *Advanced Engineering Informatics* 26(2), 349–60.

Luhn, H. P. (1961). Selective dissemination of new scientific information with the aid of electronic processing equipment. *American Documentation* 12(3), 131–8.

Marchand, D. (1985). Information management: strategies and tools in transition. *Information Management Review* 1(1), 27–37.

McInerney, C. M. & Koenig, M. E. D. (2011). *Knowledge Management (KM) Processes in Organizations*. San Rafael, CA: Morgan and Claypool.

O'Dell, C. & Jackson, C. (1998). If only we knew what we know: identification and transfer of internal best practices. *California Management Review* 40(3), 305–8.

Olszak, C. M. & Ziemba, E. (2010). Knowledge management curriculum development: linking with real business needs. *Issues in Informing Science and Information Technology* 7(1), 235–48.

Poshyvanyk, D., Gethers, M., & Marcus, A. (2013). Concept location using formal concept analysis and information retrieval. *ACM Transactions on Software Engineering and Methodology (TOSEM)* 21(4), 1–34.

Prusak, L. (1999). Where did knowledge management come from? *Knowledge Directions* 1(1), 90–96.

Rahman, M. M. & Roy, C. K. (2017, February). STRICT: Information retrieval based search term identification for concept location. In *2017 IEEE 24th International Conference on Software Analysis, Evolution and Reengineering (SANER)* (pp. 79–90). IEEE.

Riloff, E. (1995, July). Little words can make a big difference for text classification. In *Proceedings of the 18th Annual International ACM SIGIR Conference on Research and Development in Information Retrieval* (pp. 130–36).

Roknuzzaman, M. & Katsuhiro, U. (2010). KM education at LIS schools: an analysis of KM masters programs. *Journal of Education for Library and Information Science* 51(4), 267–80.

Schaffert, S. (2006, June). IkeWiki: a semantic wiki for collaborative knowledge management. In *15th IEEE International Workshops on Enabling Technologies: Infrastructure for Collaborative Enterprises (WETICE'06)* (pp. 388–96). IEEE.

Sheth, A. P. & Stephens, S. (2007). Semantic web: technologies and applications for the real-world. World Wide Web Conf. tutorial, 2007. http://www2007.org/tutorial -T11.php and http://knoesis.wright.edu/library/presentations/WWW2007-Sheth -Stephens-Tutorial-Final.ppt.

Smeulders, A. W., Worring, M., Santini, S., Gupta, A. & Jain, R. (2000). Content-based image retrieval at the end of the early years. *IEEE Transactions on Pattern Analysis and Machine Intelligence* 22(12), 1349–80.

Snoek, C. G. & Worring, M. (2008). Concept-based video retrieval. *Foundations and Trends in Information Retrieval* 2(4), 215–322.

Stewart, T. (1994). Your company's most valuable asset: intellectual capital. *Fortune*, 130 (Oct. 3), 68–74.

Sveiby, K. (1989). *The Invisible Balance Sheet*. Stockholm: Affärsvärlden Förlag.

Warren, P. (2006). Knowledge management and the semantic web: from scenario to technology. *IEEE Intelligent Systems* 21(1), 53–9.

Zheng, J. & Yu, H. (2015, September). Key concept identification for medical information retrieval. In *Proceedings of the 2015 Conference on Empirical Methods in Natural Language Processing* (pp. 579–84).

2. Knowledge management placement in organizations

Ramin Assa

1.   Introduction

"Where shall we put the Knowledge Management (KM) function in our organizational structure?" and *"At what personnel level?"* are the two questions often asked by organizations that have decided to establish KM, and similarly by organizations, with existing KM functions, which are going through a re-organization.

There have been numerous books, articles and blogs written about the value of knowledge management in organizations. Many organizations, in both private and public sectors, are at various stages of exploring, adopting, maturing, evolving or retiring KM. This chapter is not about explaining what KM is. It is also not about KM's value in an organization. Rather, the chapter explores two key contributors to KM's success (location and level[1]); and invites further research in this area. Two other key KM success contributors, budget and senior championship, are often influenced by KM's location and level, which makes the placement and level decision even more critical.

An organization is a group of people gathered together to provide a service or product. They can be for-profit or non-profit. For-profit organizations can be private or public. Non-profits can be governmental or non-governmental organizations. Each of these organizations and their sub-units will have different Knowledge Management needs. There is no one KM solution that will fit all organizations. According to Nunn (2013), there is simply no one size fits all solution.

---

[1]   This refers to the location of the KM function within an organization and its staffs' level(s).

Most contemporary organizations have some or many of the following sub-unit components (often called department, team, division ...) as part of their organizational structure:[2] administration, analysis and reviews, communications, customer service, finance (accounting, and budgeting), human resources, engineering, information technology, legal, marketing, operations, production, sales, regulatory affairs, research and development, and training. (Some organizations may also have other functions such as a library, inventory, and innovations team.)

Organizations themselves and their internal departments typically have the following individual characteristics variables: (1) role (mission); (2) size (number of people and budget); and (3) culture. These characteristics impact how KM will operate and work within the given organization and selected function.

Another factor that impacts the success of a KM function is the level of its personnel. Organizations typically also have three personnel levels at the enterprise level and in each one of their units, departments and divisions: (1) leadership, (2) management, (3) staff. KM personnel can be placed in any of these roles and at any level. If the organization establishes a KM department, the KM department itself could also have a similar level structure, led by a Chief Knowledge Officer (CKO) and managers and staff.

This chapter's author has had the privilege of establishing Knowledge Management strategies in four organizations, from the ground up. Some of these organizations already had an idea where to locate Knowledge Management (either permanent or temporary). In others, after they decided they needed knowledge management, the first question they asked was: "Where shall we put the KM function?"

The purpose of this chapter is to highlight the value and challenges of placing the KM function at one of the functional units described below and the level of personnel in the KM unit. The chapter also lays the foundation for further research to analyze and determine which placement and level has the best chances of success.

For the rest of this chapter, we will explore the pros and cons of locating KM in given parts of an organization. We will start with the most likely places where Knowledge Management may seem to be a good fit.

---

[2]   Presented in alphabetical order.

2.   Possible Locations

2.1   Information Technology (IT)

Most organizations have an IT unit (a division, team, or group). Their typical role is to manage IT assets (hardware and software); obtain, install, and update software and related services (cloud computing and web hosting); and to address security access and systems protection concerns. They could have more or less roles and responsibilities and operate as a centralized or decentralized model depending on organizational variable, such as size and mission.

Clearly, in today's environment, there is certainly an element of technology in most Knowledge Management strategies and implementations. This could be in the form of online communities, web portals and wikis. Unfortunately, because of the need to use technology, many who are not familiar with the KM discipline believe KM is just an IT issue. Consequently, they believe a robust electronic document depository and a great search capability constitutes a good KM program. And, therefore, IT, they believe, is good department to place Knowledge Management. Of course, this belief has become even more prevalent with the increased interest in and use of artificial intelligence (AI).

Most IT professionals, such as a dozen chief information officers leading IT organizations whom the chapter's author has interacted with, tend not to want an enterprise-wide KM function placed in their departments. However, this does not mean that IT is not a good place for Knowledge Management. As presented earlier, there are several IT platforms and approaches that can play an important role in KM. Therefore, there needs to be strong collaboration and cooperation between the two disciplines. One advantage of placing KM in IT is first-hand access to technological resources that can help KM succeed.[3]

There could be three main disadvantages to placing KM in IT. First, it reinforces the idea that Knowledge Management is strictly a technological issue; second, most IT professionals are not fundamentally KM experts and do not believe it's within their swim lanes; and third, there could be competing priorities between staff's need and technology preferences such as cost, security and availability. It should be noted that depending on IT leadership and their level of comfort with innovation, IT can be an acceptable place for KM.

---

[3]   Success is a subjective matter and is one of the items that needs to be clearly identified in the KM strategy.

Pros:

1. First-hand access to technology support and resources.
2. Possible access to part of the IT budget.
3. Awareness of KM issues that seek IT support and applications.

Cons:

1. Reinforcement of the idea that KM is only a technology solution.
2. Knowledge Management is not a traditional IT role.
3. IT priorities can supersede and overtake KM needs.

2.2   Human Resources (HR)

In many organizations, HR is responsible for hiring, onboarding, benefits, career development, and other personnel topics, as well as sometimes training, and administrative matters such as time-keeping, handling office supplies and logistics.

Many professionals believe KM is primarily a "people"-focused topic. In fact, Wiig (2004) has written a book on this subject, called *People-Focused Knowledge Management*, and because HR is in contact with people from the moment they come onboard until they leave the organization, it may appear as a suitable place for KM. After all, on-boarding, succession planning, and exit interviews are typically within the realm of HR. Furthermore, some HR departments also lead training efforts within an organization, and learning is clearly seen as a KM activity.

Placing Knowledge Management in HR can be a viable option given all the "people" responsibilities it typically holds. However, success is highly dependent on the level of trust staff have in their HR department and its leadership's understanding and embracing of KM. Two additional benefits of placing KM in HR are the possibility of tying KM's budget as part of the learning budget and more effective incorporation of KM in learning, including adding an active KM role in on-boarding and career development activities.

Two disadvantages of placing KM in HR are, first, the possibility that it would appear just as a learning exercise for the staff and, second, the department might not appear as important as, or capable, as other leading departments in the organization. For example, staff in key departments may feel that staff in HR may not have the breadth and depth of experience and skills necessary to understand their KM challenges and needs.[4] Furthermore, HR senior leadership may be focused more on their core business functions and less on promoting and supporting KM.

Pros:

1. First-hand and frequent contact with staff during on-boarding, exit interviews, career planning and training exercises.
2. Possibility of costs being included as part of the HR/training budget.
3. Ability to stay aware of upcoming organizational changes and needs.

Cons:

1. Knowledge Management may appear to be just a "training and learning" exercise.
2. Seen as a support role in a support unit.
3. Lower influence within the organizations because it is seen as just "support."
4. Limited HR leadership involvement and championing.
5. Staff not appearing as experts in core competitive business capabilities.

2.3   Research and Development (R&D)

First, many organizations may not even have an official R&D department, which makes this option unviable. However, in organizations that do have an R&D department, the R&D staff, who typically have advanced educational degrees, often feel they are the creators and keepers of knowledge. This is true whether they are researching advanced materials, manufacturing techniques, new software and algorithms, or consumer behavior. Again, depending on the reputation, prowess, and past successes of the R&D department, this can be good department in which to place Knowledge Management.

R&D departments typically are very good at creating new knowledge and producing related publications. However, for the most part, they are not as effective in "marketing" the new-found knowledge and their findings. They also often need inspiration to apply their knowledge. This is based on the author's observations working in several R&D departments both as a researcher and as a senior research liaison officer. On the plus side, researchers, while

---

[4]   Depending on the function of an organization, different departments may appear to have a more prominent and important role than other departments. The research and development department may be the leading department, while in a manufacturing company, production has a leading role.

sometimes protective of their information, rely heavily on collaboration and inter-connectivity to conduct their work. Collaboration is one of the key tenets of KM; therefore, researchers and scientists are on the frontlines of using and benefiting from Knowledge Management.

The R&D department staff are often seen as narrowly focused experts and are sought out to answer atypical questions. However, most field staff consider R&D staff out of touch with real-life situations and may not consider them when seeking solutions to challenging issues. Consequently, an R&D-led KM may not be used widely across all organizational departments.

Pros:

1. R&D departments and staff are used to the idea of collaborating and sharing knowledge, and likely to embrace a KM strategy.
2. R&D departments and staff are often seen as creators and keepers of knowledge.

Cons:

1. The rest of the organization may think R&D-led KM is solely focused on R&D knowledge and may not choose to use it for operational purposes.
2. R&D budgets are often the first to be cut during "hard times," risking further cuts in KM's budget which is not a core R&D function.
3. Most organizations have a small to medium sized R&D department and they may not want to take additional responsibilities beyond their core business functions.

2.4   A Leading Department

In many organizations, one department or section may appear to have a higher role and importance than the rest of the organization. These are the primary business drivers. As such, they are likely in need of the most knowledge and information. And while they may be envied and referred to as prima donnas, they are often the role model for the rest of the organization.

One of the key benefits of placing KM in a leading department is being in closest proximity to the end-users. This is where knowledge and information are mostly created and consumed. Here, Knowledge Management will have the best perspective of information needs as well as how knowledge is generated, accessed and used. Being part of the department also will improve the chances of the department itself using the information, as they see it as part of doing business. Additionally, leading departments are likely to get a fair share of the budget and resources needed to conduct business. This is where the KM function can have the greatest impact.

On the negative side, other departments may feel the information in the KM system is solely for the use of the leading department and won't be too eager to use it. This is not unlike placing the KM function in R&D. Additionally, depending on the size of the organization and the leading department, their culture might be different than other departments and the whole organization, consequently creating friction in how information is shared and used.

Pros:

1. Closest to end-users – to better understand their needs and access preferences.
2. Improved chances of adoption – because of being part of the department.
3. Better ability to access resources and funding.

Cons:

1. The rest of the organization may think a "leading department"-led KM is solely focused on that department's knowledge and information and may choose not to use Knowledge Management systems for other purposes.
2. The leading department may direct the KM team to focus on the department's issues and topics, further alienating other departments.
3. The KM team may have restricted access to the rest of the organization, reducing its overall effectiveness.

2.5   Stand-Alone *Independent* Unit

In the previous examples, we examined placing the Knowledge Management function (or unit) under an existing program or office. This type of placement subjects the KM team not only to overall organizational governing rules and requirements, but also adds additional restrictions, limitations and requirements.

Since the early 2000s, there has been a rise of new positions with titles such as Chief Innovation Officer or Chief Data Officer which have become more prevalent in organizations. These new positions often lead to small independent offices or units. Knowledge Management is no exception, and some organizations have selected to establish a stand-alone independent KM function, which is typically led by a CKO. These chiefs usually report directly to the head of the organization or a high-level senior executive.

A stand-alone unit gives the most flexibility to the KM team to propose and implement solutions that it deems necessary (as approved by the leadership team.) A stand-alone team, when reporting directly to the head of the organization, often benefits from a high degree of influence and respect, depending on leadership's standing with the staff. Another benefit of being part of the leadership circle is the first-hand access to anticipated changes in business environment and organizational changes and KM's ability, and the voice, to influence inclusion of the KM in the future state of the organization.

There are some disadvantages with an independent unit. For example, securing funding and additional resources can be challenging. Also, success can be very closely tied to the organization's leadership's bandwidth and interest in championing the topic. And there is a risk of derailment if and when there is a leadership change. Finally, the KM team must work harder in building and maintaining relationships with other units and departments.

Pros:

1. Improved access to high-level, timely information about the organization and its operations.
2. Flexibility to propose and implement independent solutions and programs.
3. Ability to communicate directly with leadership in order to better align the Knowledge Management program with organizational strategic priorities.

Cons:

1. Subject to availability and interest level of senior executives who may have other "more important" and shifting priorities.
2. Securing funding might be more challenging, because the unit may appear as a nice-to-have option, instead of a must-have option.

Overall, an independent stand-alone unit can be the most effective way to deploy KM in many types of organizations; however, there are no empirical studies to confirm this observation – hence the need for the research proposed in this chapter. There have been several research projects on KM success factors, but few have looked at the location of KM as a variable factor. For example, Doval (2015) looked at Knowledge Management characteristics in ten different organizations, which did not include location of the program.

3.   Other Possible Locations

3.1   Library

Historically, larger organizations and some specialty organizations (such as academia, law offices and research organizations) have had internal libraries. Library staff can play a role in managing a slice of explicit knowledge (books, articles and research products). They may also assist with document management. However, there are many other aspects of KM, such as community management, and after-action-reviews, that typical libraries are not set up to offer.

Placing KM in a library or renaming a library as a Knowledge Management function, narrows the focus of KM function to where staff may not use it as broadly as needed within an organization. Most importantly, KM is directly related to business intelligence, an area in which libraries are not seen as a leading department. Therefore, it is advisable to keep the two functions separate.

3.2   Chief Financial Officer (CFO)

For Knowledge Management professionals, the Chief Financial Officer's office may not appear as a good candidate for placing KM; however, there are organizations where IT and some other non-financial functions are placed under the finance department. There are three advantages to this option. First, most projects in an organization need funding to function; therefore, the CFO typically gets advanced and broad knowledge of proposed projects and organizational needs. This will give the KM function the ability to propose alternate solutions that includes KM. Second, being part of the CFO's department will give the KM function improved access to funding availability and resources; third, most departments tend to work more cooperatively with the CFO's office, and this will give the KM improved acceptability within the organization. One major risk of placing KM in the CFO's office is the possibility of a gradual reduction in the CFO's interest, involvement and championing the Knowledge Management functions over time, depending on other priorities and urgent needs.

3.3   Chief Data Officer (CDO)

While a Chief Data Officer may not be a new function within organizations, its role and responsibilities have been evolving since the mid 2010s. Also, the number of CDOs is increasing in organizations. In fact, with the passage of the Foundations for Evidence-Based Policymaking Action in January 2019, all

U.S. government agencies were required to establish a CDO position. There are similarities between CDO and CKO functions. After all, data can be the basis for developing information which could lead to knowledge. Interestingly, while the Evidence-Based Act outlined the roles of CDOs, each agency has taken a unique approach to establishing the position, including its location within the organization and the broader roles and responsibilities of the position.

While data is the basis for knowledge, because data and knowledge are inter-connected, it may make sense, in certain circumstances, to place the KM function in the CDO's office. The advantage of this approach is the potential of better access to funding because the CDO is a statuary requirement and improved access to leverage data. However, there is a risk that like placing KM in the library, or with the Chief Information Officer (CIO) and some of the other possible places, this may limit and narrow the application of KM and its broader adoption within the organization. Also, the rest of the organization may consider KM as a resource specifically for the CDO and may not include KM in their solutions and conversations.

4.   Knowledge Management Levels and Unit Size

There have been several attempts to define knowledge management roles and levels. For example, Emory University (2020) has a list of roles and responsi-bility for professionals involved in Knowledge Management.[5] Like many other subjects, KM practitioners can range from entry level analyst all the way up to a Chief Knowledge Officer's position. The unit size can also range from a part-time one-person team, all the way up to a full department with a dozen or so staff.

What defines the role is the organization's commitment to Knowledge Management and its expectations. For example, if a KM strategy is needed, a CKO's position may be necessary. Also, if the organization is leaning toward establishing a culture of learning and sharing, it may want to have a senior level KM, who can better prepare and influence for inevitable upcoming organizational change. On the other hand, if the organization is initially interested in a basic Customer Service Management-type KM, for

---

[5]   See   http://smcc.emory.edu/itsm_process/knowledge/knowledge_roles_and _responsibilities.html.

example, it may choose to employ an analyst to collect, curate, update and maintain the CRM information.

The size of a Knowledge Management department can be directly related to the size of the organization and the variety of the work it does. For example, if the organization has a thousand people who have the same need for information, one person might be enough. On the other hand, a 200-person organization with ten lines of independent businesses may need multiple knowledge managers.

5.   Proposed Research

As discussed earlier, organizations differ in their core functions and culture, among other variables. However, there are organizations with similar functions (such as retail, or engineering, and healthcare providers) that may have similar organizational structures where they may benefit by placement of KM function in certain departments.

There is a need for empirical studies to show how placement, level and size of a Knowledge Management department can influence its success. This study can start by conducting a survey of organizations with KM and asking questions like the following:

a. Do you have a Knowledge Management function?
b. How long have you had the KM function?
c. Do you have a Knowledge Management strategy?
d. How do you define KM's success?
e. Is KM meeting its strategic goals and objectives successfully?
f. Where in the organization is Knowledge Management located?
g. Was it located elsewhere before?
h. What is the highest level of KM staff?
i. How many people are there in the KM team/department?
j. What type of business are you in?
    i. Non-profit.
    ii. For profit.
    iii. Other ——.
k. How many people work in your organization?
l. Does the location and level of Knowledge Management contribute to its success?
m. Are you planning to keep the current Knowledge Management structure and location the same, or are there any plans to change it?

6.   Closing Thoughts

There are many factors that contribute to the success of a Knowledge Management program. Two factors with a high degree of impact are placement of KM in an organization and the level of KM staff and its leadership function.

In this chapter, we have examined the values and challenges of placing the Knowledge Management function in several organizational functional units. We also briefly touched on the level of personnel in KM functions. Finally, a framework for further research was laid out to find empirical values to obtain data which can form the basis for KM placement in organizations. This information can be very helpful for organizations which are deciding where to put their new KM functions or repositioning their existing KM functions to improve their performance and effectiveness. The results can also help develop criteria for making the location decision.

It's worth repeating that there is no one location that will address all Knowledge Management situations in all organizations. Placement of KM is highly dependent on each individual organization's culture, the program objectives and goals, as well as the selected department's influence and how much it is trusted and valued by staff.

Based on personal experience, an independent team, with a team leader who sits at the organizational leadership table, has the best chances of success. But this is subject to senior leadership's commitment and championship of KM, and the level of support and funding which is allocated for Knowledge Management.

References

Doval, E. (2015). A framework for knowledge management process. *Geopolitics, History, and International Relations* 7(2), 207–16.

Emory University (2020). Knowledge Roles and Responsibilities. Service Management Competency Center. http://smcc.emory.edu/itsm_process/knowledge/knowledge _roles_and_responsibilities.html.

Nunn, R. (2013). The ten steps towards a culture of Knowledge Management. *Business Information Review* 30(3), 133–9.

Wiig, K. (2004). *People-Focused Knowledge Management*. Burlington, MA: Elsevier Butterworth–Heinemann.

3. Knowledge management: enterprise-wide strategies

Joanna Paliszkiewicz

Introduction

For organizations to remain competitive, they have to effectively manage their intellectual resources and capabilities. Organizations should apply the most appropriate knowledge management (KM) strategy that fits their culture (Liebowitz and Beckman, 1998; Awad and Ghaziri, 2004; Paliszkiewicz, 2007; Attia and Salama, 2018; Buenechea-Elberdin et al., 2018; Mothe et al., 2018). Knowledge is recognized as the driver of economic growth, leading to a new focus on the role of people, organizational culture, analytics, technology and continuous improvement in the enhancement of organizational performance (Liebowitz and Wilcox, 1997; Liebowitz, 2008; Paliszkiewicz et al., 2015; Koohang et al., 2017; Mardani et al., 2018). The essential raw material for all organizations is data, and this resource can be further refined into information and, ultimately, knowledge and wisdom, the source of all sustainable competitive advantage. A knowledge-based organization tries to apply existing knowledge effectively and to create new knowledge with the help of analytics (Paliszkiewicz, 2011).

This chapter's purpose is to present the concept of knowledge management strategies based on a literature review. The importance of choosing the right knowledge management strategy in the era of big data and analytics is emphasized, and new directions of research are indicated. In the first part of the chapter, the meaning of knowledge strategy is presented, followed by the types of knowledge strategy. Next, the main aspects of selecting and implementing the right knowledge management strategy are shown, with concluding comments.

Knowledge Management Strategies

Knowledge strategy refers to an organization's approach to aligning its knowledge resources and capabilities for enhancing organizational performance (Zack, 1999). The process has to be integrated with business strategies. Knowledge strategy is also described as the set of strategic choices that shape an organization's learning processes and subsequently determine its knowledge resources (Zack, 1999). It can be considered as the process of production, encryption and transmission of explicit knowledge into tacit knowledge. It also provides appropriate knowledge for the appropriate person and in the appropriate time and place (Halawi et al., 2006). According to Bolisani and Bratianu (2017), knowledge management strategy refers to the guidelines, goals, resources and long-term plans of knowledge management programs in an organization. An appropriate knowledge management strategy enables an organization to create, develop, transfer, access, codify and leverage knowledge promptly, positively influencing organizational performance. It enables employees to have the right information in the right format at the right time.

In organizations, knowledge often becomes embedded not only in documents or repositories but also in processes, practices and routines. Knowledge is broader, deeper and richer than data or information. Knowledge is a mixture of various elements; it is fluid as well as formally structured; it is intuitive and, therefore, hard to capture in words or understand completely in logical terms. It is defined as an individual's experiences, beliefs, values, culture and know-how (Davenport and Prusak, 1998).

Knowledge can be categorized into two types: explicit and tacit (Polanyi, 1966; Nonaka and Takeuchi, 1995). Explicit knowledge is described as any knowledge that can be codified, verbalized, transferred and articulated (Duffy, 2000). It can have written forms, such as reports, procedures, articles, books and manuals (Ooi, 2014). According to Cheng (2015), it is transmittable via formal, systematic language and removed from the original context of its creation or use. Tacit knowledge exists in people's minds, behaviors and perceptions, and is described as hidden and unwritten (Maravilhas and Martins, 2019). It evolves with experience, people's interactions, and requires skills and practices (Riggins and Rhee, 1999; Martensson, 2000). This type of knowledge is difficult to transfer (Johnson et al., 2019).

Organizations possess two types of knowledge: external and internal. External knowledge is related to awareness of regulations, competition and market trends. Internal knowledge includes an understanding of fundamental competencies, capabilities, know-how and lessons learned from past experiences (Frappaolo, 2000).

Alavi and Leidner (2001) note that knowledge may be viewed from five different perspectives:

1. State of mind (emphasizing knowing and understanding through experience and study);
2. Object (defining knowledge as a thing to be stored and manipulated);
3. Process (focusing on knowing and acting);
4. Condition (emphasizing access to knowledge);
5. Capability (viewing knowledge as a capability with the potential for influencing future action).

These different views of knowledge lead to different perspectives of knowledge management (Borghoff and Pareschi, 1998; Becerra-Fernandez and Sabherwal, 2001; Gold and Malhotra 2001; Schultze and Leidner, 2002):

- IT perspective, focusing on the use of various technologies to develop and store knowledge resources. As knowledge is viewed as an object, knowledge management should focus on ensuring that explicit knowledge is accessible across an organization;
- Socialization perspective, focusing on supporting the processes of sharing, creating and disseminating knowledge among people;
- Integrated perspective, focusing on both IT and socialization perspective. The right knowledge management strategy should be implemented to develop organizational capabilities and create intellectual capital and emphasize the use of knowledge management systems.

These approaches are related to three types of knowledge management strategies: codification, personalization and integration.

The Codification Strategy

The codification strategy is a "people-to-documents" approach that involves securing explicit knowledge in the form of databases for others to access and reuse (Hansen et al., 1999). According to the broader definition of Choi and Lee (2003), it is a system-oriented approach for managing knowledge by codifying, storing and formally sharing knowledge through implementing the information technology. It depends on the capabilities of organizations and employees to perform these processes (transferring, storing, sharing and using knowledge), and it involves investments in information technology (Liao, 2007).

Companies using a codification approach put more emphasis on reusing knowledge to provide standardized information (Hansen et al., 1999; Nightingale, 2000; Markus, 2001). The codification strategy stresses knowledge transfer through documented records, and it can be an excellent mechanism to store organizational memory (Boh, 2007). All authorized employees can retrieve the codified knowledge and share their expertise via electronic devices (Hansen et al., 1999). It can help with acquiring, reusing, saving, refining and creating knowledge. The codification strategy focuses on explicit knowledge (Davenport and Volpel, 2001; Greiner et al., 2007). It is useful for organizations whose business strategy requires reusing existing knowledge, i.e., manufacturing, consulting, business process outsourcing, and franchising (Greiner et al., 2007).

The Personalization Strategy

The personalization strategy is based on a "person-to-person" approach and delivers customized services (Hansen et al., 1999). It applies contacts and interactions between people in a social learning process. Knowledge can be obtained from experienced and skilled people (Swan et al., 2000). According to Smith (2001), this strategy involves face-to-face methods, where people transfer their tacit knowledge to others. It deals with communication among people (Kumar and Ganesh, 2011; Lopez-Nicolas and Merono-Cerdan, 2011). It is beneficial in human resource development in organizations. The emphasis is on acquiring and sharing tacit knowledge and interpersonal experience (Hansen et al., 1999). Employees have to interact extensively with their colleagues to obtain such implicit knowledge. Managers in companies that have adopted this strategy have to use task-force groups, emphasize organizational learning mechanisms, and encourage employee interaction through appraisal and motivational systems (Choi and Lee, 2003). Organizations following the personalization strategy focus on managing tacit knowledge (Davenport and Volpel, 2001; Greiner et al., 2007). In this approach, organizations have a modest investment in information technology. The role of information technology is to support communication and knowledge sharing (Hansen et al., 1999; Greiner et al., 2007). The transfer of knowledge is supported through formal (organized meetings and training) and informal (coffee-break conversations) mechanisms (Storey and Kahn, 2010). A personalization strategy is often practiced by organizations that prove highly customized solutions to a unique problem (Hansen et al., 1999).

The Integrated Strategy

In the literature, integrated knowledge management strategies are proposed (Desouza and Evaristo, 2004; Sarawanawong et al., 2009; Percin, 2010; Choe, 2011). For example, Percin (2010) propose a dynamic knowledge management strategy that integrates the conceptual scope of the system (codification) and human-oriented (personalization) strategies. The research shows that the best results are found in organizations concentrating on one of these strategies (codification or personalization) and treating the second as supplementary. Desouza and Evaristo (2004) describe a hybrid approach in organizations instead of relying on a single knowledge management strategy. In the work of Sarawanawong et al. (2009) for higher education, the personalization strategy plays a leading role while the codification strategy plays a supporting role. Choe (2011) presents an integrated approach, combining both personalization and codification strategies as a mixed knowledge management strategy. Hansen et al. (1999) insist that most organizations which have used knowledge effectively pursue one predominant (80%) strategy and use the second strategy (20%) to support the first. Personalization and codification strategies are not mutually exclusive, and they support each other in implementing the knowledge processes to organizations (Gammelgaard and Ritter, 2005; Venkitachalam and Busch, 2012). According to the research presented by Mathiassen and Pourkomeylian (2003), each organization has to find a balance for the two knowledge management strategies to be dynamically adjusted as the organization matures. Using the combination of knowledge management strategies improves organizational performance (Tseng, 2010).

Knowledge Management Strategy Implementation

A knowledge management strategy is needed for the organization to be prepared for the future. It can appear that what worked yesterday may or may not work for tomorrow. Knowledge management strategy should be linked to what the organization is attempting to achieve (Jasimuddin, 2008; Oluikpe, 2012). According to suggestions by Merlyn and Välikangas (1998), it is essential to specify the purpose of the knowledge management strategy, the benefits expected to be gained, and how it will influence employees' work. In creating and implementing an appropriate strategy, the fundamental role has leadership. Leaders direct and shape the organization by providing a sense of direction, vision and purpose for all members.

Good leaders can explain and clarify the organization's purpose and priorities, develop an appropriate knowledge sharing culture, create practices to facilitate sufficient work, promote cross-boundary learning, share knowledge, and encourage employees to achieve high performance levels (Debowski, 2006). Support from top management in implementing a knowledge management strategy is essential. Human resource practices can also impact employees' attitudes towards knowledge management activities and make them committed and loyal to the organization (Hislop, 2013). As Byrne (2001, p. 325) wrote: "without loyalty, knowledge is lost." Another important aspect is the communication process, which in knowledge management has a fundamental role (Nonaka and Konno, 1998; Paliszkiewicz, 2010). It is an important element in knowledge creation. Many scholars underline also the role of people and organizational culture and describe it as the bedrock to successful knowledge management (King, 2007; Desouza and Paquette, 2011; Paliszkiewicz, 2011; Hislop, 2013).

People are critical in the success or failure of implementing a knowledge management strategy (Hislop, 2013; Liebowitz, 2016; Koohang et al., 2018). Knowledge is related to the human mind and the sharing of knowledge requires the willingness to participate in this process. One of the most important aspects is to propose and plan the right motivation process, including appropriate incentives for people to share knowledge (Hansen et al., 1999; Cabrera and Cabrera, 2005; Paliszkiewicz, 2007; Liebowitz, 2012). Knowledge management strategy should fit the organizational culture (Rai, 2011; Liao et al., 2012). It can be achieved by modifying an organization's culture in ways that support desired attitudes to knowledge management activities. Thus, in order for an organization to be successful, attention must be paid not only to information technology but also, and even more importantly, to people and organizational culture.

Conclusion

The organization should choose the right strategy to manage relevant knowledge for the organization. It is related to ensuring that people have the appropriate knowledge, where they need it, and when they need it, presented in the proper form. In the literature, various scholars have presented different knowledge management strategies (e.g., simple procedure and pure expertise (Bohn, 1994); innovators, explorers, exploiters and loners (Bierly and Chakrabarti, 1996); explicit-oriented and tacit-oriented (Jordan and Jones, 1997); conservative and aggressive (Zack, 1999); cognitive and community (Swan et al., 2000);

systems-oriented and human-oriented (Choi and Lee, 2002); and relation strategy and substitution strategy (Ravasan et al., 2013)). In this chapter, the most popular and cited have been described (codification, personalization and integrated approaches). The codification strategy mainly concentrates on information technology, personalization on human interaction, and the integrated approach is a mix of these two strategies. All strategies aim to enhance organizational performance and foster creativity and innovation within the organization. If managers overemphasize a social perspective, new ideas may be lost due to a lack of strategy and mechanism to harness them. Conversely, if the organization focuses too much on technology, a technology-based KM strategy may be biased. A balanced use of both strategies is required for success. However, the implementation of knowledge management strategies is not easy. Life is changing, especially in today's environment, and the strategy has to be adjusted to the market and the situation. If managers would like to implement a knowledge management strategy successfully, they need to find the right balance between codification and personalization strategies.

Managers should meet the following conditions: implement the right technological tools, create an appropriate organizational culture, and appropriately motivate people to share their knowledge. A review of the literature has shown that research on knowledge management should be further developed. More studies are needed to find answers for the following questions:

- How can knowledge management strategies be formulated and aligned with business strategies?
- How can an organization properly manage and protect knowledge in the era of the Coronavirus?
- How can organizations encourage people to continue to share knowledge in a pandemic time (Liebowitz, 2020)?

Qualitative and quantitative methods should also be used for the study of improving business processes in a knowledge management context.

References

Alavi, M., Leidner, D. (2001). Review: knowledge management and knowledge management systems: conceptual foundations and research issues. *MIS Quarterly*, *25*(1), 107–36.

Attia, A., Salama, I. (2018). Knowledge management capability and supply chain management practices in the Saudi food industry. *Business Process Management Journal*, *24*, 459–77.

Awad, E. M., Ghaziri, H. M. (2004). *Knowledge Management*, Upper Saddle River, NJ: Pearson Education International.

Becerra-Fernandez, I., Sabherwal, R. (2001). Organizational knowledge management: a contingency perspective. *Journal of Management Information Systems*, *18*(1), 23–55.

Bierly, P., Chakrabarti, A. (1996). Generic knowledge strategies in the U.S. pharmaceutical industry. *Strategic Management Journal*, *17*(S2), 123–35.

Boh, W. F. (2007). Mechanisms for sharing knowledge in project-based organizations. *Information and Organization*, *17*, 27–58.

Bohn, R. E. (1994). Measuring and managing technological knowledge. *MIT Sloan Management Review*, *36*(1), 61–73.

Bolisani, E., Bratianu, C. (2017). Knowledge strategy planning: an integrated approach to manage uncertainty, turbulence, and dynamics. *Journal of Knowledge Management*, *21*(2), 233–53.

Borghoff, U. M., Pareschi, R. (1998). *Information Technology for Knowledge Management*, Berlin: Springer.

Buenechea-Elberdin, M., Sáenz, J., Kianto, A. (2018). Knowledge management strategies, intellectual capital, and innovation performance: a comparison between high- and low-tech firms. *Journal of Knowledge Management*, *22*(8), 1757–81.

Byrne, R. (2001). Employees: capital or commodity? *Career Development International*, *6*(6), 324–30.

Cabrera, E., Cabrera, A. (2005). Fostering knowledge sharing through people management practices. *International Journal of Human Resource Management*, *16*(5), 720–35.

Cheng, E. C. K. (2015). *Knowledge Management for School Education*, London: Springer.

Choe, J. M. (2011). The taxonomy of knowledge management strategies in manufacturing firms: use of target costing and IT infrastructure. *African Journal of Business Management*, *5*(15), 6597–607.

Choi, B., Lee, H. (2002). Knowledge management strategy and its link to knowledge creation process. *Expert Systems with Applications*, *23*(3), 173–87.

Choi, B. Lee, H. (2003). An empirical investigation of KM styles and their effect on corporate performance. *Information & Management*, *40*, 403–17.

Davenport, T. H., Prusak, L. (1998). *Working Knowledge: How Organizations Manage What They Know*. Boston, MA: Harvard Business School Press.

Davenport, T. H., Volpel, S. C. (2001). The rise of knowledge towards attention management. *Journal of Knowledge Management*, *5*(3), 212–22.

Debowski, S. (2006). *Knowledge Management*, Milton: John Wiley & Sons Australia, Ltd.

Desouza, K. C., Evaristo, J. R. (2004). Managing knowledge in distributed projects. *Communications of the ACM*, *47*(4), 87–91.

Desouza, K. C., Paquette, S. (eds.) (2011). *Knowledge Management: An Introduction.* New York: Neal-Schuman Publishers.

Duffy, J. (2000). Knowledge management: to be or not to be? *Information Management Journal*, 34(1), 64–7.

Frappaolo, C. (2000). *Ushering in the knowledge-based economy*, The Delphi Group Symposium.

Gammelgaard, J., Ritter, T. (2005). The knowledge retrieval matrix: codification and personification as separate strategies. *Journal of Knowledge Management*, 9(4), 133–43.

Gold, A. H., Malhotra, A. (2001). Knowledge management: and organizational capabilities perspective. *Journal of Management Information Systems*, 18(1), 185–214.

Greiner, M. E., Hmann, T. B., Krcmar, H. (2007). A strategy for knowledge management. *Journal of Knowledge Management*, 11(6), 3–15.

Halawi, L. A., McCarthy, R. V., Aronson, J. E. (2006). Knowledge management and the competitive strategy of the firm. *The Learning Organization*, 13(4), 384–97.

Hansen, M. T., Nohria, N., Tierney, T. (1999). What's your strategy for managing knowledge? *Harvard Business Review*, 77(2), 106–16.

Hislop, D. (2013). *Knowledge Management in Organisations: A Critical Introduction*, Oxford: Oxford University Press.

Jasimuddin, S. M. (2008). A holistic view of knowledge management strategy. *Journal of Knowledge Management*, 12(2), 57–66.

Johnson, T. L., Fletcher, S. R., Baker, W., Charles, R. L. (2019). How and why we need to capture tacit knowledge in manufacturing: case studies of visual inspection. *Applied Ergonomics*, 74(1), 1–9.

Jordan, J., Jones, P. (1997). Assessing your company's knowledge management style. *Long Range Planning*, 30(3), 392–8.

King, W. (2007). A research agenda for the relationships between culture and knowledge management. *Knowledge and Process Management*, 14(3), 226–36.

Koohang, A., Paliszkiewicz, J., Gołuchowski, J. (2017). The impact of leadership on trust, knowledge management, and organizational performance: a research model. *Industrial Management & Data Systems*, 117(3), 521–37.

Koohang, A., Paliszkiewicz, J., Gołuchowski, J. (2018). Trust, knowledge management, and organizational performance: predictors of success in leadership. In J. Liebowitz, J. Paliszkiewicz, J. Gołuchowski, (eds.), *Intuition, Trust, and Analytics* (pp. 83–105), Boca Raton, FL: CRC Press, Taylor & Francis Group, Auerbach Publications.

Kumar, J. A., Ganesh, L. S. (2011). Balancing knowledge strategy: codification and personalization during product development. *Journal of Knowledge Management*, 15(1), 118–35.

Liao, S. H., Chang, W. J., Hu, D. C., Yueh, Y. L. (2012). Relationships among organisational culture, knowledge acquisition, organisational learning, and organisational innovation in Taiwan's banking and insurance industries. *International Journal of Human Resource Management*, 23(1), 52–70.

Liao, Y. S. (2007). The effects of knowledge management strategy and organization structure on innovation. *International Journal of Management*, 24(1), 53–60.

Liebowitz, J. (ed.) (2008). *Making Cents out of Knowledge Management*, Lanham, MD: The Scarecrow Press.

Liebowitz, J. (ed.) (2012). *Knowledge Management Handbook: Collaboration and Social Networking*, 2nd edn., Boca Raton, FL: CRC Press, Taylor and Francis Group.

Liebowitz, J. (ed.) (2016). *Successes and Failures of Knowledge Management*, Amsterdam: Elsevier Academic Press/Morgan Kaufmann.

Liebowitz, J. (ed.) (2020). *The Business of Pandemics: The COVID-19 Story*, New York: Taylor & Francis.

Liebowitz, J., Beckman, T. (1998). *Knowledge Organizations: What Every Manager Should Know*. Boca Raton, FL: CRC Press, Taylor and Francis Group.

Liebowitz, J., Wilcox, L. C. (1997). *Knowledge Management and its Integrative Elements*, Boca Raton, FL: CRC Press, Taylor & Francis Group.

Lopez-Nicolas, C., Merono-Cerdan, A. L. (2011). Strategic knowledge management, innovation and performance. *International Journal of Information Management*, *31*(6), 502–9.

Maravilhas, S., Martins, J. (2019). Strategic knowledge management in a digital environment: tacit and explicit knowledge in Fab Labs. *Journal of Business Research*, *94*, 353–9.

Mardani, A., Nikoosokhan, S., Moradi, M., Doustar, M. (2018). The relationship between knowledge management and innovation performance. *The Journal of High Technology Management Research*, *29*(1), 12–26.

Markus, M. L. (2001). Toward a theory of knowledge reuse: types of knowledge reuse situations and factors in reuse success. *Journal of Management Information Systems*, *18*(1), 57–93.

Martensson, M. (2000). A critical review of knowledge management as a management tool. *Journal of Knowledge Management*, *4*(3), 204–16.

Mathiassen, L., Pourkomeylian, P. (2003). Managing knowledge in a software organization. *Journal of Knowledge Management*, *7*(2), 63–80.

Merlyn, P. R., Välikangas, L. (1998). From information technology to knowledge technology: taking the user into consideration. *Journal of Knowledge Management*, *2*(2), 28–35.

Mothe, C., Nguyen-Thi, U. T., Triguero, A. (2018). Innovative products and services with environmental benefits: design of search strategies for external knowledge and absorptive capacity. *Journal of Environmental Planning and Management*, *11*(61), 1934–54.

Nightingale, P. (2000). Economics of scale in experimentation: knowledge and technology in pharmaceutical R&D. *Industrial and Corporate Change*, *9*, 315–59.

Nonaka, I., Konno, N. (1998). The concept of "Ba": building a foundation for knowledge creation. *California Management Review*, *40*(3), 40–55.

Nonaka, I., Takeuchi, H. (1995). *The Knowledge-Creating Company: How Japanese Companies Create the Dynamics of Innovation*, Oxford: Oxford University Press.

Oluikpe, P. (2012). Developing a corporate knowledge management strategy. *Journal of Knowledge Management*, *16*(6), 862–78.

Ooi, K. B. (2014). TQM: a facilitator to enhance knowledge management? A structural analysis. *Expert Systems with Applications*, *41*, 5167–79.

Paliszkiewicz, J. (2007). Knowledge management: an integrative view and empirical examination. *Cybernetics and Systems*, *38*(8), 825–36.

Paliszkiewicz, J. (2010). The relationship between social perspective and knowledge management. *International Journal of Innovation and Learning*, *7*(4), 450–66.

Paliszkiewicz, J. (2011). The knowledge management processes in medium enterprises: an example of Polish enterprises. *International Journal of Innovation and Learning*, *4*(9), 435–50.

Paliszkiewicz, J., Gołuchowski, J., Koohang, A. (2015). Leadership, trust, and knowledge management in relation to organizational performance: developing an instrument. *Online Journal of Applied Knowledge Management*, *3*(2), 19–35.

Percin, S. (2010). Use of analytic network process in selecting knowledge management strategies. *Management Research Review, 33*(5), 452–71.

Polanyi, M. (1966). *The Tacit Dimension*, London: Routledge & Kegan Paul.

Rai, K. (2011). Knowledge management and organisational culture: a theoretical integrative framework. *Journal of Knowledge Management, 15*(2), 779–801.

Ravasan, A. Z., Naghizadeh, R., Naghizadeh, M. (2013). A new approach to knowledge management strategies: relation strategy and substitution strategy. *International Journal of Knowledge and Systems Science, 4*(3), 55–69.

Riggins, F. J., Rhee, H. (1999). Developing the learning network using extranets. *International Journal of Electronic Commerce, 4*(1), 65–83.

Sarawanawong, J., Tuamsuk, K., Vongpraset, C., Khiewyoo, J. (2009). Development of a strategic knowledge management model for Thai universities. In *Proceedings of the Asia-Pacific Conference on Library & Information Education & Practice, Japan*, pp. 288–98.

Schultze, F., Leidner, D. E. (2002). Knowledge management in IS research. *MIS Quarterly, 26*(3), 213–42.

Smith, E. A. (2001). The role of tacit and explicit knowledge in the workplace. *Journal of Knowledge Management, 5*(4), 311–21.

Storey, C., Kahn, K. B. (2010). The role of knowledge management strategies and task knowledge in stimulating service innovation. *Journal of Service Research, 13*(4), 397–410.

Swan, J., Newell, S., Robertson, M. (2000). Limits of IT-driven knowledge management initiatives for interactive innovation processes: towards a community-based approach. In Sprague R. H. (ed.), *The Proceedings of the Annual Hawaii International Conference on System Sciences, IEEE Computer Society, Washington, DC*, pp. 237–41.

Tseng, M. L. (2010). An assessment of cause and effect decision making model for firm environmental knowledge management capacities in uncertainty. *Environmental Monitoring and Assessment, 161*, 549–64.

Venkitachalam, K., Busch, P. (2012). Tacit knowledge: review and possible research directions. *Journal of Knowledge Management, 16*(2), 357–72.

Zack, M. H. (1999). Developing a knowledge strategy. *California Management Review, 41*(3), 125–45.

4. Knowledge management from a technology perspective

Vincent Ribiere, Cheng Gong and Kaiyu Yang

> Ask not only what it is that technology CAN do FOR you;
> ask also what it MAY do TO you![1]

Introduction

The three commonly accepted pillars of Knowledge Management (KM) are people, process, and technology. They work hand in hand and are equally important to make KM happen. But technology is often defined as the enabler of KM, meaning that it helps to support knowledge flows as well as the knowledge-enabled business processes. Without technology, KM would still exist, but its value and impact would be much more limited. Before getting into more detail about what kind of technologies enable KM and what new emerging technologies can bring to KM, it is important to offer a quick historical overview of the different knowledge management eras. As Dixon (2018) presents in Figure 4.1, KM has gone through three main eras.

The first era started in the mid-1990s (the early stage of KM), when a large number of software vendors saw an easy opportunity to sell their information system solutions under the new label of KM tools, without making fundamental changes to them. This situation created some confusion and disillusionment among the first adopters and portrayed a bad/false image of KM. Organizations became rapidly disappointed by KM/IT tool capabilities, and they realized that it was an over-simplistic IT understanding of knowledge.

---

[1]   A saying of Dr. Francesco Calabrese, who has inspired the authors of this chapter over the years, and to whom this chapter is dedicated.

The main focus of KM tools was then on leveraging explicit knowledge by capturing it, storing it in knowledge repositories (e.g., lessons learned, best practices) and redistributing it to those who might need it. This is what we will further describe later on as a codification approach, a document-centered approach to KM. Nevertheless, without advanced collaborative and supportive technologies, the KM movement could have never started and grown so fast.

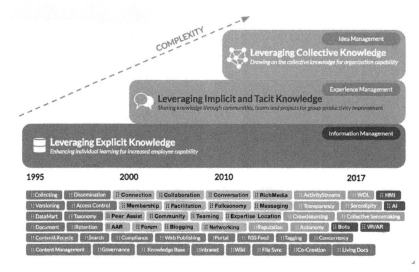

Figure 4.1   The three knowledge eras

Source: Dixon, 2018.

The second era of Knowledge Management started around the year 2000. Organizations realized the value of leveraging implicit and tacit knowledge, the types of knowledge that cannot or that can hardly be codified into documents since it is mainly based on know-how and experience. It is estimated (Mohajan, 2016) that 80% to 90% of organizational knowledge remains tacit, so when employees return home in the evening, the organization loses a large part of its knowledge! So what can be done to reduce the knowledge loss risks associated with this high percentage of uncodified but extremely useful knowledge? This might be the right opportunity for us to share our views on what knowledge is/is not. For us, IT can only manage information (tangible); on the other hand knowledge is intangible and it can be defined as the human capability to take effective action (Bennet & Bennet, 2008), so it can only exist in a human's brain. Consequently, IT cannot "manage" knowledge per se, but it can help to provide an environment where information relevant to us flows and generates knowledge in us (learning) and new ideas (creativity).

The second KM era was people-centric. Since tacit knowledge cannot be codified, it has to be transferred directly from people to people. The main focus in this period shifted to knowledge sharing/transfer activities, like Communities of Practice, tutoring/mentoring programs, knowledge cafés, storytelling, and so on. Technologies can help to support such knowledge exchanges (e.g., video conferencing, expertise locator), but they are less predominant than they used to be in the first KM era, despite the fact that they are still active in the second era. The emergence of social technologies (often referred to as corporate social media, social intranet, social tools, social software, social networks, enterprise 2.0, enterprise social networks, social collaboration, or social KM platforms), facilitated discussions and sharing/exchanging of contributions among employees, and also their interactions with customers and suppliers. They made KM systems more user-friendly and more integrated into daily work activities and smoothed the flow of knowledge.

We are currently positioned in the third era, labeled "leveraging collective knowledge"; new approaches to KM are directly influenced by the fast changes happening in society, in technologies, and in organizations, for instance, by digital transformations that will be further developed later on in this chapter. The focus of KM and KM technologies is no longer just on the internal issues of an organization; it goes outside its boundaries, expanding to support various inbound and outbound flows of knowledge. These knowledge flows are supportive of the innovation process (closed and open) as well as acting as the source of collective intelligence. Artificial Intelligence (AI) and deep learning systems have now reached a level of maturity that makes them applicable in almost every organizational process. A section of this chapter is later dedicated to the linkage between KM and AI (as well as other chapters presented in this book). It is important to mention that the two previous eras of KM are still active and benefit from each other and that new, emerging technologies are also improving the efficiency of past technologies that originally used to support each KM era.

BOX 4.1 FUTURE RESEARCH ISSUES, GAPS, CHALLENGES, OPPORTUNITIES AND TRENDS

- Will there be a fourth era of KM and, if so, what will it be like?
- Will a fourth KM era be a purely techno-centric era or a human-techno powered era?
- Are we entering a KM 3.0 (cognitive) area in an industry 4.0 context?

Categorizing KM Technologies

When it comes to categorizing KM technologies, there are different ways to classify them. The common way is to categorize them based on what KM sub-process(es) they support. If we take, for instance, the APQC Knowledge Flow Process Framework, we can define what technologies can support each of the seven steps of the cycle (APQC, 2018), that is, to create, identify, collect, review, share, access and use knowledge (Figure 4.2).

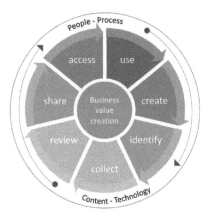

Figure 4.2   APQC Knowledge flow framework

Source: APQC, 2018.

Another way to organize KM technologies is through codification and personalization approaches (Hansen et al., 1999). Through the level they enable, we could also look at them on individual, team, organizational and intra-organizational levels. We could also organize them based on how they enable the popular four steps of the Nonaka and Takeuchi (1995) SECI model (socialization, externalization, combination, internalization). Other categorizations can be used, based on the type of data that the technology deals with (unstructured, semi-structured or structured), or based on where they fit in an IT/KM architecture (e.g., in the resources/repositories layer, in the information architecture layer, in the integration layer (i.e., navigation methods, communication tools, processes (business rules))), in the user interface layer (including visualization, personalization and customization), or in other transversal layers, like in the security layer, or metrics layer. We are certain that there might be other ways to categorize all these IT tools, based, for instance, on their maturity (i.e., Gartner hype cycles), the industry they serve, or any other view.

To present our categorizations, we will not get into particular vendor solutions, but we will use the family type of technologies, also allowing this chapter not to become obsolete rapidly since a lot of vendors' IT solutions emerge and disappear very rapidly! By reviewing the academic literature and various KM vendors lists (e.g., *KMWorld Buyers' Guide*), we have identified 41 technologies that can support KM. There are, certainly, other technologies that could fit into each category, but we believe we have covered the main ones. As mentioned earlier, we could categorize them using different approaches/views, but due to space limitations here we have decided to present two of them: technologies supporting the KM seven sub-processes (Table 4.1), and the same technologies organized in the way they mainly support a codification or a personalization approach (Table 4.2). Please note that these tables only include KM IT-related tools and do not include KM practices (e.g., tutoring, mentoring, peer assists, after action reviews, storytelling). Some technologies are used in multiple steps (e.g., online/virtual communities and networks).

Table 4.1   Technologies supporting the seven KM sub-processes

KM sub-process	Technologies
Create **The creation of new knowledge,** **including creativity/innovation**	Knowledge discovery systems Big data analytics Idea management systems Online/virtual communities & networks Crowdsourcing platforms
Identify **Identify what is known (and** **unknown), who knows what** **and critical knowledge**	Expertise locator Knowledge mapping/audits Big data analytics Online/virtual communities & networks Knowledge discovery systems Business intelligence Social network analysis
Collect **Capture, document, store and** **protect knowledge**	Natural language processing Image, forms, document capture Speech recognition Online/virtual communities & networks Content/document management system Data warehouse/data lakes Knowledge asset repositories (best practices, lessons learned, knowledge artifacts) Knowledge security

Table 4.1   Technologies supporting the seven KM sub-processes (continued)

KM sub-process	Technologies
Review **Evaluate, curate and regularly assess knowledge for its relevance and accuracy**	Social tagging & rating Wikis (peer editing) Online/virtual communities & networks Workflow systems
Share **Transfer, disseminate, communicate knowledge to others**	Collaboration platforms Online/virtual communities and networks Video/audio conferencing Instant messaging apps Content/document management systems Cloud computing Podcasting/videocasting/webinars Blogs & Wikis Enterprise social networking/social media Email
Access **Find/discover knowledge, using both push and pull techniques**	Semantic & cognitive search Cloud-based systems Knowledge visualization Virtual an augmented reality Taxonomy & metadata Natural language processing/chatbots Expertise location Mobile apps Predictive analytics AI & intelligent automation Cognitive computing Syndicated newsfeed
Use **Apply, learn, reuse, adapt/ adopt knowledge to make a decision, solve a problem etc.**	Cognitive computing Decision support systems Expert systems Learning management system/e-learning Virtual and augmented reality KM value/use measurement system (analytics)

The other categorization we used, which is more strategic, is the one articulated by Hansen et al. (1999) based on two KM complementary approaches/ strategies, the codification and the personalization approaches.

Codification tools and practices intend to collect, codify, and disseminate information and knowledge artifacts. One of the benefits of the codification approach is the reuse of knowledge. "The aim of codification is to put organizational knowledge into a form that makes it accessible to those who need it. It literally turns knowledge into a code (though not necessarily a computer code) to make it as organized, explicit, portable, and easy to understand as possible" (Davenport & Prusak, 1998, p. 68). Personalization tools and practices focus on developing networks for linking people so that tacit knowledge can be shared/transferred. This approach corresponds to the Nonaka and Takeuchi personalization phase of their popular SECI Model (Nonaka & Toyama, 2003). As can be seen in Table 4.2, technologies moderately support the personalization approach, due to its emphasis on tacit knowledge transfer.

Table 4.2   KM tools based on their support for codification and/or personalization approaches

Codification	Personalization
AI & intelligent automation	Collaboration platforms
Blogs & Wikis	Email
Business intelligence	Enterprise social networking/social media
Cloud computing	Instant messaging apps
Cloud-based systems	Online/virtual communities & networks
Cognitive computing	Podcasting/videocasting/webinars
Content/document management system	Video/audio conferencing
Data warehouse/data lakes	
Decision support systems	
Expert systems	
Image, forms, document capture	
KM value/use measurement system (analytics)	
Knowledge asset repositories (best practices, lessons learned, knowledge artifacts)	
Knowledge mapping /audits	
Knowledge security	
Knowledge visualization	
Learning management system/e-learning	
Natural language processing/chatbots	
Predictive analytics	
Semantic & cognitive search	

Table 4.2
(continued)   KM tools based on their support for codification and/or personalization approaches

Codification	Personalization
Social tagging & rating	
Speech recognition	
Syndicated newsfeed	
Taxonomy & metadata	
Virtual and augmented reality	
Wikis (peer editing)	
Workflow systems	
Codification and Personalization	
Crowdsourcing platform	
Expertise location	
Mobile apps	
Social network analysis	

Some technologies could be used for both codification and personalization approaches; for example, using a crowdsourcing platform will help to identify people with some novel ideas/knowledge/solutions that can solve problems. The platform will help make the connection and capture the knowledge, but it is very likely that the person who submitted the idea will also be contacted to further share their expertise/experience on the topic; as a result, tacit knowledge transfer will happen indirectly. The same ideas apply to the expertise locator system for the social network analysis (who knows what? followed by direct interaction with the subject matter expert). Mobile apps/KM can also be used for various KM-related purposes (see Box 4.2).

The codification and personalization approaches are expected to be complementary. Hansen et al. (1999) originally postulated that companies trying to excel at both risked failing at both. They referred to a 20–80 (80–20) split between codification and personalization emphasis. Their 20–80 proposition has been the source of many debates in the literature (e.g., Venkitachalam & Willmott, 2017), and we also believe, based on our experience and research, that this ratio is too extreme and that a balanced approach is more suitable (see Ribiere & Arntzen, 2010).

It is interesting to note that the Gartner group, until 2003, used to publish a knowledge management hype cycle (Gartner, 2003) with all its associated technologies, as it does for many other IT-related disciplines, but they decided to remove it from all hype cycles in 2007, after it was first integrated with other hype cycles (high performance workplace, collaboration and communication, and content management), for the following reason: "We believe that the KM concept has matured sufficiently and gained enough enterprise penetration that it has moved well into the Plateau of Productivity and therefore of the Hype Cycles. Going off the Hype Cycle is by no means an indication that KM is no longer important or useful; on the contrary, achieving maturity makes the potential benefits of effective KM even greater" (Gartner, 2007). They also acknowledged that "KM is something you do, not something you buy." Nevertheless, by looking at the current hype cycles, we can still find many KM technologies mentioned in more than 20 of them (e.g., digital workplace, artificial intelligence, emerging technologies).

The American Productivity & Quality Center (APQC) has released what they believe to be the eight main KM emerging technologies for 2020. They are based on in-depth interviews with more than 20 knowledge management practitioners and thought leaders (APQC, 2019):

- **Autotagging and autoclassification.** Tools that automatically generate items relevant metadata tags for content based on information about the content's source and/or analysis of the content itself through natural language processing (NLP).
- **Chatbots**. Software application that acts as a virtual agent and conversationally responds to human enquiries.
- **Cognitive computing and Artificial Intelligence (AI).** Technology that uses data mining and machine learning to simulate human thought processes.
- **Cognitive search.** Integrates information about a user's current and past behavior across multiple applications and systems to deliver customized, highly relevant search results.
- **Integrated digital productivity and collaboration platforms.** Suite of interconnected applications—including email, chat, document management, database management, word processing, spreadsheets, and presentation programs—that employees use for everyday work.
- **Natural language processing.** Machine learning software that enables computers to understand human language and detect patterns therein.
- **Smart recommendation systems.** Integrates information about users and their past behavior to filter items and predict which will be most relevant or appealing to a particular user.
- **Virtual and augmented reality.** Technology that superimposes computer-generated visual and other sensory elements onto the user's environment.

As we can observe, most of these emerging technologies are enabled by Artificial Intelligence and are targeted toward finding relevant information, improving customer experience (self-service technologies), and extending human capabilities (cognitive computing). For this reason, we have decided to dedicate the next section of this chapter to the integration of KM and AI.

BOX 4.2 FUTURE RESEARCH ISSUES, GAPS, CHALLENGES, OPPORTUNITIES AND TRENDS

- As we see less and less publications about KM systems architecture, are KM systems architecture still needed? Are KM systems themselves still needed, or should KM functionality be integrated into other systems/ platforms?
- How can (emerging) technologies better enable some of the less supported knowledge flow steps like tacit knowledge capture, knowledge maintenance, knowledge audits, e-learning, lessons learned management, knowledge embedding, KM metrics, and serendipity management for innovation?
- How can technologies be developed that bridge the gap/integrate codification and personalization approaches (knowledge collaboration/ collaborative KM)?

Artificial Intelligence (AI) and Knowledge Management (KM)

One of the early oversimplified definitions of Knowledge Management was to be able to provide the right information to the right person at the right time and in the right format so they could make the right decision. While this definition is very limited/incomplete and could also be used as an information management definition (since KM should also provide insight, guidance, experience and know-how), it has been a continuous challenge for organizations to be able to deliver such service while the amount of information available is exponentially growing in various locations and formats. AI is not a new technology, since computer scientists have been working on trying to develop machines that think like humans since the late 1950s. However, its integration in various types of common applications has slowly grown and matured, until around 2010, when its activity started to outperform other computer science activities (Shoham et al., 2018) and when the combination of technologies, like cloud technology and big data analytics, became available. AI allows machines to make more intelligent responses and, associated with machine learning tools, helps them to learn and adjust, and not only follow pre-defined algorithms created by humans. Until recently, AI projects were conducted separately from KM projects. We are now seeing a strong convergence among these two families of technologies supporting the digital workplace. One example of such integration is the Cortex project by Microsoft presented in Box 4.3.

BOX 4.3 OVERVIEW OF THE PROJECT CORTEX BY MICROSOFT

Based on preexisting intelligence like Microsoft Graph, Teams, and SharePoint, etc., Project Cortex is a new service in Microsoft 365 devised with a specific aim to connect people to knowledge and knowledge to people in an organization and facilitate knowledge sharing across an organization.

Going beyond searching for information throughout the entire Office 365 suite, Cortex creates a knowledge network through building connections among people, contents and topics (Debroy, 2020). It automatically creates topic pages and knowledge centers based on content. The AI-powered product ingests both structured and unstructured content, including all of the Office documents, email, chat logs and transcripts from meeting recordings that an organization generates (Lardinois, 2019), and organizes them into topics like projects, products, processes and customers (Hanley, 2019), which can be easily accessed by employees.

The "just-in-time" pop-up topic cards (Middleton, 2020) that can appear in various daily-used Microsoft products like the Office apps, Outlook and Teams surface the right kind of information and offer users a quick overview of what is happening by providing relevant information (Mechanics, 2019). Users can then further retrieve knowledge from topic pages that comprise connected parts, including a description of the topic, people who are referenced, and resources (relevant documents) involved and present a visual view that helps users to understand the context of the topic across the organization (Mechanics, 2019). In this way, Topic pages assist in locating expertise and leveraging existing work and prior experiences in the organization. And the knowledge center that serves as an organizational knowledge database helps users to manage projects, campaigns and initiatives inside an organization, based on topics. Given the knowledge baseline built by AI, what project owners/managers need to do is refine the information and apply it to how to get work done (Mechanics, 2019).

Topics can be enhanced through being edited by subject-matter experts incorporating their knowledge and additional resources, and new topics can be created with Wiki-like simplicity. Alongside ongoing people-centric curation, AI enables the holistic topic-based knowledge network to stay updated by learning from human curation how best to process the content it handles (Middleton, 2020).

With AI doing all the heavy lifting—mining all content and extracting, analyzing and organizing information behind the scenes, and delivering collective knowledge and experience to every engaging employee in the organization—Project Cortex helps organizations to know what they know and may create a possible way for individual employees to acquire tacit knowledge by constructing a common frame of reference just as Communities of Practice (CoP) does.

Project Cortex can be deemed an innovative step in knowledge management in the sense that it incorporates AI learning with human curation. And it allows us to catch a glimpse into the future of knowledge management software.

We now summarize how AI will mainly benefit KM.

Improved Search and Findability

As previously mentioned, due to a large amount of information currently available in (and outside) an organization, stored in various systems/departments (often siloed) and spread through a multitude of apps that employees are now using, it is difficult for the traditional search engine to provide concise and relevant results. AI can help to search and make linkages through this plethora of data/information and provide smarter and more predictive search capabilities and suggest other related/relevant resources (e.g., documents, experts, Communities of Practice (CoPs)).

Improved Expertise Location

Since the early days of KM, expertise location (quickly identifying who knows what) has been a good way to find and transfer experiential knowledge. Original expertise locator systems used to ask employees to fill in a profile that was rarely updated later on, and that was usually incomplete. With the use of AI, dynamic employee profiles can be generated based on the document they create/access, and on their emails/virtual discussions, etc.

Assisting Digitally Enabled Communities

CoPs often use a community space, allowing them to collaborate and to store their community-developed knowledge (i.e., tools, manuals, documents). The collaboration tools have evolved over the years, from conversation to communication, to coordination, to cooperation, to collaboration, and we now even talk about co-evolution. Most of the collaboration tools now embed some AI components allowing users to be more effective, which could be exceedingly helpful under such a situation as the COVID-19 pandemic crisis experienced in 2020 and beyond, when some employees were suddenly forced to work from home. Without such collaborative and knowledge sharing platforms, it would have been difficult for individuals and teams to remain connected and productive.

Enabling a (Remote) Digital Workplace

AI-enabled workspace tools help knowledge workers perform better, faster, and be more innovative. They include collaborative work management, content collaboration, workstream collaboration and meeting solutions. They are helping workers become digitally dexterous within the context of the employee experience. The Gartner hype cycle for digital workspace presents some of the emerging technologies in this field (Gartner, 2019).

Providing Real-Time Human-Like Answers to Questions/Queries from Customers

AI chatbots associated with natural language processing tools allow real-time answers to customers'/employees' questions/queries, like a human customer service representative will do. AI chatbots are able to learn and adapt to individual requirements/preferences since they often have the capability to analyze sentiments and to understand behavioral patterns.

Knowledge Visualization

AI-enabled visualization tools help to create smarter and more accessible ways of presenting and graphically displaying datasets, information and knowledge links on virtually any topics to users across the enterprise. Based on the number of tutorial videos available on platforms like YouTube and learning platforms like MOOCs, it is evident that our society prefers to watch short videos rather than read manuals! Unfortunately, this preference that we have in visuals is being implemented rather slowly as part of KM solutions. Nevertheless, some dedicated tools like maps, charts, and cloud and graph tools already exist, and they facilitate, through the display of visual elements, the identification of trends, patterns and ideas embedded in data. It is sometimes referred to as visual analytics. An interesting website that presents a classification of visualization tools is the "Periodic Table of Visualization Tools" (Visual Literary, 2020). Other chapters in this book present data visualization concepts in more detail.

Improved User Interface/Experience

Intelligent user interfaces better understand users' needs and personalize or guide the interaction. The interface uses simulated cognitive functions to facilitate the interaction between humans and machines. An example of an AI user interface is Amazon's Alexa.

Supporting Knowledge-Based Innovation

If we agree that any new knowledge is the re-combination of previously existing knowledge, AI can help to look for potentially meaningful relationships between existing knowledge. For example, a tool like Invention Machine Goldfire helps engineers and scientists to dig into patent databases and other documents to find potential existing solutions to problems and to validate their ideas.

Providing Cognitive Insights

KM and AI can predict and profile customer behaviors and preferences, and accordingly adjust ads and offers. They can do the same for employees by predicting their knowledge needs and by presenting them with some relevant knowledge sources.

Increased Process Automation

Due to their ability to learn and improve, KM and AI technologies can more efficiently and smartly automate digital and physical tasks using robotic process automation technologies.

Augmented Employee Knowledge Productivity

By eliminating repetitive tasks and data-heavy activities, KM and AI tools free knowledge workers, allowing them to use their time to solve more complex tasks, to have the time for quiet thinking, to reflect, and to innovate, all high-value cognitive activities that knowledge workers currently struggle to find time to do properly (Forbes Insights, 2019; Forrester Consulting, 2019).

As we have seen, the combination of KM and AI technologies is very powerful and applies to various areas, providing a wide range of benefits at the individual, team/CoP and organizational levels. These tools are just in their infancy and we can already feel they are making a positive difference. The integration of KM and AI is happening in a broader context of digital transformation, which we will now further describe.

BOX 4.4   FUTURE RESEARCH ISSUES, GAPS, CHALLENGES, OPPORTUNITIES AND TRENDS

- How can AI and KM projects become more integrated (since they are unfortunately often run in parallel)?
- Who should be in charge of the integration of KM and AI? The KM teams or the AI/IT/knowledge engineer teams?
- AI (+ machine learning) can learn from its mistakes; it will soon also be able to learn from the real world through the Internet of Things (IoT), smart cities, etc. and it can also demonstrate some level of creativity, so does it potentially have any cognitive limits?
- What could be the potential problems brought about by machine learning? A new perspective is needed to view knowledge workers' job responsibilities and job routines.

New Opportunities and Challenges for Embedding Knowledge Management (KM) in Digital Transformation (DT)

As we just have seen, AI and digital technologies, in general, do not eliminate the need/input of human knowledge and intelligence; in contrast, human insight and experience remain in high demand. Technologies open up new opportunities for KM to identify context-sensitive and situation-dependent knowledge (Bennet et al., 2015) and patterns within the chaos, and offer support in innovation (i.e., knowledge creation), collaborative work (i.e., knowledge transfer), and other activities within the knowledge process value chain in our fast-changing environment/a VUCA (volatility, uncertainty, complexity, and ambiguity) world.

Defining Digital Transformation

As there was no consensus concerning a KM definition until the KM ISO 30401 standard was published in November 2018, similarly, there still exists some confusion of understanding around the concepts of digital transformation (DT), digitalization and digitization. These three terms are often used interchangeably in both academic and practitioner communities. Digitization reduces paper clutter and improves efficiency by making it easier to store, search and find information, whereas digitalization involves using digital technologies to automate processes for better outcomes and to optimize value (NCMM, 2020). A unified definition of DT has been developed by Gong and Ribiere (ms.) to differentiate the concept from other related terms: "A fundamental change process, enabled by the innovative use of digital technologies accompanied by the strategic leverage of key resources and capabilities, aiming to radically improve an entity [e.g., an organization, a business network, an industry, or society] and redefine its value proposition for its stakeholders."

The Role of KM in Times of Digital Transformation

As far as the impact of DT on KM is concerned, studies cover, on the one hand, the whole spectrum of scenarios of the widespread use of digital technologies (Liebowitz, 2020), e.g., ABCDMR technologies in the KM domain,[2] and, on the other hand, significant changes to KM programs brought about by DT across various entities.

According to a 2020 APQC survey on 294 KM professionals' response to people, process and technology changes, 54% said broad DT across the business is having a significant impact on their KM programs, and 97% of respondents are confident that technology will play a role in helping KM respond to change and meet evolving needs. Today's KM programs are dealing with forces beyond their control—transformative new technologies, significant changes to business leadership and strategy, dramatic market swings and disruption, mergers and acquisitions, reorganizations, and demographic turnover in the workforce (APQC, 2020).

---

[2]   A = artificial intelligence, autoclassification; B = blockchain; C = cloud platforms for content management and collaboration, cognitive search, content recommendation algorithms, cybersecurity; D = data analytics; M = mobile apps; R = robotic process automation.

Two Levels of KM and Knowledge Process Value Aligning with Digital Technologies

At the core of KM is empowering people to make better decisions. Therefore, the innovative use of digital technologies and strategic leverage of critical knowledge and expertise of human resources to create new value for stakeholders in the emerging knowledge ecosystem of work and organization can bolster confidence in embracing digital change and further the impact of DT. Considering personal knowledge management (PKM) for all organization members as a starting point to improve the daily work performance, and change the knowledge culture of the organization as a whole, can function as a basis for successful organizational knowledge management (OKM). With an expanding scope of KM programs, digital technologies can assist knowledge workers on personal and organizational levels in acquiring, categorizing and classifying, storing, and sharing their knowledge within their communities of practice (CoP) and the knowledge process value chain (KPVC) to solve standardized and non-standardized problems. Furthermore, knowledge services are now accessible anywhere at any time through mobile KM (see Box 4.5).

BOX 4.5   MOBILE KNOWLEDGE MANAGEMENT

Mobile KM

Mobile KM is a mobility solution to generate affordance along different dimensions (spatial, contextual, temporal and social) for supporting and facilitating KM. The practice of making KM in a mobile environment and its cross-boundary characteristic make the knowledge process and social learning more accessible than ever in the current era of the Internet and smartphones, where a growing number of people get internet access from a smartphone rather than from a laptop browser. Productivity drain and information siloes are just some of the results of poor KM. Incorporating Mobile KM into business improves real-time collaboration and efficiency, employee onboarding, and customer support for knowledge capturing, storing and sharing that currently resides in people and apps. It enables organizational information and experience to be accessed remotely on employee's terms. Mobile KM through a mobile application that boasts features as attractive as corporate social media applications, which provide a clear measure of work progress, facilitate the integration of knowledge across departments, unite various departments (Marufi, 2019), or apps that engage remote collaborators (i.e., customers, experts, etc.), will get people to voluntarily sign up, enter and maintain their personal information, expand their network continually, and more importantly, link their key knowledge initiatives, such as sharing, innovating, reusing, collaborating and learning, to the app (Garfield, 2019).

Drawing on the resource-based view, the capability-based view of the organization, and more generally, the knowledge-based view, which considers knowledge as drivers for developing an organizational strategy, the strategies of personalizing organizational knowledge (POK) and "organizationalizing" personal knowledge (OPK) can work as the effective linkage between PKM and OKM to take full advantage of the knowledge resources of competitiveness to optimize workflow and work processes in organizations and invariably leads to improvement, which equates with an increase in value generated for organizational stakeholders. This also resonates with the APQC's KPVC that includes the identification, collecting, reviewing, sharing, accessing, utilization and creation of knowledge resources (see Figure 4.2). The use of digital technologies has changed the way KPVC actors communicate and operate, as well as the nature and forms of knowledge assets and processes of managing strategic knowledge resources and defining core competencies and dynamic capabilities of organizations.

New Opportunities and Challenges in Integrating Digital Technologies in KM

New technologies are both a disruptor and a tool to digitalize KM and to respond to change. Many digital technologies discussed in this chapter disrupt an established trajectory of performance improvement and redefine value propositions and value creation strategies to stakeholders in the digital workplace and in their market. However, KM programs have widely implemented digitalization projects to automate routine knowledge processes and analysis, to enable virtual collaboration and large-scale knowledge transfer, and to enable content management and knowledge creation. Machines have the cognitive and computational power to perform both repetitive and highly complex "knowledge" work in some industries, and they will shortly be aggressively penetrating the job market. Then, what will the role of KM, KM managers, and knowledge workers be in organizations and societies where machines or humanoids can replace humans in knowledge-related tasks? Nonetheless, such a situation is just like what the word "crisis" in Chinese describes, which consists of two characters, literally meaning "risk and opportunity." Coherent with the notion of DT, the value of automation and AI lies not in the ability to replace human labor with machines, but in augmenting the workforce and enabling human work to be reframed in terms of problem-solving and the ability to create new knowledge (Deloitte, 2019).

Note that even though digital technologies have made abundant explicit knowledge available to advance decision-making and action-taking, there is a remaining gap in capturing knowledge workers' tacit knowledge. The role of tacit knowledge must be further recognized, and its value to the organization better understood and appreciated. Challenges remain, posed by unclear knowledge mapping for prioritizing critical knowledge and managing change, and massive upskilling to work alongside and collaborate with machines. Organizations need workforces both qualified in their knowledge domain and equipped with digital skills to ensure smooth and successful DT implementation, which results in further implications for HR and its capabilities and competencies. More future research effort is needed in these fields.

With increasing reliance on digitalized knowledge, organizations are faced with the risk of knowledge leakages that will put their intellectual assets/advantage in jeopardy. Consequently, knowledge security should also be seriously considered to mitigate such risks (see Box 4.6).

BOX 4.6 KNOWLEDGE MANAGEMENT SECURITY

Research on knowledge management security can be traced back to the early years of KM when it was claimed that KM security was about analyzing risk and protecting knowledge assets appropriately, and that KM security was an important KM critical success factor (Jennex & Zyngier, 2007).

It is logical that KM incorporates security, considering the fact that knowledge is the greatest asset of an organization. Protection of knowledge is of critical significance in KM security areas with involvement in maintaining knowledge integrity, confidentiality and availability (Jennex & Zyngier, 2007), and it plays a critical part in sustaining an organization's competitive advantage (Manhart & Thalmann, 2015). With the belief that any knowledge protection strategy should always be linked to an organization's information security strategy (Manhart & Thalmann, 2015) come several questions: (1) How can the value of every single piece of information be identified? (2) How can they be categorized into various sensitivity levels to ensure proper security strategies are in place and technologies are applied? (3) How can authorization and access control be decided? (4) And is there any room for technology to come into play to get these processes done? Things can also go to another extreme when the ease of purchase of some piece of technology creates an attraction to knowledge managers, making them neglect possible threats and risks of bringing the new technology into existing systems or networks.

Witnessing the interconnectedness in the digital working environment, including intertwined networks, complicated systems, various (mobile) devices/platforms working in a combined effort, and information flowing in and out through multiple formal and informal channels/apps, knowledge managers could probably find that the practice that used to work ideally ceases to function. Traditional information security technological solutions can be used like encryption, and new technologies are also emerging like decentralized blockchain data storage. From a KM perspective, the challenges go beyond having technologies in place to protect stored knowledge and getting some technicians to ensure the maintenance of some technology.

Things may get even more complicated when looking at a knowledge management system as a whole. Besides protecting the basic technical system components, knowledge managers are supposed to take security awareness education and management support and direction into account, focus on organizational processes and individuals involved in each process, and assess the overall risk in terms of KM security. In this context, a KM security plan needs to be generated based on KM governance/management support and KM strategy/process, and the key enabler of this process is the incorporation of risk management into KM governance/management support (Jennex & Zyngier, 2007).

Finally, from the perspective of technology development, innovations in technology, particularly those that are designed to ensure security, should be driven by market-pull. It is not difficult to predict the failure of a technology that fails to meet the market demand. But here comes another paradox— how can we expect an organization that hopes to prevent network attack to share information on its vulnerabilities?

Regardless of time and space, DT provides enormous opportunities and challenges for organizations to synergize with KM activities by leveraging internal strategic knowledge into new (intelligent) activities/value propositions, and to connect entities holistically with external knowledge ecosystems. As a result, organizations can capitalize on their "organizational intelligence" to maintain their competitive edge (Liebowitz, 1999).

BOX 4.7   FUTURE RESEARCH ISSUES, GAPS, CHALLENGES, OPPORTUNITIES AND TRENDS

- How can KM respond to fundamental changes and meet evolving needs in the context of DT?
- How can digital technologies assist knowledge workers in transferring tacit knowledge effectively on a larger scale?
- How can KM bring the process of DT to different levels?
- How can we further interpret DT following a knowledge-based view?
- What kind of performance metrics can be used for assessing the strategic impact of KM on DT?
- How can KM security and KM sharing/availability be balanced properly to support (open) innovation while protecting an organization's intellectual capital?
- How does digital risk protection integrate with KM security?

Conclusion

Through this chapter, we have tried to provide a general overview and understanding of what roles technology is playing in Knowledge Management, particularly in a digital transformation context. It is interesting to note that not all KM subprocesses are equally supported by KM technologies; for instance, if we look at the connection between KM and e-learning systems, which should be naturally/directly fed by the knowledge and experience gained and shared by employees, we can identify some serious gaps (Liebowitz & Frank, 2016). As we have presented in this chapter, AI and emerging technologies will continue to empower knowledge workers as well as KM tools and KM practices. We cannot claim that they are revolutionizing the field of KM, but they are, for sure, helping to make KM more powerful, simpler, and embedded/transparent in the daily working routines of knowledge workers/communities in their digital workspaces.

The challenge of knowledge security remains important to protect organizations' intellectual capital and should be considered seriously. Human–machine interactions will remain, but they will look more like an exchange/a conversation rather than keyword queries. Cognitive computing will help to create some intelligent virtual assistants capable of answering directly any question one might have, as well as providing one with recommendations and advice. In the near future, we may not need to have access to a book chapter presenting a topic like this one; we might just need to ask Amazon's Alexa to tell us all that is known about KM technologies, taking into consideration what we already know and what is of particular interest to us. Academics like us may, perhaps, be missed.

References

APQC (2018). *APQC Knowledge Flow Process Framework.* Retrieved from https://www.apqc.org/resource-library/resource-listing/apqcs-knowledge-flow-process-framework.

APQC (2019). *Guide to Emerging Technologies for Knowledge Management.* Retrieved from https://www.apqc.org/resource-library/resource-listing/guide-emerging-technologies-knowledge-management.

APQC (2020). *Innovation in the Face of Disruption: 2020 KM Trends Survey Report.* Retrieved from https://www.apqc.org/resource-library/resource-listing/innovation-face-disruption-2020-km-trends-survey-report.

Bennet, A., Bennet, D. & Avedisian, J. J. F. (2015). *The Course of Knowledge.* Frost, WV: MQI Press.

Bennet, D. & Bennet, A. (2008). The depth of knowledge: surface, shallow or deep? *VINE: The Journal of Information and Knowledge Management Systems, 38*(7), 405–20.

Davenport, T. & Prusak, L. (1998). *Working Knowledge: How Organizations Manage What They Know.* Boston, MA: Harvard Business School Press.

Debroy, S. (2020). Microsoft's Project Cortex at a glance, January 20. Retrieved from https://www.kmworld.com/Articles/Editorial/ViewPoints/Microsofts-Project-Cortex-at-a-glance-136021.aspx.

Deloitte (2019). Leading the social enterprise: reinvent with a human focus. Retrieved from https://www2.deloitte.com/content/dam/insights/us/articles/5136_HC-Trends-2019/DI_HC-Trends-2019.pdf.

Dixon, N. M. (2018). The three eras of knowledge management. In J. P. Girard & J. L. Girard (eds.), *Knowledge Management Matters: Words of Wisdom from Leading Practitioners* (pp. 21–47). Macon, GA: Sagology.

Forbes Insights (2019). Everyday AI: harnessing artificial intelligence to empower the knowledge worker. Retrieved from https://www.forbes.com/forbes-insights/our-work/everyday-ai/.

Forrester Consulting (2019). Extending the Value of AI to Knowledge Workers. Retrieved from https://info.microsoft.com/rs/157-GQE-382/images/EN-CNTNT-AnalystReport-ForresterExtendingtheValueofAItoKnowledgeWorkers.pdf.

Garfield, S. (2019). Find a killer KM app. Retrieved from https://lucidea.com/blog/find-a-killer-km-app/.

Gartner (2003). *Hype Cycle for Knowledge Management* (R-20-0010). Retrieved from https://www.bus.umich.edu/KresgePublic/Journals/Gartner/research/115400/115434/115434.html.

Gartner (2007). *Why Knowledge Management Is No Longer on the Gartner Hype Cycles*. Retrieved from https://www.gartner.com/en/documents/517706/why-knowledge -management-is-no-longer-on-the-gartner-hype.

Gartner (2019). *Hype Cycle for the Digital Workplace*. Retrieved from https://www .gartner.com/en/documents/3953515/hype-cycle-for-the-digital-workplace-2019.

Gong, C. & Ribiere, V. (ms.). Developing a unified definition of digital transformation.

Hanley, S. (2019). Introducing Project Cortex: the future of enterprise knowledge gets a big boost at Ignite, November 4. Retrieved from https://www.computerworld.com/ article/3451364/introducing-project-cortex-the-future-of-enterprise-knowledge -gets-a-big-boost-at-ignite-2019.html.

Hansen, M. T., Nohria, N. & Tierney, T. (1999). What's your strategy for managing knowledge? *Harvard Business Review*, *77*(2), 106–16.

Jennex, M. E. & Zyngier, S. (2007). Security as a contributor to knowledge management success. *Information Systems Frontiers*, *9*(5), 493–504.

Lardinois, F. (2019). Microsoft launches Project Cortex, a knowledge network for your company, November 4. Retrieved from https://techcrunch.com/2019/11/04/ microsoft-launches-project-cortex-a-knowledge-network-for-your-company/.

Liebowitz, J. (1999). *Building Organizational Intelligence: A Knowledge Management Primer*. Boca Raton, FL: CRC Press.

Liebowitz, J. (2020), The ABCDEs for digital transformation, but don't forget the FGHIJs. *INFORMS Analytics*, May/June. Retrieved from https://pubsonline.informs .org/do/10.1287/LYTX.2020.04.02/full/.

Liebowitz, J. & Frank, M. (2016). *Knowledge Management and e-Learning*. Boca Raton, FL: CRC Press.

Manhart, M. & Thalmann, S. (2015). Protecting organizational knowledge: a structured literature review. *Journal of Knowledge Management*. doi:10.1108/JKM-05-2014 -0198.

Marufi, M. (2019). Testing the strength of knowledge management apps in the era of disruption. Retrieved from https://www.thejakartapost.com/life/2019/12/12/testing -the-strength-of-knowledge-management-apps-in-the-era-of-disruption.html.

Mechanics, M. [producer] (2019). Project Cortex deep dive | Intelligent knowledge management built on SharePoint (Microsoft Ignite) [video], November 12. Retrieved from https://www.youtube.com/watch?v=sWAaq2R6TtY.

Middleton, B. (2020). What is Project Cortex?, February 26. Retrieved from https:// www.avepoint.com/blog/office-365/project-cortex-explained/.

Mohajan, H. (2016). Sharing of tacit knowledge in organizations: a review. *American Journal of Computer Science and Engineering*, *3*, 6–19.

NCMM (2020). Digital transformation creates middle market growth and opportunity. Retrieved from https://www.middlemarketcenter.org/research-reports/case -for-digital-transformation.

Nonaka, I. & Takeuchi, H. (1995). *The Knowledge Creating Company*: Oxford University Press.

Nonaka, I., & Toyama, R. (2003). The knowledge-creation theory revisited: knowledge creation a synthesizing process. *Knowledge Management Research and Practice*, *1*(1), 2–10.

Ribiere, V. & Arntzen, A. (2010). Knowledge management technologies. In A. Green, M. Stankosky & L. Vandergriff (eds.), *In Search of Knowledge Management: Pursuing Primary Principles* (pp. 221–44). Bingley: Emerald.

Shoham, Y., Perrault, R., Brynjolfsson, E., Clark, J., Manyika, J., Niebles, J. C., ... and Bauer, Z. (2018). *The AI Index 2018 Annual Report*. Retrieved from http://cdn .aiindex.org/2018/AI%20Index%202018%20Annual%20Report.pdf.

Venkitachalam, K. & Willmott, H. (2017). Strategic knowledge management—insights and pitfalls. *International Journal of Information Management*, *37*(4), 313–16.

Visual Literary (2020). A periodic table of visualization methods. Retrieved from https://www.visual-literacy.org/periodic_table/periodic_table.html.

5. Knowledge management and artificial intelligence analytics: a bibliometric study of research trends

Francisco J. Cantu-Ortiz

1.   Introduction

With the advent and success of machine and deep learning methods and the capacity to store and mine huge amounts of data in the order of terabytes and beyond, along with the advancement of cloud computing, the Internet of Things, web semantics, natural language processing and other information and artificial intelligence (AI) technologies, the swell of data in human activity has evidenced an exponential behavior. This phenomenon has offered up and opened the door to new challenges in the learning of knowledge from large repositories and data warehouses which have brought great opportunities for the testing and application of powerful AI analytics and learning algorithms (Kaput, 2019).

A vast amount of knowledge learned from digging into large datasets found in both databases and the worldwide web is being produced on a regular basis, and is waiting for someone to apply it in meaningful ways to business and other human activities, which is the essence of the analytics approach. Sometimes, this knowledge is automatically applied in some type of autonomous system, while at others, it is put in a queue for a human analyst or decision maker to take advantage of it. One way or another, knowledge generated by modern AI technologies represents a great opportunity to revise and update traditional Knowledge Management (KM) practice in firms and institutions known and positioned as knowledge-based organizations (Chang et al., 2019; Kahn and Vorley, 2017).

Although originating as a mathematics and computer science discipline, AI has become a multidisciplinary field with its nexus to various disciplines ranging from the human sciences to natural, art, health, and social sciences, including business management. It is in the area of business management that KM has its provenance in the mid-1980s as a multidisciplinary field, thanks to an influx of AI subdiscipline knowledge-based systems and expert systems that emerged in the 1960s and 1970s with the work of Feigenbaum and co-workers at Stanford University (Lindsay et al., 1980) and that have evolved during the last four decades. Technologies such as AI, cloud computing, the Internet of Things, data science, natural language processing and speech recognition, combined with storage capacity, mobile technologies, smart cities, and sensor-based data gathering have been enablers in creating the fourth industrial revolution and digital transformation of society on which modern firms that have built competencies on the use of KM find themselves in the third decade of the new millennium.

This chapter is organized as follows: Section 2 presents a brief historical account and a bibliometric analysis of AI and KM interaction in the period 1986–2019. Section 3 gives a bibliometric analysis of interaction between AI, KM and analytics circa 2020, with articles published in the last decade (2011–19) in the main AI subdisciplines, and ideas about how KM could take advantage of AI analytics with the management of knowledge that is potentially present and that can be obtained by mining big datasets coming from real-time transactional systems and other sources. Section 4 discusses AI, KM and analytics research opportunities for young scientists in future years, and presents specific topics of research in their intersection. Section 5 offers some concluding remarks.

2.   KM and AI 1986–2019

In this section, we present an overview of KM and AI interaction in the 35-year period from1986 to 2019. We should say that KM and AI have interacted closely since the birth of KM in the mid-1980s and both have benefited mutually from the adoption and use of methods and techniques in each discipline.

2.1   Tracking the Origins of AI and KM

Since its inception in the early 1950s through the seminal work of Alan Turing (1950) and the coining of the term by John McCarthy et al. (1956), modern Artificial Intelligence (AI) has experienced ups and downs over the years with prosperity and success stories interspersed with lean times. One of the AI peaks occurred in the late 1960s and 1970s with the emergence of expert systems and knowledge-based systems originated by Edward Feigenbaum and colleagues at Stanford University from his work on Dendral and Mycin which were the first rule-based systems with a forward and backward chaining reasoning capability, programmed in Lisp (Lindsay et al., 1980). The rule based paradigm comprised knowledge representation and reasoning, and launched the appearance of the first large-scale knowledge-based system applications, the AI subfield of knowledge engineering, and set the ground for an incipient industry that reached its pinnacle in the 1980s with the Japanese fifth-generation computer program, which did not show first symptoms of decay until the 1990s.

One of the offshoots of the knowledge-based systems breakthrough paradigm that is encapsulated in the adage "knowledge is power" is Knowledge Management as an interdisciplinary field that arises not just from AI's knowledge-is-power paradigm, but from other areas, mainly business management and decision theory in terms of promoting the adage, "knowledge sharing is power." KM has been defined in multiple ways, but a commonly accepted definition is that it is the process of creating, sharing, using and managing the knowledge and information of an organization (Girard and Girard, 2015). To the best of our knowledge, the concept was coined and first used by Karl Wiig (1993) in 1986, although some believe that the term was employed and had even been utilized before in the 1960s (Lambe, 2007). Independently of attribution, Karl Wiig's work has been highly influential in the shaping and diffusion of KM as an essential business strategy at the corporate level as demonstrated by his prolific writing displayed in the three-volume series on KM (Wiig, 1993, 1994, 1995) and other KM seminal and influential works (Wiig, 1997, 2004). In volume 1, Wiig presents the fundamentals of KM and the concept of meta-level thinking, or thinking about thinking, as well as an analysis on how people and organizations create, represent and use knowledge (Wiig, 1993). In volume 2, Wiig argues that the central management focus for intelligent-acting organizations is KM (Wiig, 1994), whereas volume 3 is about KM methods seen as practical approaches to managing knowledge (Wiig, 1995). Another early and seminal work is Liebowitz's *Knowledge Management Handbook* that compiles KM strategies, methods, human elements, intellectual capital, application, and AI technologies commonly used during the 1980s and 1990s (Liebowitz, 1999, 2012).

2.2   Bibliometric Analysis of KM and AI Research

As a result of the foundational research outlined above, KM and AI communities have been collaborating during the last 35 years. Applying the analytics method, Figure 5.1 presents the trend of publications related to Knowledge Management and Artificial Intelligence from 1986 to 2019.

Documents by year

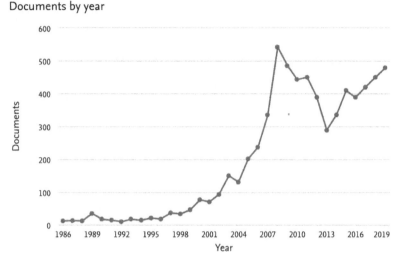

Figure 5.1   Publications on Knowledge Management and Artificial Intelligence 1986–2019

Source: Elsevier's Scopus database, May 9, 2020 (https://www.scopus.com/).

The total number of research publications found for the period 1986–2019 that treat KM and AI combined is 8,873. We can see that there is a growing trend with a peak in 2008, then a decline, followed by a resurgence after 2013 and a second peak in 2015 followed by growth until 2019.

Figure 5.2 displays trends for the number of publications in Knowledge Management for the same period 1986–2019. The total number of documents is 74,140.

Similarly, Figure 5.3 shows Artificial Intelligence documents published in the same period with a total of 483,871 publications and 501,801 since 1954 up to May 9, 2020.

The analysis shows that the number of AI research publications in the last 35 years has been steadily growing during this period and seems to be keeping to this trend at least for following years. On the other hand, KM documents, after a constant growth until 2009, show a decline during 2010–14 with signs of recovery since 2015 to date. As a result, the number of KM and AI joint works have declined and revived in the same period of time, following a pattern similar to the one displayed in Figure 5.2.

Documents by year

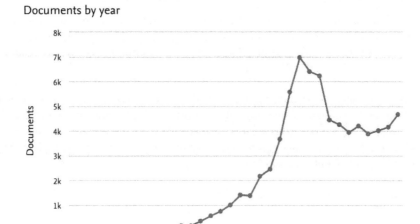

Figure 5.2   Publications on Knowledge Management 1986–2019

Source: Elsevier's Scopus database, May 9, 2020 (https://www.scopus.com/).

Documents by year

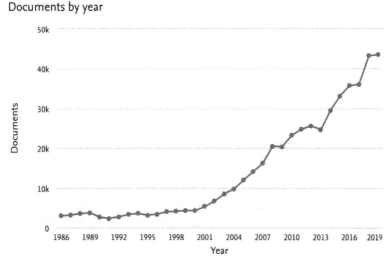

Figure 5.3   Publications on Artificial Intelligence 1986–2019

Source: Elsevier's Scopus database, May 9, 2020 (https://www.scopus.com/).

2.3   A Glimpse of KM and AI Joint Research Works

To obtain an idea of how KM and AI have collaborated in the past, and in order to learn lessons from this interaction for the following years, here we present an analysis of works on AI and KM for the period 1997–2019, a decade after the coining of the KM term.

Jakubczyc and Owoc published an article to introduce and discuss the use of AI as an essential technology to support knowledge management goals of organizing human knowledge in organizations in the early 1990s, where various AI techniques are pointed out as an effective way of supporting KM in corporations (Jakubczyc and Owoc, 1998).

At the dawn of the millennium, Liebowitz wrote about KM and AI and he pointed out that KM practitioners and theorists were overlooking the role of AI in its methods and practice (Liebowitz, 2001). Aguirre et al. (2001) reported the use of multi-agent systems (MAS) as a way of representing and reasoning about knowledge with interacting intelligent agents organized as a knowledge-based network. Hoeschl and Barcellos (2006) performed an analysis of AI and KM from the perspective of the dualism between mind and body in order to represent human knowledge in computational terms and the filtering and analysis of the information contained in databases and open and unstructured source such as the Internet.

Arcos and colleagues introduced the concept of an electronic institution modeled on a society of interacting multi-agent systems (Arcos et al., 2005). Robles et al. applied the concept of electronic institutions to model working processes in a business environment and applied them to the enterprise sector including hotel chains with knowledge representation, reasoning and decision making capabilities (Robles et al., 2009).

Nonaka and von Krogh (2009) introduced the concepts of tacit knowledge and knowledge conversion that shape the development of organizational knowledge creation theory and argue that tacit and explicit knowledge can be conceptually distinguished along a continuum and that knowledge conversion explains, theoretically and empirically, the interaction between tacit and explicit knowledge.

Cantu and Ceballos (2010) describe a knowledge and information network approach for managing research assets in a knowledge-oriented organization using an MAS. The purpose of the approach is to provide decision makers a knowledge management framework to assist them in generating benefits from the knowledge assets developed by the research groups in a knowledge institution.

Neururer (2015) addresses the problem of how AI technology can boost Knowledge Management goals. Starting from Liebowitz's concept of KM as "creating value from an organization's intangible assets," he argues that it is challenging to grasp intangible assets, to address them, turn them into tangible pieces and make them accessible for the organization as a whole, and that the process of knowledge transformation has to undergo another innovation cycle. Besides bringing to the surface the role of the chief knowledge officers (CKOs) in organizations, he points to drivers for dealing with this change that include technological infrastructure to bring processing power, global connectivity, and AI technologies like natural language processing, web technologies, speech recognition, intelligent agents, knowledge workers, and others. However, this approach does not tackle the elusive problem of converting intangible into tangible assets (Neururer, 2015).

Sanzogni et al. (2018) explore the theoretical and practical limitations of AI and KM and provide an epistemological understanding of both disciplines as a means of furthering the knowledge debate, with particular emphasis on the role of tacit knowledge within this jurisdiction.

Rhem (2017) sees KM as a multidisciplinary field that encompasses psychology, epistemology, and cognitive science, where the goals of KM are to enable people and organizations to collaborate, share, create, use and reuse knowledge. In understanding KM this way, it allows people to improve performance, increase innovation and expand what we know both from an individual and organizational perspective. He argues that the connection of KM and AI has led the way for the fermentation of cognitive computing to simulate human thought processes using AI technologies like deep learning neural networks, text and data mining, pattern recognition and natural language processing to mimic the way the human brain works. He considers that cognitive computing is leading the way for future applications involving AI and KM.

Martin (2018) says that the combination of scalable cloud technology, faster micro-processing, and big data analytics has finally led us to take AI concepts and build AI solutions that can solve key business challenges, and that executives responsible for their organization's Knowledge Management processes are looking for ways to improve how their employees can capture, find, and use knowledge to increase productivity and efficiency. He concludes that the use of cognitive computing is the needed connection between AI and KM.

Pushpa (2019) points out that during the second industrial revolution, society got "electrified" whereas in the fourth industrial revolution it will end up being "cognified." To understand the linkage between KM and AI, he asks what exactly organizations do with knowledge and distinguishes between critical and routine tasks and whether they are performed by humans or by machines, and between know-how or procedural knowledge and know-why or causal knowledge to determine the best way to design business solutions.

Hoffman and Freyn (2019) address the issue of how competitive intelligence, as a subset of the management consulting industry along with business intelligence and KM, can benefit from AI, considering that big data, big data analytics, and other AI technologies are transforming innumerable industries in such a way that they will disrupt the management consulting world and could even render the role of the human analyst obsolete. Greene (2020) asserts that adding AI to KM drastically reduces the amount of oversight required to manage the program, and he proposes to explore the ways in which AI may help KM.

The works presented above are just a few examples of the way in which KM and AI have interacted during the 35 years since the introduction of the term Knowledge Management by Wiig in 1986. In the following sections, we provide an overview of research opportunities in which KM and AI may interplay in the next decade (2021–30) and consolidate themselves as two key disciplines that have had a growing influence in modern organizations and will continue to do so in the future.

3.   KM and AI circa 2020 and Beyond

In this section we explore the connection and potential synergies between AI and KM for the following decade in the context of the fourth industrial revolution and the digital transformation phenomena brought by disrupting modern technologies.

The history of science covers three industrial revolutions in the 18th–20th centuries. The first industrial revolution, between 1750 and 1850, was characterized by a transition from agricultural and commercial hand production methods to steam-powered machines; the rise of chemical, iron and textile industries; new transportation methods like the railways; and the appearance of mechanized factory systems. The second industrial revolution, between 1870 and 1914, featured the discovery and industrialization of electricity to replace candles and gas lamps, and the internal combustion engine that revolutionized factories and transportation with the introduction of automobiles and airplanes to replace horses, tumbrils and human physical work. The discovery of electricity and radio communication led to the invention of the telephone, the telegraph, the light bulb and other innovations. This era also witnessed the emergence of petroleum and steel industries. The initiation of the third industrial revolution is debated, but it can be traced to the appearance of computers and nuclear energy after World War I and up to the emergence of the first computer networks in the 1970s and 1980s. It is commonly believed that society is at the dawn of the fourth industrial revolution, characterized by the proliferation of the Internet, the world wide web, the Internet of Things, social networks, cloud computing, smart cities, autonomous vehicles, robotics, industry 4.0, big data and, specifically, AI, along with other cyber technologies. Thus, AI is an enabler and the driving force of the fourth industrial revolution and of the digital transformation phenomenon society is going through in the new millennium.

In an initiative orchestrated by the Association for the Advancement of Artificial Intelligence (AAAI), a panel of experts was assembled in 2015 to make an assessment of the state of the art of AI and perform a study of the possible impact of AI by 2030 (AAAI, 2016). The panel issued a report in September 2016, "Artificial Intelligence and Life in 2030" as part of the One-Hundred Year Study on Artificial Intelligence (AI100). The study is about recent advances in AI as well as the potential social impact on jobs, environment, transportation, public safety, healthcare, community engagement, government and other areas. The committee considered various ways to focus the study, including surveying AI subfields and their status, examining a particular AI technology and studying particular application areas such as healthcare or transportation. In the end, the committee chose a thematic focus on "AI and Life in 2030" to recognize that AI will have an important impact on economies, societies, and the way people live and interact (AAAI, 2016, pp. 1–2).

Olley et al's. 2018 study "Artificial Intelligence: How Knowledge is Created, Transferred, and Used. Trends in China, Europe, and the United States" identifies key AI research, outlines how AI is being used in education, industry and media, and offers a taxonomy and word-map of seven crucial AI clusters: (1) search and optimization, (2) fuzzy systems, (3) natural language processing and knowledge representation, (4) computer vision, (5) machine learning and probabilistic reasoning, (6) planning and decision making, and (7) neural networks. The report points out that key AI technologies are migrating from academia to the corporate sector through an outflow of talented people being recruited by industry, transferring knowledge and skills to enrich companies' capabilities to scale up current AI practices.

Finally, CBInsights 2018 "Top AI Trends to Watch in 2018" presents 13 artificial intelligence trends that are reshaping industries and economies in areas ranging from agriculture to cybersecurity to commerce to healthcare, and more. The report shows trends in equity deals by quarters from 2012 to 2017 in 26 industry sectors, including healthcare, cybersecurity, education, travel, real estate and sports. The report concludes by saying that Amazon, Google and Microsoft seem to dominate enterprise AI.

3.1   KM and AI 2011–19

With the context presented above, we now present an overview of how advancements in AI and analytics can leverage the development of KM in the following decade. We do this by revising key AI technology reports discussed in AAAI (2016), Olley et al. (2018) and CBInsight (2018), and their possible impact and uses in KM theory and practice. Due to their influence in digital transformation, we have added cloud computing and the Internet of Things to the listing. The AI and IT technologies considered in this study are displayed in Table 5.1.

The approach we have used is as follows: First, we undertook a bibliometric analysis of research articles published during the period 2011–20 that use KM and each of the technologies listed in Table 5.1. Then we estimated how the patterns displayed in 2011–19 may extrapolate to the 2020 and 2030 decades, based on trends found in the three intelligence reports. The underlying assumption is that high-quality AI research applied to KM in meaningful ways will permeate into corporate environments via an effective technology transfer strategy. The AI research quality criterion is taken from Elsevier's Scopus database.

Table 5.1 displays the statistics of the articles published in the period 2011–19 in 15 AI/IT technologies given in the first column. The second column shows the number of articles published; the third column exhibits the number of articles that combine KM and AI; and the last column indicates the percentage of KM and AI inclusive articles with respect to the total number of articles published for each technology during 2011–19.

Table 5.1 is sorted in descending order according to the percentage of KM and AI documents for each technology, and we distinguish three patterns in the table grouped in tiers: Tier 1 represents technologies with less than 1%; Tier 2 is technologies with between 0.9% and 2%; and Tier 3 is technologies with greater than 2%. The interpretation of the percentages is as follows: Tier

Table 5.1   AI/IT and KM/AI publications 2011–19

Technology AI/IT	Articles	KM and AI combined	%
Robotics	149,679	437	0.29
Voice recognition	32,755	136	0.42
Computer vision	74,840	362	0.48
Internet of Things	77,689	462	0.59
Machine learning	149,735	1,390	0.93
Big data	77,577	783	1.01
Multi-agent systems	18,105	220	1.22
Cloud computing	70,950	873	1.23
Data science	131,671	2,000	1.52
Cognitive computing	813	13	1.60
Natural language processing	40,704	758	1.86
Soft computing	15,993	299	1.87
Expert systems	12,565	259	2.06
Knowledge-based systems	26,802	3,099	11.56
Semantic web and ontologies	23,498	3,276	13.94
Knowledge engineering	8,407	1,724	20.51

Source: Elsevier's Scopus database, May 7, 2020 (https://www.scopus.com/).

1, with a number of publications in the thousands for a given technology, points towards a potential opportunity to contribute to KM research goals. Robotics, voice recognition, computer vision, Internet of Things, and related technologies are in Tier 1. Tier 2, with a significant number of publications, suggests another potential opportunity to contribute to KM research objectives. AI analytics and, specifically, machine learning, big data, data science, neuro-linguistic programming (NLP), multi-agent systems (MAS), soft, cognitive, and cloud computing, and related technologies follow this pattern and are in this group. Tier 3, with knowledge-based systems, semantic web and knowledge engineering, follow a third pattern and look less likely to influence KM since they are mature technologies that have already made important contributions in the last two decades and contributed to shaping KM goals.

But the question now is how can technologies such as robotics, voice recognition, computer vision, and the Internet of Things make a contribution to KM in 2020–30? We know that KM is the process of creating, sharing, using and managing the knowledge and information of an organization, and that it is performed mainly by humans supported by computers systems which interact with them in various ways. Nonetheless, based on trends on autonomous systems, we can imagine a scenario in which it is not just humans and machines that interact with each other, but humans; computer systems; mobile, smart machines like robots, chatbots and office appliances; wearable devices with vision, speech, learning and reasoning capabilities; and smart walls, rooms, buildings, lighting, surveillance and car parking, in an environment enabled by IoT and monitored by a network of MAS. In such a scenario, there are many opportunities to conduct doctoral research and we can imagine ways in which KM theory and practice would have to be revised and updated to reflect the new ways in which companies will conduct their business.

3.2   KM and AI in 2020-30: Analysis of Scenarios from 2011-19 Research Trends

We now proceed to study the various AI and IT technologies from a bibliometric point of view looking at how KM and AI research publications have behaved in the period 2011 to 2019 and suggest manners of which these interactions could look like during 2020-2030.

Figure 5.4 shows joint publications for Tier 1 of KM and robotics, computer vision, voice recognition and IoT from 2011 to 2019, with the number of joint publications shown in parentheses. In this period, we observe a growing trend in KM and IoT documents which should keep rising in 2020–30 to the extent that sensor-based technologies become ubiquitous and economy of scale reaches the marketplace. Robotics, computer vision and voice recognition show ups and downs and seem somewhat dormant from 2011 to 2019, but we believe that they will have a renaissance in 2020–30 as more opportunities will emerge in this decade with the dissemination of IoT systems and their integration into business' operations.

Figure 5.5 displays joint publications for Tier 2 of KM and data science, machine learning, big data and soft computing in 2011–19, with the number of joint publications shown in parentheses. In this period, we observe a growing trend in KM and data science, machine learning and big data documents,

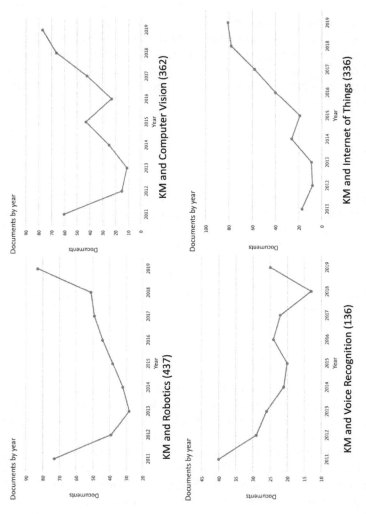

Figure 5.4   Publications of Knowledge Management and Tier 1 technologies 2011–2019

Source: Elsevier's Scopus database, May 6, 2020 (https://www.scopus.com/).

which also should keep rising in 2020–30 to the extent that data generated from business operation and transactions will keep growing, and cloud storage and cloud computing will permeate corporate and business lives. Soft computing is about approximate reasoning and learning, and embraces fuzzy logic, genetic algorithms, swarm intelligence and ant colony optimization. Neural nets are sometimes regarded as soft or intelligent computing, but these papers are counted in machine learning and deep learning; they show a variable publication rate and seem to have been dormant in 2011–19, but we believe that they will show a resurgence in 2020–30 as more opportunities will emerge in this decade. Soft computing also seems to be dormant in 2011–19, but has a high potential to increase machine learning methods with a positive impact for KM in the short term.

Figure 5.6 displays the second part of joint publications for Tier 2 of KM and natural language processing, multi-agent systems, cloud computing and cognitive computing in 2011–19, with the number of joint publications shown in parentheses. In this period, we observe a growing trend in KM and NLP documents, although 2015 is atypical as the search displayed zero documents, which is strange; but aside from that, this trend should keep rising in 2020–30 to the extent that speech recognition and human computer interaction will grow and become robust in most digital devices. Cloud computing shows ups and downs, but indicates a growth since 2016 that should increase for the next decade. MAS shows a decline during 2011–19, but we believe that it has good potential to contribute to KM, in combination with other networked technologies that expect an increase in 2020–30 as more opportunities will emerge for concurrency and task coordination. Cognitive computing seems not to have attracted attention during 2011–19, but involves high potential to increase rapidly in other Tier 2 and Tier 1 technologies in the following years.

Finally, Figure 5.7 depicts the joint publications for Tier 3 of KM and expert systems, knowledge-based systems, semantic web and ontologies, and knowledge engineering in 2011–19, with the number of joint publications shown in parentheses. In this period, we observe a decline in the number of publications in semantic web/ontology and knowledge-based systems and erratic activity in knowledge engineering which exhibits ups and downs, and very low work in KM and expert systems, also with ups and downs. This behavior of Tier 3 technologies was to be expected and it seems that it will keep showing a low profile during 2020–30.

This review concludes the analysis of KM and AI interaction between 2011 and 2020 using a bibliometric approach and the outline of possible scenarios and trends for the period 2020–30.

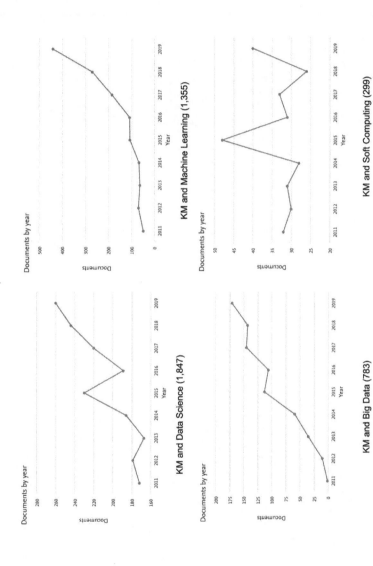

Figure 5.5   Publications of Knowledge Management and Tier 2a technologies 2011–2019

Source: Elsevier's Scopus database, May 6, 2020 (https://www.scopus.com/).

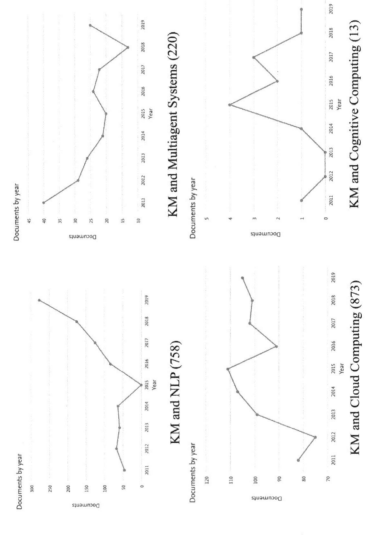

Figure 5.6   Publications of Knowledge Management and Tier 2b technologies 2011–2019

Source: Elsevier's Scopus database, May 6, 2020 (https://www.scopus.com/).

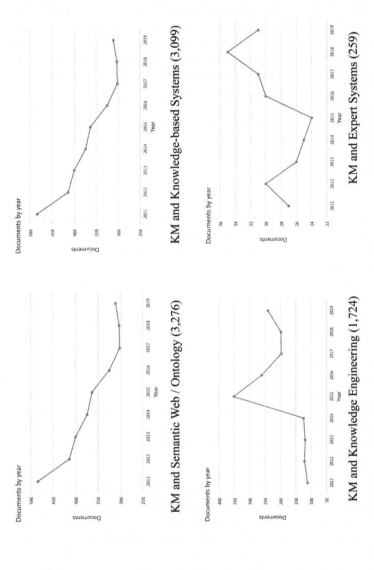

Figure 5.7   Publications of Knowledge Management and Tier 3 technologies 2011–2019

Source: Elsevier's Scopus database, May 6, 2020 (https://www.scopus.com/).

4.   Discussion

AI documents amount to 483,871 in the period 1986–2019, whereas KM output totals 74,140, 15% of AI production. AI and KM joint documents total 6,678, 1.3% of AI and 9% of KM. Thus, there seems to be ample room for joint work in both fields. By breaking down AI into 16 subfields or technologies, we found the total number of articles in each subfield and identified those papers that report joint work with KM and the corresponding percentage. The listing was sorted from smallest to largest according to percentages, and three patterns were found that were grouped in tiers.

These patterns seem to resemble the future, the present and near future, and the past of KM and AI interaction. We analyze each of these patterns and provide pointers into a KM and AI future research agenda in specific areas of both disciplines following an analytics-based approach.

We start with knowledge-based technologies in Tier 3. We know that these technologies have had a key role in spreading AI applications and collaborating with KM for the last 30 years. They may need to be reinvented, although the spirit within them (knowledge-based systems, expert systems, knowledge engineering, web semantics) is present in other AI and IT subdisciplines and will, silently, keep on inspiring 2020–30 innovations in KM and AI.

The pattern found and wrapped into the second tier hinges around adopting and extending a data thinking and AI analytics approach encompassing data science, data analytics, data mining, data engineering, data management and big data, along with AI technologies like machine learning, NLP, MAS, soft computing and related fields. These subfields are ripe areas in which to dig around data following analytic methods and for finding useful knowledge for practical decision making. These technologies show a growing trend in 2015–19 and will definitely have an important impact on KM and many other disciplines during 2020–25 with a consolidation in 2026–30 once integrated with Tier 1 technologies.

We observe a rich research agenda in this tier with many specific research questions that need to be investigated involving many applications of AI analytics related to practically any aspect of human life. We have explored a few of them. One of them has brought analytics and big data to develop strategic models that connects KM with intellectual capital acquisition and retention for business use (Harlow, 2018). Also, big data and AI analytics have been leveraged for the discovery of trends (using an analysis of large numbers of patents in intellectual property repositories) to provide competitive advantage to companies who own them, or to trends that need to built upon what already exists and developed with appropriate KM strategies which will bring economic value to firms (Aristodemou and Tietze, 2018).

KM and AI analytics can also pump value into traditional functional areas of companies, be these manufacturing, purchasing, marketing, sales, customer relationship management, and others. For instance, the B2B sales process with human-centered funnel processes has been enriched with the incorporation and integration of AI analytics with human roles (Paschen et al., 2020). Big data, analytics, and KM have been used in the accounts payable domain in the public sector (Edwards and Rodriguez, 2016). Data-driven design has also benefited with the use of AI analytics to systems engineering design and trade-space exploration (Fitzgerald and Ross, 2019). Another area of applied research is procurement, a core business function that plays a key in generating value for a firm. For instance, a new enterprise architecture that proposes to leverage emerging technologies to guide procurement organizations in their digital transformation using analytics, business rules and complex event processing has been explored and adapted to the world of procurement for reducing costs (Barrad et al., 2020). An important issue in the digital transformation age is in the domain of cybersecurity. AI analytics is being applied to firms within the KM context to address issues and risks raised by cyber-attacks via the Internet (Petrenko et al., 2020). Other firms that have implemented knowledge management technologies have shown limited capabilities to effectively process and analyze big data. Studies about how companies are protecting themselves from cyber-attacks so that managers can receive pertinent information to make better-informed security decisions already exist, but more research is needed to equip them with integrated solutions (Obitade, 2019).

Finally, the patterns found in the first tier indicate that autonomous systems and other AI technologies comprising robotics, computer vision, voice recognition, IoT and other related fields have little KM interaction for now, but high potential to fertilize KM especially in 2026–30 after an incubation period spanning 2020 to 2025. An example of this interaction is the design of a governance environment of automated image analysis and artificial intelligence analytics in the domain of healthcare (Ho et al., 2019). Regarding robotics, analytics, digitization and blockchain, which are considered critical to enabling agility, optimizing efficiency and driving sustainability for next generation sourcing enterprises, these are ripe areas to continue pursuing (Kishorepuria et al., 2019).

5. Conclusion

We have presented a bibliometric study of Knowledge Management and Artificial Intelligence analytics research as both independent and joint fields for the period 2011–19, as well as the possible trends based on this analysis for the decade 2020–30. With this work, we intend to provide motivation and insights on a potential research agenda for young scientists who will be embracing thesis or postdoctoral projects in the forthcoming years around the interdisciplinary intersection of both AI and KM in the age of analytics, and its potential application to knowledge-based and intelligent organizations. This forthcoming research aims to provide novel ways about how institutions could take advantage of the research outcomes of KM, AI and analytics synergy through suitable technology transfer strategies in future years.

References

AAAI (2016). Artificial Intelligence and Life in 2030. https://ai100.stanford.edu/sites/g/files/sbiybj9861/f/ai_100_report_0831fnl.pdf.

Aguirre, J.L., Brena, R., Cantu, F.J. (2001). Multiagent-based knowledge networks. *Expert Systems with Applications* 20(1), pp. 65–75.

Arcos, J.L., Esteva, M., Noriega, P., Rodriguez-Aguilar, J.A., Sierra, C. (2005). Engineering open environments with electronic institutions. *Engineering Applications of Artificial Intelligence* 18, pp. 191–204.

Aristodemou, L., Tietze, F. (2018). The state-of-the-art on Intellectual Property Analytics (IPA): a literature review on artificial intelligence, machine learning and deep learning methods for analysing intellectual property (IP) data. *World Patent Information* 55, pp. 37–51.

Barrad, S., Gagnon, S., Valverde, R. (2020). An analytics architecture for procurement. *International Journal of Information Technologies and Systems Approach* 13(2), pp. 73–98.

Cantu, F.J., Ceballos, H. (2010). A multiagent knowledge and information network approach for managing research assets. *Expert Systems with Applications* 37(7), pp. 5272–84.

CBInsights (2018). Top AI Trends to Watch in 2018. https://www.cbinsights.com/research/report/artificial-intelligence-trends-2018/.

Chang, H.-C., Wang, C.-Y., Hawamdeh, S. (2019). Emerging trends in data analytics and knowledge management job market: extending KSA framework. *Journal of Knowledge Management* 23(4), pp. 664–86.

Edwards, J.S., Rodriguez-Taborda, E. (2016). Using knowledge management to give context to analytics and big data and reduce strategic risk. *Procedia Computer Science* 99, pp. 36–49.

Fitzgerald, M.E., Ross, A.M. (2019). Artificial intelligence analytics with multi-attribute tradespace exploration and set-based design. *Procedia Computer Science* 153, pp. 27–36.

Girard, John P., Girard, JoAnn L. (2015). Defining knowledge management: toward an applied compendium. *Online Journal of Applied Knowledge Management* 3(1): 14.

Greene, J. (2020). 4 key benefits of adding AI to your knowledge management program. https://www.askspoke.com/blog/knowledge-management/ai-helps-knowledge -management/.

Harlow, H.D. (2018). Developing a knowledge management strategy for data analytics and intellectual capital. *Meditari Accountancy Research* 26(3), pp. 400–419.

Ho, C.W.L., Soon, D., Caals, K., Kapur, J. (2019). Governance of automated image analysis and artificial intelligence analytics in healthcare. *Clinical Radiology* 74(5), pp. 329–33.

Hoeschl, H.C., Barcellos, V. (2006). Artificial intelligence and knowledge management. In *TFTP International Federation for Information Processing, Volume 217, Artificial Intelligence in Theory and Practice*, ed. M. Bramer, Boston, MA: Springer, pp. 11–19.

Hoffman, Fred P., Freyn, Shelly L. (2019). The future of competitive intelligence in an AI-enabled world. *International Journal of Value Chain Management*, 10(4), pp. 278–89.

Jakubczyc, J.A., Owoc, M.L. (1998). Knowledge management and artificial intelligence. *Argumenta Oeconomica* 1–2(6), pp. 155–70.

Kaput, M. (2019). How is artificial intelligence used in analytics? https://www .marketingaiinstitute.com/blog/how-to-use-artificial-intelligence-for-analytics.

Khan, Z., Vorley, T. (2017). Big data text analytics: an enabler of knowledge management. *Journal of Knowledge Management* 21(1), pp. 18–34.

Kishorepuria, P., Madane, A., Sharma, N., Salmon, K. (2019). Next-generation sourcing: winning with agility and innovation. *Apparel*, 61(4), pp. 16–23.

Lambe, P. (2007). The prehistory of knowledge management. http://www .greenchameleon.com/gc/blog_detail/the_prehistory_of_knowledge_management/.

Liebowitz, J. (ed.) (1999). *The Knowledge Management Handbook*, Boca Raton, FL: CRC Press.

Liebowitz, J. (2001). Knowledge management and its link to artificial intelligence. *Expert Systems with Applications*, 20(1), pp. 1–6.

Liebowitz, J. (ed.) (2012), *The Knowledge Management Handbook: Collaboration and Social Networking*, 2nd edition, Boca Raton, FL: CRC Press.

Lindsay, R.K., Buchanan, B.G., Feigenbaum, E.A., Lederberg, J. (1980). *Applications of Artificial Intelligence for Organic Chemistry: The Dendral Project*, New York: McGraw-Hill Book Company, 1980.

Martin, M. (2018). How is artificial intelligence changing knowledge management? https://www.ikaun.com/2018/09/04/how-is-artificial-intelligence-changing -knowledge-management/.

McCarthy, J., Minsky, M., Rochester, N., Shannon, C.E. (1956). A proposal for the Dartmouth summer research project on artificial intelligence. http://raysolomonoff .com/dartmouth/boxa/dart564props.pdf.

Neururer, M. (2015). Artificial intelligence in knowledge management. https://medium .com/artificial-intelligence-ai/the-role-of-artificial-intelligence-in-knowledge -management-309973209cfd.

Nonaka, I., von Krogh, G. (2009). Perspective – tacit knowledge and knowledge conversion: controversy and advancement in organizational knowledge creation theory. *Organization Science* 20(3), pp. 635–52.

Obitade, P.O. (2019). Big data analytics: a link between knowledge management capabilities and superior cyber protection. *Journal of Big Data* 6(71). https://doi.org/10 .1186/s40537-019-0229-9.

Olley, D., Perrault, R., Motta, E. (2018). *Artificial Intelligence: How Knowledge is Created, Transferred, and Used: Trends in China, Europe, and the United States*. New York: Elsevier.

Paschen, J., Wilson, M., Ferreira, J.J. (2020). Collaborative intelligence: how human and artificial intelligence create value along the B2B sales funnel. *Business Horizons* 63(3), pp. 403–14.

Petrenko, S., Makoveichuk, K., Olifirov, A. (2020). New methods of the cybersecurity in knowledge management analytics. *Communications in Computer and Information Science* 1140CCIS, pp. 296–310.

Pushpa, R. (2019). Artificial intelligence and knowledge management: understanding how they are linked. https://www.linkedin.com/pulse/artificial-intelligence -knowledge-management-how-linked-pushpa/.

Rhem, A.J. (2017). The connection between artificial intelligence and knowledge management. A.J. Rhem & Associates, Inc. KM Institute. https://www.kminstitute.org/ blog/connection-between-artificial-intelligence-and-knowledge-management.

Robles, A., Noriega, P., Cantu, F. (2009). An agent-oriented hotel information system. *Proceedings of the 8th International Conference on Autonomous Agents and Multiagent Systems*, Volume 2, pp. 1415–16.

Sanzogni, L., Guzman, G., Busch, P. (2018). Artificial intelligence and knowledge management: questioning the tacit dimension. *Prometheus* 35(4), pp. 1–20.

Turing, A. (1950). Computing machinery and intelligence. *Mind* 59(236), pp. 433–60.

Wiig, K.M. (1993). *Knowledge Management Foundations: Thinking about Thinking – How People and Organizations Create, Represent, and Use Knowledge*, Volume 1, Arlington, TX: Schema Press.

Wiig, K.M. (1994). *Knowledge Management: The Central Management Focus for Intelligent-Acting Organizations*, Volume 2, Arlington, TX: Schema Press.

Wiig, K.M. (1995). *Knowledge Management Methods: Practical Approaches to Managing Knowledge*, Volume 3, Arlington, TX: Schema Press.

Wiig, K.M. (1997). Knowledge management: an introduction and perspective. *The Journal of Knowledge Management* 1(1), pp. 6–14.

Wiig. K.M. (2004). *People-Focused Knowledge Management: How Effective Decision Making Leads to Corporate Success*. New York: Routledge.

6. Knowledge management and measurement

Anthony J. Rhem

Introduction

This chapter details metrics and KPIs (key performance indicators) by first detailing input and output measures, as well as outcome measures. Metrics dealing with Knowledge Management (KM) program elements such as community of practice (CoP), search, lessons learned, knowledge continuity, and KM value analysis will then be examined.

Input, Output and Outcome Measures

Metrics used by organizations often influence which product and/or service to initiate or what feature and/or capability to launch. Metrics, in turn, are a powerful tool used by organizations to drive the direction of an organization, and getting the right metrics is an important and difficult task. Creating good metrics that capture long-term organizational goals often starts with identifying input measures, output measures and outcome measures (Dmitriev and Wu, 2016; Liebowitz and Suen, 2000).

Input Measures

Input measures provide measurements of the resources that are put into a process in order to achieve an output, including labor, capital, equipment, and raw materials. Input measures, along with measurements of outputs, process time, and other factors, are used to develop Six Sigma process improvement plans. Input measures will be used to monitor the amount of resources being used to develop, maintain, or deliver the KM solution (product, activity or service). Examples include:

- Money spent on system-related software, hardware and services
- Number of employee hours worked
- Facility costs
- Total operating expenditures
- Number of full-time employees
- Number of contractual employees.

Output Measures

Output measures describe what was produced (i.e., number of software features) or the service(s) that is/are being delivered. Output measures are the result of the KM project plan work breakdown structure (WBS). However, output measures do not address the value or impact of work to either internal or external stakeholders. An example of an output measure is velocity. Output measures monitor "how much" was produced or provided. They provide a number indicating how many items, referrals, actions, products, etc. were involved. Examples include:

- Number of software features ready for customer use
- Number of people trained
- Number of knowledge assets used
- Number of users accessing the Knowledge Management System (KMS)
- The amount of Knowledge rated as "high."

Outcome Measures

Outcome measures provide baseline data. There are three types of outcome measures: performance based, self-reported, and a hybrid that contains both. These measures are primarily used to gauge performance of the KMS and how the KMS improved the overall employee performance, as well as other possible organizational effectiveness outcomes. To measure the outcomes of knowledge management, there are five essential metrics (Krob, 2015):

1. Buy-in of your Knowledge Management Program.

This focuses on the employees understanding of why KM is being initiated. This includes an understanding of how KM will benefit them, how KM will change the way they work and how KM will support the access to knowledge.

2. How Well You Fulfill the Need for Knowledge.

This focuses on employee adoption of KM at the organization (i.e., program, initiatives, KMS, etc.). This examines how well individuals and teams integrate and adopt KM.

3. Knowledge Quality.

This focuses on how easy is the knowledge to find and is it easy to consume. Also, is the knowledge accurate and up to date. The knowledge quality will directly affect the ability for the knowledge to be reused.

4. Time to Competency.

Time to competency is a single measure capturing whether the behavioral changes necessary to adopt KM are resonating. According to Krob (2015), "time to competency is determined by the number of days it takes a new team member to work independently."

5. Rework Effort.

Rework effort is an additional measure that shows both the quality and usefulness of the knowledge. This is essentially a measure of time. Rework effort is the amount of time spent on a repeat customer need and is determined by capturing the amount of time spent on all work and categorizing the work as new or rework.

Output vs Outcome Measures

Output measures tell the story of what you or your organization produced. It also tells the story of the activities that occur in that production. Output measures do not address the value or impact of your product or service to your customer. However, outcome measures are measurements that address the level of performance or achievement that occurred because of the product or service that was provided.

Community of Practice (CoP) Metrics

A community of practice (CoP) represents gatherings of people to share their knowledge around a common expertise or area of interest. Sharing knowledge is one of the pillars of knowledge management. In the community, learning from each member and the creation of new knowledge will take place. This occurs within the context of social learning within the community. This form

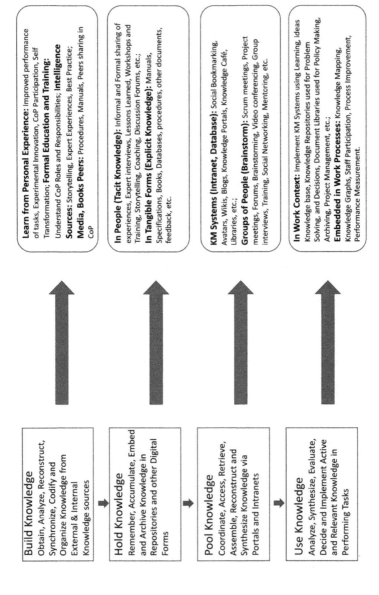

Build Knowledge
Obtain, Analyze, Reconstruct, Synchronize, Codify and Organize Knowledge from External & Internal Knowledge sources

Learn from Personal Experience: Improved performance of tasks, Experimental Innovation, CoP Participation, Self Transformation; **Formal Education and Training:** Understand CoP Roles and Responsibilities; **Intelligence Sources:** Storytelling, Expert Experiences, Best Practice; **Media, Books Peers:** Procedures, Manuals, Peers sharing in CoP

Hold Knowledge
Remember, Accumulate, Embed and Archive Knowledge in Repositories and other Digital Forms

In People (Tacit Knowledge): Informal and Formal sharing of experiences, Expert interviews, Lessons Learned, Workshops and Training, Storytelling, Coaching, Discussion Forums, etc.; **In Tangible Forms (Explicit Knowledge):** Manuals, Specifications, Books, Databases, procedures, other documents, feedback, etc.

Pool Knowledge
Coordinate, Access, Retrieve, Assemble, Reconstruct and Synthesize Knowledge via Portals and Intranets

KM Systems (Intranet, Database): Social Bookmarking, Avatars, Wikis, Blogs, Knowledge Portals, Knowledge Café, Libraries, etc.; **Groups of People (Brainstorm):** Scrum meetings, Project meetings, Forums, Brainstorming, Video conferencing, Group interviews, Training, Social Networking, Mentoring, etc.

Use Knowledge
Analyze, Synthesize, Evaluate, Decide and Implement Active and Relevant Knowledge in Performing Tasks

In Work Context: Implement KM Systems using Learning, Ideas Knowledge base, Knowledge Repositories used for Problem Solving, and Decisions, Document Libraries used for Policy Making, Archiving, Project Management, etc.; **Embedded in Work Processes:** Knowledge Mapping, Knowledge Graphs, Staff Participation, Process Improvement, Performance Measurement.

Figure 6.1   Community of practice (CoP) using the Karl Wiig knowledge management (KM) cycle

Source: Venkatraman and Venkatraman, 2018.

of social learning through the exchange of knowledge leads each member in becoming a better practitioner, while being an integrated part of a community.

In measuring the effectiveness of knowledge sharing through communities of practice, examining the CoP from the perspective of the knowledge management cycle will assist in identifying what should be measured (Figure 6.1).

Typical CoP metrics include average posts per day, unique contributors (people posting at least once), repeat contributors (people posting more than once) and majority contributors (minimum people for greater than 50% of posts). Some points to consider:

1. Recognize the diversity of interests in those participating in the group, and that this is a voluntary undertaking for all involved.
2. Develop a stakeholder classification and perform a RACI (responsible, accountable, consulted, and informed) assessment for each stakeholder group.
3. Through a collaborative process, arrive at coherent goals, objectives, principles and strategies for the group.
4. Develop a CoP plan with agreed upon moderator criteria and stakeholders that influence group behavior in ways that are congruent with the group's goals and objectives (Rhem, 2018).

Search Engine Optimization and Search Metrics

Search Engine Optimization

Search Engine Optimization (SEO) drives the establishment and tracking of search metrics and KPIs. Utilizing the technical SEO hierarchy of needs (Figure 6.2) will guide you into establishing metrics for your KMS. The following provides brief details of each section of the hierarchy:

- *Crawlability*: Crawlability refers to the ability for the URL's of the KM application (site) to be discovered by the search engine bots. URLs that are not crawlable may still be accessible to users only through navigation; because the site is invisible to bots, it will not appear in the search results (Search Engine Land, 2019).
- *Indexability*: Indexability refers to the ability of the site URLs of the KM application (site) to be indexable. Indexable URLs are URLs that a search engine can include in a catalog of pages that are available to be presented in search results pages. Although a URL has been crawled, there are various properties that can prevent it from being added to the index (such as security, duplicate pages, redirections) (Search Engine Land, 2019).

- *Accessibility*: Accessibility refers to the ability of the URL of the KM application (site) to be displayed. A URL that is both crawlable and indexable might still be inaccessible at the moment when a search engine attempts to crawl it. This can be due to pages and sites that have persistent accessibility problems (Search Engine Land, 2019).
- *Rankability*: Rankability refers to the ability of the KM application (site) URL and pages to appear higher in the search result. Rankability is the first part of the pyramid that deals with optimization. Improving the position of a site and/or page rankings often includes semantically interlinking related content and expanding keywords (Search Engine Land, 2019).
- *Clickability*: Clickability refers to the ability on the KM application (site) URL and pages being accessible to be selected within the search result page. Content structure, which includes lists, tables, headings and user selected labels, will assist search engines to understand page content and facilitate dynamic creation of featured (faceted) results. This is the final level of technical SEO optimization that makes it more likely for a user to click on your results from the search page (Search Engine Land, 2019).

Some of the important search metrics to track include: keyword rankings, keyword growth, search engine usage, number of searches performed, number of highly rated searches performed, user rankings, information currency, user feedback, traffic by landing page and location, organic clicks, click-through rate, top three pages by performance, new vs. returning visitors, bounce rate, and average session duration (Search Engine Land, 2019).

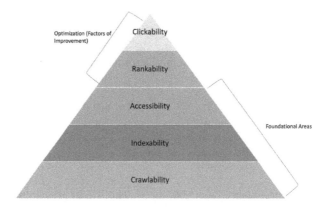

Figure 6.2   Technical SEO hierarchy of needs

Source: Search Engine Land, 2019.

Search Metrics

Search metrics are determined through tuning and optimization. Administrators should constantly observe and evaluate effectiveness of search results. Administrators should be able to gather search results reports from the KMS administrator periodically (for example, every two weeks). From these reports, they can analyze the type of keywords users are searching for and from which sites most of the search queries come from. Based on this, administrators can add "synonyms" for their sites. If any newly added metadata column needs to be available in advanced search filters, then the request must be sent to the KMS administrator.

Search Engine Usage

Search engine logs can be analyzed to produce a range of simple reports, showing usage, and a breakdown of search terms. Also, other measures like number of searches performed (within one's own area and across areas) and number of highly rated searches performed could be useful (Rhem, 2018).

Knowledge Use (Rating of Knowledge)

A more direct measure of many KM initiatives is whether the information is being *used in practice*. As usage normally happens outside of the system, it must be reported by the staff. Providing a simple mechanism for rating and notifying when information is used records insights on knowledge usage (Rhem, 2018).

Number of Users

Directly related to system usage is the total number of staff accessing the system. This should clearly grow as the system is rolled out across the organization. This can be tracked via security login in order to determine accurate staff numbers (Rhem, 2018).

User Rankings

This involves asking the readers themselves to rate the relevance and quality of the information being presented. Subject matter experts or other reviewers can directly assess the quality of material in the content management system, or KM platform (Rhem, 2018).

Edits Required

This can be done by utilizing workflow capability. Audit trails generated by this can be analyzed to determine how many edits or reviews were required for each piece of content. If the original material is of a high quality, it should require little editing (Rhem, 2018).

Links Created

A popular page with useful information will be more frequently linked to other parts of the system. By measuring the number of links, the effectiveness of individual pages can be determined (Rhem, 2018).

Information Currency

This is a measure of how up-to-date is the information stored within the system. The importance of this measure will depend on the nature of the information being published, and how it is used. The best way to track this is using the metadata stored within the KMS, such as publishing and review dates. By using this, automated reports showing a number of specific measures can be generated:

- Average age of pages
- Number of pages older than a specific age
- Number of pages past their review date
- Lists of pages due to be reviewed
- Pages to be reviewed, broken down by content owner or business group
- The KM system will allow variable review periods (or dates) to be specified, depending on the nature of the content. This metric is a tool for ongoing knowledge asset management.

User Feedback

A feedback mechanism will be established for the KM system. Use of such a feedback system is a clear indication that staff are using the knowledge. While few feedback messages may indicate the published knowledge is entirely accurate, it is more likely that the system is not being accessed, or that the feedback mechanism is not recognized as useful. Alternatively, while many feedback messages may indicate poor quality of knowledge, it does indicate strong staff use. It also shows they have sufficient trust in the system to commit the time needed to send in feedback.

Distributed Authoring

The extent to which the business as a whole takes responsibility for keeping content up to date is a metric in itself. At the most basic level, the number of KM system authors can be tracked against a target. A more rigorous approach uses statistics from the workflow capabilities to determine the level of activity of each author.

Transaction Costs

A process analysis activity can also determine costs involved in completing tasks. This allows direct cost savings made by implementing and leveraging the KM system. Multiplied out by the number of times the activity is completed in a year, the whole-of-business savings can be determined.

Lessons Learned Metrics

Lessons learned are documented results that include reflections on both positive and negative results of projects and initiatives at all stages. Lessons learned metrics are determined and organized by responses gathered during a lesson learned session (i.e., after-action review or retrospective) session. Lessons learned should be identified by type of lesson learned captured (resource, time, budget, system, content, etc.). Summarize the lesson learned by creating a brief summary of the findings and providing recommendations for correcting the findings (i.e., findings – a summary of the issues found during the review process; recommendations – recommended actions to be taken to correct findings). In order to provide accurate metrics, the approved actions should be documented and tracked to completion. In some cases, the approved action may become a project due to high level of resources required to address the finding (Rhem, 2018). Some metrics include impact analysis (time (increased/decreased), improper resourced, budget constraints, software/system limitations, lack of available content, etc.); applying the lesson learned – that is, the percentage of problem/issue solved with the lesson learned per category and overall (Rhem, 2018).

Knowledge Continuity

Knowledge continuity refers to ensuring that no critical knowledge is lost to the organization or to its employees due to employees leaving the organization (e.g., retirement, resignation or other reason) or moving to another part of the organization. The keys at the heart of knowledge continuity include:

- What constitutes mission-critical knowledge that should be preserved?
- Where is the targeted mission-critical knowledge and is it accessible and transferable?
- What decisions and action are required to stem the loss of valuable knowledge, and in many cases, irreplaceable knowledge?
- Successfully obtaining, transferring and storing the lessons learned and best practices from their most experienced and valuable workers to a knowledge base or (KM application) before employees depart or retire.

Metrics to capture for knowledge continuity include:

- Percentage of knowledge harvested and stored from key employees
- Percentage of knowledge transferred to successor employees
- Cost associated with preventing corporate mission-critical knowledge from loss
- A structured framework and system to store, update, access, enrich and transfer to employees to support their work activities
- The amount of ramp-up time of new hires, moving them rapidly up their learning curves and making them more productive sooner.

ROI and Value Analysis for KM

From the outset, calculating a return on investment (ROI) for a knowledge management effort is not easy, especially when compared to a more traditional situation like a new piece of equipment, such as a computer color photocopier or other capital equipment. Investing in a piece of equipment can be directly tied to increases in product quality and/or quantity through multiple metrics (e.g., lower defect rates, finished products per hour). However, calculating the ROI for investments in knowledge management efforts is not that simple or direct.

The ROI for KM should be measured by how well it supports the mission and/or objectives of the organization. Essentially, did the KM initiative increase the performance of its users or how well did it support the strategic mission of the organization?

When we are looking at achieving a return on our KM initiatives historically, it can take a considerable amount of time to show results or a visible ROI for an organization. An approach to use involves the Knowledge Value Equation (KVE). This states that the value created from managing knowledge is a function of the costs, benefits and risks of the KM initiative (Rhem, 2016). Mathematically stated: KM Value = F(cost, benefit, risk), which equals total Discounted Cash Flow (DCF) created over the life of the KM investment (Rhem, 2016). This formula attempts to quantify the intangible impacts of KM, relating it back to cash flow. This includes improved problem solving, enhanced creativity, and improved relationships with customers and other performance-related activities.

Three common indicators of the viability of the KM initiative are: net present value (NPV), internal rate of return (IRR), and the payback period. NPV helps us normalize future cash flows (both cash we intend to spend and cash we expect to receive) into their present value. As a general rule, if the NPV of a KM initiative is greater than zero than you invest in the KM initiative. If the NPV is negative, you should not invest in the KM initiative. The reason for this is simple: the future cash flows do not justify the present investment. The IRR is the discount rate (also called investment yield rate) for the KM initiative. The IRR is the rate at which the NPV for a KM initiative is equal to zero. When comparing two KM initiatives, the one with the higher IRR is preferred (Rhem, 2016). Another option to the IRR is to present the ROI. This value represents, as the name implies, the savings (benefit) one will get out of the KM initiative for the investment (cost) outlays.

The payback period helps one estimate how quickly the investment will be recouped. Put another way, it is the time required for the savings to equal the cost. When comparing two nearly similar alternatives, the rational person will choose the KM initiative with the shorter payback period. The important thing to bear in mind is that no single financial metric will be adequate for evaluating a KM initiative's feasibility or its value proposition in comparison to other uses of the funds. Metrics are best used in conjunction with each other, as each one provides a slightly different value perspective.

Unlike traditional (e.g., manufacturing) KM initiatives, financial analysis for a KM initiative has additional complications. For example, many of the KM initiative benefits from the knowledge management effort will be based on soft facts. That is, quantifying intangible assets may create some difficulties.

Knowledge management efforts lead to changes in behaviors, approaches and methods that, on their own may not have direct bottom-line impacts. However, when these are mapped and traced to organizational processes, the impacts can be measured and articulated. Needless to say, this is often a more time-consuming and creative effort than simply measuring direct impacts as in the case of outcomes from a new piece of manufacturing equipment. Equally important is that there is a lag time between when one invests in a KM effort and when one achieves outcomes that result in payoffs. Accounting for this time lag is not easy, yet it is essential to building an adequate business case.

Investing in KM is akin to a group as a whole investing in a common effort. Consider the case of investing in initiatives such as the prevention of global warming by lowering greenhouse gas emissions or the promotion of fair trade practices. Most people agree that preventing global warming or increasing the adoption of fair trade practices benefits society. The challenge arises when we ask who wants to take responsibility for investing in these efforts. If taxes were raised to support these efforts, would you be happy? Rational individuals often want others to bear the cost of these common efforts and gladly enjoy the benefits, yet hesitate to initiate responsibility. A similar predicament faces knowledge management efforts. Departments within an organization want their peer units to invest in a common effort. Each department might see knowledge management as an effort someone else should put up resources for and hence defers spending its own resources. In some organizations, KM efforts might be viewed as a "tax" levied across the departments and enterprise.

KM Strategy Metrics and Key Performance Indicators (KPIs)

KM strategy will link the best practices to initiatives to expected benefits (best practice → KM initiative → benefit). At every phase in the KM tactical delivery of initiatives, metrics should provide a valuable means for focusing attention on desired behaviors and results. Each KM initiative and KM activity should have its own set of metrics.

KM performance measures have several objectives:

- Help make a business case for implementation or sustainment and expansion
- Provide targets or goals to drive desired behavior
- Guide and tune the implementation process by providing feedback

- Retrospectively measure the value of the initial investment decision and the lessons learned
- Develop benchmarks for future comparisons and for others to use
- Aid learning from the effort and developing lessons learned.

KPIs and metrics to track for the KM strategy include:

- Customer Satisfaction: Customer satisfaction can be improved, specifically in contact centers and agencies where there is constant interaction with the customer. Customer satisfaction is best measured using standard market research techniques, such as:
  - Surveys
  - Follow-up telephone calls
  - Focus groups.

Benefits, Goals and Measurement Criteria for KM/KMS

One of the obvious benefits described will be that the business problem/opportunity outlined above will be addressed. To help in this regard, completing the benefit-value table (Table 6.1) is a recommended approach. Please note that the benefits are examples only; refer to your established KM metrics and KPIs, including your performance figures for specific benefit information (Rhem, 2016).

Table 6.1   Benefit-Value table

Category	Benefit	Value
Financial	New revenue generated	$ x
	Reduction in costs	$ x
	Increased profit margin	$ x
Operational	Improved operational efficiency	x %
	Reduction in product time to market	x hrs
	Enhanced quality of product / service	x %
Market	Increased market awareness	x %
	Greater market share	x %
	Additional competitive advantage	Describe
Customer	Improved customer satisfaction	x %
	Increased customer retention	x %
	Greater customer loyalty	Describe
Staff	Increased staff satisfaction	x %
	Improved organizational culture	Describe
	Longer staff retention	x %

Costs and Funding Plan

Describe the tangible and intangible costs to the company upon implementation of the solution. The costs of the *actual* KM initiative should be included as well as any negative impact to the business resulting from the *delivery* of the KM initiative. A way to capture these costs is by completing the cost–value table (Table 6.2).

Table 6.2   Cost–Value table

Category	Cost	Value	Budgeted
People	Salaries of KM initiative staff Contractors / outsourced parties Training courses	$ x $ x $ x	YES NO YES
Physical	Building premises for KM initiative team Equipment and materials Tools (e.g., computers, phones)	$ x $ x $ x	NO NO NO
Marketing	Advertising/branding Promotional materials PR and communications	$ x $ x $ x	YES NO NO
Organizational	Operational down-time Short-term loss in productivity Cultural change	$ x $ x Describe	NO NO NO

Feasibility

Describe the feasibility of the solution. To adequately complete this section, a feasibility study may need to be initiated to quantify the likelihood of achieving the desired KM initiative result. To assess the overall feasibility of this option, break the solution down into components and rate the feasibility of each component using the component–feasibility table (Table 6.3).

To ensure that the feasibility ratings are accurate, use all appropriate methods possible to identify the likely feasibility of the solution. For example, if adopting new KM technology, develop a small prototype and test it to see if the resultant benefits match those expected from the exercise.

Table 6.3   Component–Feasibility table

Component	Rating (1 (low)–10 (high))	Method used to determine feasibility
New KM technology	5	A KM technology prototype was created to assess the solution
New people	8	A survey was completed to identify skill-set availability
New processes	3	Processes within similar organizations were reviewed
New assets	9	Physical assets were inspected

Risks

Summarize the most apparent risks associated with the adoption of this solution. Risks are defined as "any event which *may* adversely affect the ability of the solution to produce the required deliverables." Risks may be strategic, environmental, financial, operational, technical, industrial, competitive or customer-related. Completing a risk–mitigation table is the recommended approach (Table 6.4).

To complete this section thoroughly, it may be necessary to undertake a formal risk assessment (by documenting a *Risk Management Plan*). To reduce the likelihood and impact of each risk's eventuating, clear "mitigating actions" should be defined.

Table 6.4   Risk-Mitigation table

Risk description	Likelihood	Impact	Mitigating actions
Inability to recruit skilled resource	Low	Very high	Outsource KM initiative to a company with proven industry experience and appropriately skilled staff
Technology solution is unable to deliver required results	Medium	High	Complete a pilot KM initiative to prove the technology solution will deliver the required results
Additional capital expenditure may be required in addition to that approved	Medium	Medium	Maintain strict cost management processes during the KM initiative

Issues

Summarize the highest priority issues associated with the adoption of this option. Issues are defined as "any event which *currently* adversely affects the ability of the solution to produce the required deliverables." Completing an issue–resolution table is the recommended approach (Table 6.5).

Table 6.5 Issue–Resolution table

Issue description	Priority	Resolution actions
Required capital expenditure funds have not been budgeted	High	Request funding approval as part of this proposal
Required computer software is only at "beta" phase and has not yet been released live	Medium	Design solution based on current software version and adapt changes to solution once the final version of the software has been released
Regulatory approval must be sought to implement the final solution	Low	Initiate the regulatory approval process early so that it does not delay the final roll-out process

Conclusion

Knowledge management metrics are critical to convince senior management as to the value of their KM efforts. Many organizations simply use input and output measures, but it's the outcome measures which should be the most important to the organizational goals and strategic mission. This chapter provides some food for thought in this area. Future research issues deal with how best to further quantify intangible assets in an organization, how to best align KM strategies to the overall strategic mission of the organization, and how to apply other costing techniques to provide more clarity on the outcome metrics for KM initiatives.

References

Dmitriev, P., Wu, X. (2016). Measuring metrics. *CIKM '16: Proceedings of the 25th ACM International Conference on Information and Knowledge Management*, pp. 429–37.

Krob, A. (2015). Five metrics for assessing knowledge sharing outcomes. Retrieved from https://www.thinkhdi.com/library/supportworld/2015/knowledge-sharing-outcomes.aspx.

Liebowitz, J., Suen, C. (2000). Developing knowledge management metrics for measuring intellectual capital. *Journal of Intellectual Capital* 1(1), pp. 54–67.

Rhem, A. (2016). *Knowledge Management in Practice*. Auerbach Publications.

Rhem, A. (2018). Measuring the effectiveness of your knowledge management program. Retrieved from https://www.kminstitute.org/blog/measuring-effectiveness-your-knowledge-management-program.

Search Engine Land (2019). The technical SEO hierarchy of needs. Retrieved from https://searchengineland.com/the-technical-seo-hierarchy-of-needs-312670.

Venkatraman, S., Venkatraman, R. (2018). Communities of practice approach for knowledge management systems. Retrieved from https://www.mdpi.com/.

7. Knowledge management and innovation: issues, gaps, applications and opportunities

Vida Skudienė

Introduction

Today's turbulent, uncertain and unpredictable global business environment forces companies to constantly innovate in order to gain competitive advantage or just to survive. The significance of innovativeness to economic growth and a successful firm performance is evident (Ruppel & Harrington, 2000; Wang & Ahmend, 2004). Knowledge is widely considered to be the main resource of innovation as innovation implies the "creation of new knowledge and ideas to facilitate new business outcomes" (Du Plessis, 2007, p. 21). This interplay of knowledge and innovation has led to a large amount of research into the knowledge management–innovation relationship. It has been observed that most studies support the assumption that knowledge management promotes innovation outcomes (Du Plessis, 2007; Chen et al., 2010; Jimenez et al., 2014; Scuotto et al., 2017). The findings of these studies show that organizations have to prioritize Knowledge Management (KM) activities if they want to foster innovation. In turn, a growing body of literature suggests that effective knowledge exploration provides necessary conditions for open innovation to thrive (Vrontis et al., 2017; Che et al., 2018; Wu & Hu, 2018). Scholars have analyzed widely different KM dimensions, such as knowledge creation, knowledge sharing, knowledge sourcing, and knowledge implementation relationships with innovation. The variety of innovation modes (performance, capability, success, improvement, etc.) have also been considered in their link with KM activities. The proliferation of studies in this field calls for a systemized review that could identify gaps, enable new research trends and advance the KM-innovation research agenda.

This chapter aims to further the understanding of knowledge management's role and significance for the development of firm innovation performance. The study reviews the empirical evidence on how various KM practices impact innovation performance and addresses the research gaps and trends. Based on an extensive academic analysis, opportunities are highlighted for organizations that strive to increase their capacity to innovate by exploring and exploiting the potential of knowledge management. The chapter begins with an overview of the relevant academic literature on the interplay between KM and innovation performance. Then, a discussion is offered on advancing a research agenda for scholarly inquiry. Finally, useful insights are provided into how managers may foster innovation performance by effectively managing knowledge.

KM: Innovation Relationship Research

Considering the importance of knowledge management to an organization's innovative performance, many researchers have explored the link between the two phenomena. According to Calantone, Cavusgil and Zhao (2002), the tricky and complicated issue of innovativeness can be tackled through knowledge management as an instrument (Chen et al., 2010) which helps new information to be included into the existing organizational memory and resource capital (Chen & Huang, 2011) or existing, old information to be converted into new knowledge. Thus, even though the knowledge management primary task is not innovation creation, it generates an environment favorable for innovation to happen (Du Plessis, 2007) and is viewed as a process where knowledge can be leveraged as a useful resource to accomplish or increase the innovation (Yahya & Goh, 2002).

Because knowledge management is said to stimulate the combination of existing and newly obtained knowledge, which together enable new connections and associations (Tsai, 2001), a company with proper KM capabilities is able to use its resources more effectively and efficiently in order to become more innovative (Darroch, 2005). Chen and Lin (2004) noted that KM practices increase organizational innovativeness in climates that are known as innovative and supportive. In fact, KM plays an invaluable role in innovations; that is, it is said to facilitate collaborations, assist in tacit knowledge transformation to explicit knowledge, help identify knowledge gaps and ensure that needed knowledge is available and accessible to everyone (Du Plessis, 2007). Yahya and Goh (2002) claim that KM as a process allows the control of knowledge so that it can become an instrument for achieving or increasing the innovation of process, products or services, by increasing effective decision-making and organizational adaptation to the market. When knowledge is shared among employees, it encourages collective learning and generates beneficial collaborations that improve the core knowledge available to a company (Chen et al., 2010), and provides opportunities for new knowledge creation leading to innovative solutions.

In general, knowledge management is claimed to positively affect an organization's innovation performance (Subramaniam & Youndt, 2005) because KM practices give direct access to collective organizational know-how, knowledge and skills, which create new organizational and individual competencies (Gloet & Terziovski, 2004).

Based on the reviewed literature, the KM processes (creation, sharing, sourcing, implementation) relationship with innovation are viewed from three perspectives: knowledge exploration processes link with innovation, knowledge exploitation processes link with innovation, and an ambidextrous KM perspective incorporating both exploratory and exploitatory processes (Gupta et al., 2006) links with innovation. Knowledge exploration is related to new knowledge acquisition using external sources. Knowledge exploitation activities enable organizations to adopt and apply the existing knowledge (He & Wong, 2004). Innovation construct has been investigated by scholars referring to several outcomes: innovation performance and capacity, innovation success, innovation improvement, innovative employee/work behavior, open innovation, and technological and organizational innovation.

Knowledge Creation and Innovation

The most prominent research in the knowledge creation–innovation link was conducted by Esterhuizen, Schutte and Toit (2012). Based on Nonaka's SECI model on knowledge creation (see Nonaka & Takeuchi, 1995), the scientists developed an innovation maturity model that provides a platform for knowledge creation alignment to innovation capability across maturity levels. The main findings of this research confirmed that knowledge creation enables innovation and that the ability to generate new knowledge plays a vital role in creating sustainable competitive advantage. The original outcome of this research is that the tangible link between knowledge creation and innovation capability maturity was confirmed.

Several researchers have examined and confirmed multilevel knowledge aspects, like knowledge creation and sharing (Chen et al., 2010) or knowledge creation, sharing, acquisition and storage (Andreeva & Kianto, 2011), which impact company innovation performance.

The findings of Shu, Page, Gao and Jiang's (2012) study on knowledge creation's firm link with innovation conducted within 270 Chinese cross-sectional companies demonstrate that knowledge creation impacts process and product innovations. The survey by Zelaya-Zamora and Senoo (2013) developed a multidimensional knowledge creation concept encompassing six dimensions: absorptive capacity, SECI performance, external ties, inter-unit ties, members' commitment, cooperation and trust, to explore their link with innovation performance. The positive and significant relationship between these constructs was confirmed.

An interesting study by Spaeth, Stuermer and von Krogh (2010) presented external contributors' knowledge creation as a benefit to open innovation process. The researchers focused on knowledge creation sources employing an open approach to accelerate innovation performance. Wang, Chin and Lin (2019) indicated that external knowledge can be a critical catalyst spurring innovation performance. The authors proposed that an ambidextrous knowledge strategy has a positive impact also on innovation implemented management.

In summary, in the studies on the knowledge creation–innovation link, scholars have proposed that knowledge creation could be approached from exploitatory, exploratory and ambidextrous perspectives. Recent research supports the multichannel, that is, an ambidextrous KM strategy to enhance innovation capabilities. Particular attention is drawn to external knowledge creation domains' opportunities to enhance innovation opportunities. It is acknowledged that companies are not taking proper advantage of global, digitalized and technologically embedded business environments that offer a means for unorthodox knowledge creation initiatives.

Knowledge Sharing and Innovation

An extensive body of research is devoted to investigation of the knowledge sharing–innovation relationship. It has been proposed by many researchers that knowledge sharing is a managerial priority in the 21st century (Hansen et al., 1999; Radaelli et al., 2011) and is the most important determinant of a successful innovation capability (Lin, 2007). The studies support knowledge-sharing value for promoting innovation (Andreeva & Kianto, 2011; Saenz et al., 2012; Wand & Wang, 2012; Lee et al., 2013; Akhavan & Mahdi, 2016), and argue that development of a knowledge-sharing culture is expected to facilitate creativity, generate new ideas and enhance innovation.

Soto-Acosta, Popa and Palacios-Marques (2018) and Ganguly, Tlukdar and Chatterjee (2019) found a positive relationship between knowledge sharing and innovation performance. These studies exhibit the critical role that knowledge sharing plays in developing organizational innovation performance and capability. Ganguly, Tlukdar and Chatterjee (2019) observe that social capital, tacit knowledge sharing and knowledge quality are positively associated with innovation capability. The study findings regarding knowledge quality and innovation interdependence are consistent with Zubielqui, Lindsay, Lindsay and Jones's (2018) and Yoo's (2014) empirical research results.

A recent study by Keszey (2018) focused on the boundary spanners' knowledge sharing impact on innovation success in turbulent environments. The study results indicate that boundary spanners' willingness to share their knowledge has an impact on new product development innovativeness and performance. Scholars have also indicated that knowledge-sharing and knowledge dissemination may moderate the link between organizational factors and innovation capability and performance (Akhavan & Mahdi, 2016; Ferraris et al., 2017).

Knowledge sharing research addresses both internal and external perspectives. Although, the majority of research is devoted to the potential of internal company resources to enable innovation by effective knowledge sharing among employees and departments, the current studies focus on external knowledge sharing opportunities (Ritala et al., 2017). According to Serenko and Bontis (2016), external knowledge sharing is beneficial for firms' innovation performance. The studies in general indicate the positive effect of knowledge sharing internally and externally on innovativeness; however, referring to external knowledge sharing, the researchers pay attention to the risks of knowledge leaking which might be detrimental to innovation (Ritala et al., 2017).

Knowledge Sourcing/Acquisition and Innovation

The literature on knowledge sourcing (sourcing others' knowledge), both tacit and explicit, states that it plays an important role in innovative performance of an organization (Li et al., 2004; Johnson et al., 2006; Huggins et al., 2010; Xu et al., 2010). The results of Che, Wu, Wang and Yang's (2018) study indicate that knowledge sourcing influences employee innovative behavior. The research also indicates that the link between knowledge sourcing and employee innovative behavior is strongly moderated by information transparency.

Open innovation paradigm and open innovation models suggest that knowledge should be acquired from internal and external resources and integrated to seek improved organizational performance (Chesbrough, 2003; West &

Borgers, 2014). The results of Papa, Dezi, Gregori, Mueller and Miglietta's (2017) empirical research is in line with Leiponen and Helfat's (2011) and Dahlander, O'Mahony and Gann's (2016) studies indicating that integrated knowledge acquisition positively impacts innovation performance.

Knowledge acquisition is mainly discussed either taking into consideration internal sources or external sources, or both (Liao et al., 2012; Marvel, 2012; Chen et al., 2016). Some scholars highlight social capital (Martinez-Canas et al., 2012; Parra-Requena et al., 2013; Molina-Morales et al., 2014); others explore networks (Zheng et al., 2011), or focus on technological resources and market knowledge acquisition's (Marvel, 2012) role in an organization's innovation performance. A growing body of studies investigates external knowledge sources as innovation determinants (Chen et al., 2016; Ferraris et al., 2017; Scuotto et al., 2017; Vrontis et al., 2017; Simao & Franco, 2018) taking into account globalization and information technologies' development contexts as benefits for external knowledge acquisition (Cassiman & Veugelers, 2006; Laursen & Salter, 2006). Some studies explore other external knowledge sourcing channels, such as licencing, spin-outs, contracts, patents and licencing (Tidd & Bessant, 2009). Consequently, the studies prove that external and internal knowledge usage may improve innovation performance (Chesbrough, 2003; Ferraris et al., 2017). According to Rass, Dumbach, Danzinger, Buillinger and Moeslein (2013), an organization's social relations and networks positively impact its open innovation capability. However, the study conducted by Ham, Choi and Lee (2017) reveals some contradictory findings that an external knowledge-oriented approach does not have an effect on innovation performance in a large company context.

Knowledge Management Implementation and Innovation

Knowledge implementation processes refer to application of new knowledge created inside a company (Wu & Hu, 2018). However, based on a dynamic capability concept of knowledge management, external and internal knowledge acquisition processes may interact with each other to reach maximal benefits (Motta, 2013; Tseng & Lee, 2014; Lee, 2015). Recent studies explore the evaluation of knowledge management implementation as an integral process influencing open innovation process (Gretsch et al., 2012; Karami et al., 2015; Wu & Hu, 2018). According to Wu and Hu (2018), empirical research findings on open innovation processes (outside-in, inside-out, coupled) are correlated with KM implementation processes. This research proposes a novel framework defining an open innovation process as the driver of KM implementation performance. Several studies have explored knowledge management implementation success factors (Farzin et al., 2014; Karami et al., 2015) and measured its architecture composed of different steps (Gretsch et al., 2012). However, many studies have contended that organizational and demographic factors may positively correlate with KM implementation success. Very few investigations have been performed on the knowledge implementation–innovation relationship.

Gaps and Future Research Opportunities

A stream of contemporary research devoted to ambidextrous knowledge management effects on innovation performance indicate that internal and external knowledge management processes can enhance a firm's innovative efforts and performance. The studies assert that both knowledge exploration and exploitation have a positive impact on innovation (Gupta et al., 2006; Miller et al., 2007; Chen & Huang, 2009; Zack et al., 2009; Donate & Guadamillas, 2011; Secundo, Toma, Schiuma & Passiante, 2019; Wang et al., 2019). In addition, knowledge-centered culture, leadership and HR practices have been found to play a moderating role in the link between knowledge exploration and exploitation practices with innovation (Donate & Guadamillas, 2011). An analytical literature review of the ambidextrous KM role in supporting open innovation activities based on 39 articles published between 2006 and 2017 highlights that knowledge management has to integrate internal and external knowledge elements in order to enhance open innovation opportunities (Natalicchio et al., 2017). Moreover, the studies indicate that the switch between KM exploration and exploitation contributes to inbound, outbound and coupled open innovation capabilities and emphasizes the significance of a balanced KM architecture facing today's global dynamic environment.

Considering the vast breadth of investigations on knowledge management and innovation, there is still a lack of research on the interplay between KM modes and innovation drive (Björkman & Lervik, 2007; Brock & Siscovick, 2007; Evans et al., 2010; Espedal et al., 2012; Oparaocha, 2016). According to Terziovski and Gloet (2004), the blind side in extant literature is the analysis of the knowledge management process in relation to the innovation process, as a large number of authors focus their research solely on improvement of innovativeness in organizations or knowledge management issues. Meanwhile, investigation of the supportive role that KM plays in innovation process and its effects remains under-researched (Darroch, 2005; Du Plessis, 2007). Additionally, Quintane, Casselman, Reiche and Nylund (2011) identify that current measurement and interpretations of innovation as an outcome based on knowledge, lacks clarity, and call for theoretical justification of a knowledge-based approach to innovation that could be operationalized in future empirical studies. According to an international expert panel of the Global KM Network, coordinated by Dr. Peter Heising, the key research gap is a better understanding of the relationship between KM and company performance (Heising, 2014).

To date, there is a need for more studies into the ambidextrous perspective of KM and innovation processes. Future studies should explore the effects of firms' openness to external knowledge and its effect on innovation outcomes. Further investigation is necessary to explore the complex KM role for promoting innovation in specific organizational realities, in particular taking into consideration business environment changes moving from office-bound to home-bound work conditions and from closed to open business systems.

Another stream of research should address knowledge creation and sharing, and acquiring mechanisms' relations with *open innovation* processes in different sets of ecosystems. Furthermore, network and inter-partner knowledge sharing and creation contributions to *collaborative innovation* could be explored in more depth. In terms of research methodology, more accurate ways to measure the KM–innovation link are encouraged.

There is still need for research on the implications of the role of external knowledge sources in organizational innovation development processes (Simao & Franco, 2018). Given the need for innovative solutions to manage the turmoil in our contemporary business world, researchers are encouraged to explore the *collaborative knowledge management* potential in dynamic economic uncertainty and unpredictable social environment contexts. Future studies could investigate the collaborative KM strategy linkages with open and collaborative innovation.

Practical Applications

In fostering their companies' innovation capabilities, it is suggested that managers develop first of all a sustainable KM strategy integrating internal and external systems. They should develop the organizational social network architecture to ensure transparent knowledge flow and create an innovative organization culture fostering ambidextrous KM processes in order to stimulate innovation capacities. For innovations to succeed, openness is crucial (Cammarano et al., 2017); therefore, managers have to reconsider the conservative approach to knowledge management and start experimenting with implementation of novel KM practice, techniques, processes and structures by providing more opportunities for new and unorthodox ideas to enhance company innovation.

Social, economic and business environments have substantially changed from "closed" to more "open" interaction patterns that are caused by fundamental technological and societal evolution. An explorative approach to KM processes may reduce uncertainty and avoid failures through the implementation of new ideas (Karasek & Theorell, 2016). Therefore, it is suggested that companies invest in development of a cooperation and collaboration mindset, and seek to increase their innovation capacity. Innovation is becoming an increasingly open process (Chesbrough, 2007); thus, companies must create an open business culture that enables them to receive knowledge from the outside and share their ideas with outside market players.

A company's future depends on its ability to build ambidexterity into its organization (Birkinshaw & Gibson, 2004) that will enable the company to succeed in the long run. Companies need to manage both exploratory and exploitatory knowledge processes. Exploiting existing knowledge and exploring new external knowledge possibilities will allow them to achieve long-term success. Knowledge exploration and exploitation require different managerial approaches and processes (Chen, 2017). A new approach to a KM strategy is necessary to build complementary interactions internally and externally for improving organizational performance. The emerging business environment demands that organizations adapt knowledge management (Liebowitz & Paliszkiewicz, 2019) to align it with the changing innovation development architecture.

References

Akhavan, P. & Mahdi, H.S. (2016). Social capital, knowledge sharing, and innovation capability: an empirical study of R&D teams in Iran. *Technology Analysis & Strategic Management*, 28 (1), 96–113.

Andreeva, T. & Kianto, A. (2011). Knowledge processes, knowledge-intensity and innovation: a moderated mediation analysis. *Journal of Knowledge Management*, 15 (6), 1016–34.

Birkinshaw, J. & Gibson, C. (2004). Building ambidexterity into an organization. *MIT Sloan Management Review*, 45 (4), 46–55.

Björkman, I. & Lervik J.E. (2007). Transferring HR practices within multinational corporations. *Human Resource Management Journal*, 17 (4), 320–35.

Brock, D.M. & Siscovick, I.C. (2007). Global integration and local responsiveness in multinational subsidiaries: some strategy, structure, and human resource contingencies. *Asia Pacific Journal of Human Resources*, 45 (3), 353–73.

Calantone, R.J., Cavusgil, S.T. & Zhao, Y. (2002). Learning orientation, firm innovation capability, and firm performance. *Industrial Marketing Management*, 31(6), 515–24.

Cammarano, A., Caputo, M., Lamberti, E. & Michelino, F. (2017). Open innovation and intellectual property: a knowledge-based approach. *Management Decision*, 55(6), 1182–208.

Cassiman, B. & Veugelers, R. (2006). In search of complementarity in innovation strategy: internal R&D and external knowledge acquisition. *Management Science*, 52 (1), 68–82.

Che, T., Wu, Z., Wang, Y. & Yang, R. (2018). Impacts of knowledge sourcing on employee innovation: the moderating effect of information transparency. *Journal of Knowledge Management*, DOI 10.1108/JKM-11-2017-0554.

Chen, C., Huang, J. & Hsiao, Y. (2010). Knowledge management and innovativeness. *International Journal of Manpower*, 31(8), 848–70.

Chen, C. & Lin, B. (2004). The effects of environment, knowledge attribute, organizational climate, and firm characteristics on knowledge sourcing decisions. *R&D Management*, 34 (2), 137–46.

Chen, C.J. & Huang, J.W. (2009). Strategic human resources practices and innovation performance – the mediating role of knowledge management capacity. *Journal of Business Research*, 62, 104–14.

Chen, C.W. & Huang, S.H. (2011). Implementing KM programs using fuzzy QFD. *Total Quality Management*, 22(4), 387–406.

Chen, Y. (2017). Dynamic ambidexterity: how innovations manage exploration and exploitation. *Business Horizons*, 60, 385–94.

Chen, Y.M., Liu, H.H. & Wu, H.Y. (2016). Reputation for toughness and anti-dumping rebuttals: competitive rivalry, perceived benefits, and stage of the product life cycle. *Journal of Business Research*, 69(6), 2145–50.

Chesbrough, H. (2003). *Open Innovation: The New Imperative for Creating and Profiting from Technology*. Boston, MA: Harvard Business School Press.

Chesbrough, H. (2007). *Why Companies Should Have Open Innovation Business Models*. Boston, MA: Harvard Business School Press.

Dahlander, L., O'Mahony, S. & Gann, D.M. (2016). One foot in, one foot out: how does individuals' external search breath affect innovation outcomes? *Strategic Management Journal*, 37(2), 280–302.

Darroch, J. (2005). Knowledge management, innovation and firm performance. *Journal of Knowledge Management*, 9 (3), 101–15.

Donate, M.J. & Guadamillas, F. (2011). Organizational factors to support knowledge management and innovation. *Journal of Knowledge Management*, 15 (6), 890–914.

Du Plessis, M. (2007). The role of knowledge management in innovation. *Journal of Knowledge Management*, 11 (4), 20–29.

Espedal, B., Gooderham, P. & Evensen, H. (2012). The impact of global leadership development programs on social networks and knowledge sharing in multinational enterprises. *Human Resources Management & Ergonomics*, 6(2), 235–44.

Esterhuizen, D., Schutte, C.S.L. & Toit, A.S.A. (2012). Knowledge creation processes as critical enablers for innovation. *International Journal of Information Management*, 32 (4), 354–64.

Evans, P., Pucik, V. & Björkman, I. (2010). *The Global Challenge: International Human Resource Management*. New York: McGraw-Hill Higher Education.

Farzin, M.R., Kahreh, M.S., Hesan, M. & Khalouei, A. (2014). A survey of critical success factors for strategic knowledge management implementation: applications for service sector. *Procedia – Social and Behavioral Science*, 109 (8), 595–9.

Ferraris, A., Santoro, G. & Dezi, L. (2017). How MNC's subsidiaries may improve their innovative performance? The role of external sources and knowledge management capabilities. *Journal of Knowledge Management*, 21 (3), 540–52.

Ganguly, A., Tlukdar, A. & Chatterjee, D. (2019). Evaluating the role of social capital, tacit knowledge sharing, knowledge quality and reciprocity in determining innovation capability of an organization. *Journal of Knowledge Management*, 23 (6), 1105–35.

Gloet, M. & Terziovski, M. (2004). Exploring the relationship between knowledge management practices and innovation performance. *Journal of Manufacturing Technology Management*, 15(5), 402–9.

Gretsch, S., Mangl, H. & Schatz, R. (2012). Implementation process of a knowledge management initiative: yellow pages. *New Research on Knowledge Management Models and Methods*, 14, 311–32.

Gupta, A., Smith, K. & Shalley, C. (2006). The interplay between exploration and exploitation. *Academy of Management Journal*, 49 (4), 693–706.

Ham, J., Choi, B. & Lee, J.N. (2017). Open and closed knowledge sourcing. *Industrial Management and Data Systems*, 117(6), 1166–84.

Hansen, M.T., Nohria, N. & Tierney, T. (1999). What's your strategy for managing knowledge? *Harvard Business Review*, 77 (2), 106–16.

He, Z.L. & Wong, P.K. (2004). Exploration vs exploitation: an empirical test of the ambidexterity hypothesis. *Organization Science*, 15 (4), 481–94.

Heising, P. (2014). Knowledge management – advancements and future research needs – results from global knowledge research network study. *Proceedings of the British Academy of Management Conference (BAM2014)*, Belfast, September 9–11.

Huggins, R., Izushi, H., Clifton, N., Jenkins, S., Prokop, D. & Whitfield, C. (2010). Sourcing knowledge for innovation: the international dimension, DOI: 10.13140/2.1.3488.2246.

Jimenez, D., Martínez-Costa, M. & Sanz-Valle, R. (2014). Knowledge management practices for innovation: a multinational corporation's perspective. *Journal of Knowledge Management*, 18 (5), 1–22.

Johnson, M.D., Hollenbeck, J.R., Humphrey, S.E., Ilgen, D.R., Jundt, D. & Meyer, C.J. (2006). Cutthroat cooperation: asymmetrical adaptation to changes in team reward structures. *Academy of Management Journal*, 49(1), 103–19.

Karami, M., Alvani, S.M., Zare, H. & Kheirandish, M. (2015). Determination of critical success factors for knowledge management implementation using qualitative and quantitative tools (case study: Bahman automobile industry). *Iranian Journal of Management Studies*, 8 (6), 882–90.

Karasek, R. & Theorell, T. (2016). Healthy work: stress, productivity, and the reconstruction of working life. *Quarterly Review of Biology*, 19(4), 671–81.

Keszey, T. (2018). Boundary spanners' knowledge sharing for innovation success in turbulent times. *Journal of Knowledge Management*, 22 (5), 1061–81.

Laursen, K. & Salter, A. (2006). Open for innovation: the role of openness in explaining innovation performance among UK manufacturing firms. *Strategic Management Journal*, 27 (2), 131–50.

Lee, K. (2015). A measurement model of operational capabilities in application software firms. *International Journal of Business Management*, 10 (12), 89–102.

Lee, V.H., Leong, L.Y., Hew, T.S. & Ooi, K.B. (2013). Knowledge management: a key determinant in advancing technological innovation. *Journal of Knowledge Management*, 17 (6), 848–72.

Leiponen, A. & Helfat, C.E. (2011). Location, decentralization and knowledge sources for innovation. *Organizational Science*, 22 (3), 641–58.

Li, X., Hong, P., Nahm, A.Y. & Doll, W.J. (2004). Knowledge sharing in integrated product development. *European Journal of Innovation Management*, 7 (2), 102–12.

Liao, S., Chang, W.J., Hu, D.C. & Yueh, Y.L. (2012). Relationships among organizational culture, knowledge acquisition, organizational learning, and organizational innovation in Taiwan's banking and insurance industries. *International Journal of Human Resource Management*, 23 (1), 52–70.

Liebowitz, J. & Paliszkiewicz, J. (2019). The next generation of knowledge management: implications for LIS educators and professionals. *Online Journal of Applied Knowledge Management*, 7 (2), 16–28.

Lin, H.F. (2007). Knowledge sharing and firm innovation capability: an empirical study. *International Journal of Manpower*, 28 (3–4), 315–32.

Martinez-Canas, R., Saez-Martinez, F.J. & Ruiz-Palomino, P. (2012). Knowledge acquisition's mediation of social capital-firm innovation. *Journal of Knowledge Management*, 16 (1), 61–76.

Marvel, M. (2012). Knowledge acquisition asymmetries and innovation radicalness. *Journal of Small Business Management*, 50 (30), 447–68.

Miller, B., Bierly, P. & Daly, P. (2007). The knowledge strategy orientation scale: individual perceptions of firm-level phenomena. *Journal of Managerial Issues*, 19 (3), 414–35.

Molina-Morales, F.X., Garcia-Villaverde, P.M. & Parra-Requena, G. (2014). Geographical and cognitive proximity effects on innovation performance in SMEs: a way through knowledge acquisition. *International Entrepreneurship and Management Journal*, 10 (2), 231–51.

Motta, E. (2013). 25 years of knowledge acquisition. *International Journal of Human-Computer Studies*, 75 (2), 131–4.

Natalicchio, A., Ardito, L., Savino, T. & Albino, V. (2017). Managing knowledge assets for open innovation: a systematic literature review. *Journal of Knowledge Management*, 21 (6), 1362–83.

Nonaka, I. & Takeuchi, H. (1995). *The Knowledge Creating Company: How Japanese Companies Create Dynamics of Innovation*. Oxford: Oxford University Press.

Oparaocha, G.O. (2016). Towards building internal social network architecture that drives innovation: a social exchange theory perspective. *Journal of Knowledge Management*, 20 (3), 534–56.

Papa, A., Dezi, L., Gregori, G.L., Mueller, J. & Miglietta, N. (2017). Improving innovation performance through knowledge acquisition: the moderating role of employee retention and human resource management practices. *Journal of Knowledge Management*, DOI 10.1108/JKM-09-2017-0391.

Parra-Requena, G., Ruiz-Ortega, M.J. & Garcia-Villaverde, P.M. (2013). Social capital and effective innovation in industrial districts: dual effect of absorptive capacity. *Industry and Innovation*, 20 (2), 157–79.

Quintane, E., Casselman, R.M., Reiche, B.S. & Nylund, P.A. (2011). Innovation as a knowledge-based outcome. *Journal of Knowledge Management*, 15(6), 928–47.

Radaelli, G., Mura, M., Spiller, N. & Lettieri, E. (2011). Intellectual capital and knowledge sharing: the mediating role of organizational knowledge-sharing climate. *Knowledge Management Research and Practice*, 9, 342–52.

Rass, M., Dumbach, M., Danzinger, F., Bullinger, A.C. & Moeslein, K.M. (2013). Open innovation and firm performance: the mediating role of social capital. *Creativity and Innovation Management*, 22 (2), 177–94.

Ritala, P., Husted, K., Olander, K. & Michailova, S. (2017). External knowledge sharing and radical innovation: the downsides of uncontrolled openness. *Journal of Knowledge Management*, 22 (5), 1104–23.

Ruppel, C.P. & Harrington, S.J. (2000). The relationship of communication, ethical work climate and trust to commitment and innovation. *Journal of Business Ethics*, 25 (4), 313–28.

Saenz, J., Aramburu, N. & Blanco, C.E. (2012). Knowledge sharing and innovation in Spanish and Colombian high-tech firms. *Journal of Knowledge Management*, 16(6), 919–33.

Scuotto, V., Del Giudice, M., Bresciani, S. & Meissner, D. (2017). Knowledge driven preferences in informal inbound open innovation modes: an explorative view on small to medium enterprises. *Journal of Knowledge Management*, 21 (3), 640–55.

Secundo, G., Toma, A., Schiuma, G. & Passiante, G. (2019). Knowledge transfer in open innovation: a classification framework for healthcare ecosystems. *Business Process Management Journal*, 25(1), 144–63.

Serenko, A. & Bontis, N. (2016). Negotiate, reciprocate, or cooperate? The impact of exchange modes on inter-employee knowledge sharing. *Journal of Knowledge Management*, 20 (4), 687–712.

Shu, C.L., Page, A.L., Gao, S.X. & Jiang, X. (2012). Managerial ties and firm innovation: is knowledge creation a missing link? *Journal of Product Innovation Management*, 29(1), 125–43.

Simao, L. and Franco, M. (2018). External knowledge sources as antecedents of organizational innovation in firm workplaces: a knowledge-based perspective. *Journal of Knowledge Management*, 22(2), 237–56.

Soto-Acosta, P., Popa, S. & Palacios-Marques, D. (2018). Social web knowledge sharing and innovation performance in knowledge-intensive manufacturing SMEs. *The Journal of Technology Transfer*, 42 (2), 425–40.

Spaeth, S., Stuermer, M. & von Krogh, G. (2010). Enabling knowledge creation through outsiders: towards a push model of open innovation. *International Journal of Technology Management*, 52(3–4), 411–31.

Subramaniam, M. & Youndt, M.A. (2005). The influence of intellectual capital on the types of innovative capabilities. *Academy of Management Journal*, 48(3), 450–63.

Terziovski, M. & Gloet, M. (2004). Exploring the relationship between knowledge management practices and innovation performance. *Journal of Manufacturing Technology Management*, 15(5), 402–9.

Tidd, J. & Bessant, J. (2009). *Managing Innovation: Integrating Technological, Market and Organizational Change*, 4th edn. New York: John Wiley & Sons.

Tsai, W. (2001). Knowledge transfer in intra-organizational networks: effects of network position and absorptive capacity on business unit innovation and performance. *Academy of Management Journal*, 44(5), 996–1004.

Tseng, S.M. & Lee, P.S. (2014). The effect of knowledge management capability and dynamic capability on organizational performance. *Journal of Enterprise Information Management*, 27 (2), 158–79.

Vrontis, D., Thrassou, A., Santoro, G. & Papa, A. (2017). Ambidexterity, external knowledge and performance in knowledge-intensive firms. *The Journal of Technology Transfer*, 42(2), 374–88.

Wand, Z. & Wang, N. (2012). Knowledge sharing, innovation and firm performance. *Expert Systems with Application*, 39 (10), 8899–908.

Wang, C., Chin, T. & Lin, J.-H. (2019). Openness and firm innovation performance: the moderating effect of ambidextrous knowledge search strategy. *Journal of Knowledge Management*, DOI 10.1108/JKM-0402019-0198.

Wang, C. L. & Ahmed, P.K. (2004). The development and validation of the organizational innovativeness construct using confirmatory factor analysis. *European Journal of Innovation Management*, 7(4), 303–13.

West, J. & Borgers, M. (2014). Leveraging external sources of innovation: a review of research on open innovation. *Journal of Product Innovation Management*, 31 (4), 814–31.

Wu, I.-L. & Hu, Y.-P. (2018). Open innovation based knowledge management implementation: a mediating role of knowledge management design. *Journal of Knowledge Management*, 22 (8), 1736–56.

Xu, J., Houssin, R., Caillaud, E. & Gardoni, M. (2010). Macro process of knowledge management for continuous innovation. *Journal of Knowledge Management*, 14 (4), 573–91.

Yahya, S. & Goh, W.K. (2002). Managing human resources toward achieving knowledge management. *Journal of Knowledge Management*, 6 (5), 457–68.

Yoo, D.K. (2014). Substructures of perceived knowledge quality and interactions with knowledge sharing and innovativeness: a sense-making perspective. *Journal of Knowledge Management*, 18 (3), 523–37.

Zack, M., McKeen, J. & Singh, S. (2009). Knowledge management organizational performance: an exploratory survey. *Journal of Knowledge Management*, 13 (6), 392–409.

Zelaya-Zamora, J. & Senoo, D. (2013). Synthesizing seeming incompatibilities to foster knowledge creation and innovation. *Journal of Knowledge Management*, 17 (1), 106–22.

Zheng, S.L., Zhang, W., Wu, X.B. & Du, J. (2011). Knowledge-based dynamic capabilities and innovation in networked environments. *Journal of Knowledge Management*, 15 (6), 1035–51.

Zubielqui, G.C., Lindsay, N., Lindsay, W. & Jones, J. (2018). Knowledge quality, innovation and firm performance: a study of knowledge transfer in SMEs. *Small Business Economics*, 53 (1), 1–20.

8. Serendipitous encounters to support innovations via knowledge visualizations

Simon Li and Eric Tsui

1.   Introduction

Every researcher usually needs to deal with an ocean of documents. It is necessary to have some tools to help us "digest" the documents to give us a convenient way to survive the ocean of paperwork and make some sense of it all. Then we don't need to read all of them. It is too time consuming and the linkages between documents may not easily be discovered. Text mining can help in this situation by analyzing a collection of documents and providing useful information to facilitate comprehension of the text without reading everything manually. Topic modeling is one of the useful text extraction methods to pluck related "themes" from a collection of documents as "topics." Each topic would contain related terms from the documents. The situation would look like connecting the "dots." The "dots" can be any terms extracted from a document or any other possible things learned from the real world. There can be static or dynamic patterns out there, depending on your prior knowledge and imagination. Therefore, it is important to begin by studying the relationship between the connections of "dots" and serendipity. Later in the chapter, the computational/algorithmic tools used (KeyGraph and LDAvis) are explained, followed by a description of the data collection for this research. The chapter concludes with the presentation of a testbed that supports data visualization, narrative generation, and scenario planning for users to explore serendipitous discoveries of new knowledge.

2.   Serendipity and Connection of "Dots"

This research is about serendipitous encounters in information seeking via data visualization. The connection of the "dots" (Figure 8.1), inspired by Steve Jobs, is the most important element and the connection of this idea to serendipity is a significant idea of this research using computational/algorithmic models. Serendipity is about finding useful deviations from expected patterns so as to provide new insights (Foster & Ford, 2003; Foster, 2004; de Rond, 2014; Yaqub, 2018). The serendipitous results of text mining using existing literature and a suite of tools called Chance Discovery (CD) (Wang & Ohsawa, 2011) with some computational algorithms (e.g., KeyGraph) (Ohsawa et al., 1998; Wang et al., 2013; Zhang et al., 2013) were examined to experience serendipity. Latent Dirichlet Allocation (LDA) (Blei et al., 2003; Hoffman et al., 2010) is a generative topic discovery algorithm (Ponweiser, 2012) which builds probabilistic models of latent topics for a corpus of documents. The KeyGraph and LDA algorithms were accidentally found to be the long-awaited tool for detecting serendipitous findings from a large volume of text because they all build connections of "dots." They are explored in the following sections.

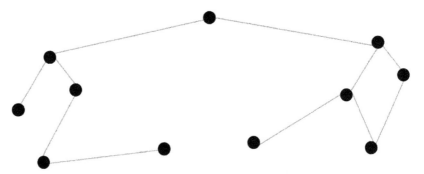

Figure 8.1   Connection of "dots" as a conceptual model of serendipity

3.   Chance Discovery and KeyGraph

Chance Discovery (CD) (Wang et al., 2011) is a suite of computational/ algorithmic and human methods. The objectives are to identify chances, not by luck, but by using both computer algorithms and human participation. It seems to facilitate the serendipity we mentioned above. CD is a suite of tools to help find the possible "signs" of chance, which may be unexpected relevance. A "chance" is described as an unnoticed, hidden, rare, potential or novel, but significant, event(s)/situation(s) which can be regarded either as an opportunity or risk (Ohsawa & Fukuda, 2002). A chance can, therefore, be defined as a piece of timely information about an event or a situation having a significant impact on decision-making. The definitions of "chance" here are like the signs of serendipity, where an unanticipated, anomalous, and strategic nature can be found (Merton & Barber, 2011).

The KeyGraph algorithm, which is the core component of CD, can be used for mainly analyzing textual data. Textual data is generally free-form and unstructured/semi-structured. Quite a number of knowledge sources from the Internet belong to this type and, as a result, most of the existing data-mining techniques and tools, which were designed for structured databases and Knowledge Discovery in Databases (KDD) (Han et al., 2011), may not be directly applicable. Some specialized computational tools, especially from the areas of text mining, would be needed, since unstructured textual content would be a significant part of Big Data. In addition to analysis, knowledge discovery over unstructured data would be difficult without using some specialized text mining, or general computational methods and associated tools (e.g., Chance Discovery). The computational/data mining/system mechanisms for facilitating serendipity would work at the macro level to filter, select and rank some information from a corpus of documents to increase the opportunity for serendipity. Even if we can successfully facilitate serendipity from the different or combined perspectives to select some potential information collection, it is still difficult for an individual to comprehend, since the potential unexpected relevance may still be hidden.

CD can work on the level of a selected corpus of documents (i.e., it can be regarded as the selected information after applying the computational model of serendipity mentioned above). An individual can then easily find signs of "chances" by seeing the unobservable events by visualization of different link structures from the selected corpus that can have high potential to experience serendipity. By integrating the features of the above models and methods from different scholars, we can try to implement the serendipity modeling mechanism as the "computation engine" to enhance the existing information retrieval mechanism. It would work on the areas of presentation of the information, its arrangement order, and the inter-linkage. For example, with the computational serendipity model in place, the distribution of connected links within a particular web page containing the information and the ranking/display order of arrangement of information regarding a serendipity index, instead of relevance, can be designed.

CD can also be defined as the awareness of a chance or risk and the explanation of its significance (Ohsawa & Fukuda, 2002). CD research, therefore, aims to offer theories, methods, strategies and tools to enable receivers to feel and obtain chances while avoiding risks in various situations. The objective is to let people understand explicitly what actions should be made to turn a discovered chance into a real benefit, or what preventive measures can be taken to reduce hazards or risks. Discovering, learning and improving human processes for CD are critical to its acceptance and implementation (Maeno & Ohsawa, 2007). To maximize the potential benefits or minimize the risks, different social, business, and technical domains would require a correct conceptual understanding and evaluation of a potential opportunity or risk from the cognitive and mental perspectives of the CD. In other words, CD is a collaborative and strategic combination of human and the computer processes toward future scenario detection and invention.

Data-/text-mining algorithms can be used to analyze the content of information and the ways the content is organized within a corpus of the document in some unexpected but relevant manner by seeing their "irrelevance" visually and mentally. It can also be useful for discourse analysis if the semantic network approach is also used together with the KeyGraph algorithm. The operating principles of the KeyGraph algorithm can be understood using an analogy of constructing a physical building (Ohsawa et al., 1998). A document, just like a typical building (Figure 8.2), has foundations (i.e., statements representing the basic concepts of the document), walls, doors and windows (just as decoration only), and so on. The roof of the building, which protects the inhabitants against rain or sunshine, represent the key ideas of the document. A roof is supported by columns (i.e., the relationships between the items in the document). The KeyGraph algorithm first generates co-occurrence graphs of terms (original points) from the document into segments (or clusters) to find the foundations (i.e., terms that hold the rest of the document together via columns) of a document. The foundations are the primary and preparatory concepts obtained from the clusters. Afterward, the columns are extracted from the relationships between the items in the document. Finally, the roof would be extracted from the nodes (representing terms) at the intersection of the strong columns for surfacing the most important ideas.

The top-ranked terms based on each term's relationship to the clusters are selected as keywords (Ohsawa et al., 1998). A concept from the author of a document would be represented as a cluster. The most frequently found items in the document would be represented as black nodes in KeyGraph. Solid black lines connect the most strongly co-occurring item pairs forming the edges in the KeyGraph, representing the co-occurrence between events.

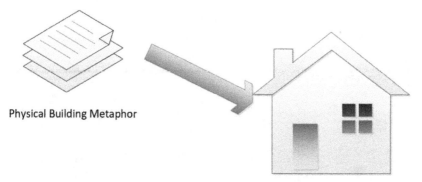

Physical Building Metaphor

Figure 8.2   Physical building metaphor of KeyGraph

As a result, these extracted terms can accurately match the points/ideas of the author of a document, although KeyGraph would be content-sensitive and domain independent. KeyGraph can visualize the relations between data items corresponding to real events in everyday human life to allow thinking inside or even outside the box. Therefore, although KeyGraph is essentially a text-mining tool, it can be used as a critical component to seek information in unanticipated, anomalous and strategic ways to nurture innovation.

The working mechanism behind CD has been illustrated to understand why it can bring such strategic advantages to discovering chances. The CD suite includes a text-mining technology called KeyGraph, which is used to visualize the connections of the important terms distributed inside a corpus of the document by detecting and extracting those key items and their relationships. The hidden/missing linkages between the terms grouped into clusters would then be found so that interesting patterns can be found visually. This method is inspiring in applying data/text-mining technologies to help humans to find the "missing links" between islands of information as "chances," as illustrated in Figure 8.3 (Maeno & Ohsawa, 2007).

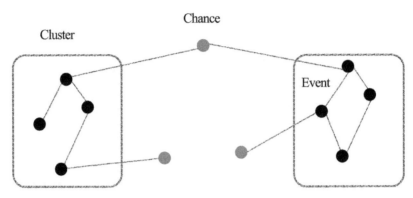

Figure 8.3   A sample KeyGraph

Source: Based on Wang et al., 2011.

Another extension tool of KeyGraph is called data crystallization (Ohsawa, 2005). In a real-world situation, only the visible parts can be represented as data in a document. However, most chances or risks may come from incomplete or ill-structured data. Data crystallization would be used to handle these obstacles by inserting dummy items, which correspond to the hidden and unobservable structures or events. The unobservable events (which can be chances or risks) and their relations with other events can be visualized by applying KeyGraph iteratively to the data donated with the dummy items by gradually increasing the number of edges in the graph. This approach works as the "crystallization of snow" during a gradual decrease in air temperature.

KeyGraph is a text-mining algorithm used to identify the co-occurrence of term pairs and their corresponding clusters (Ohsawa et al., 1998). The terms (called keywords) identified among the different clusters can be regarded as connectors bridging them together, and different clusters can be regarded as different concepts. The connecting keywords can be regarded as "chances" since an individual can probably move from one concept to others. It would provide the paths for an individual to "make things happen." Ideagraph (plus) (Wang et al., 2013; Zhang et al., 2013) is one of the descendants of KeyGraph, which was developed to overcome some of the limitations of KeyGraph. Co-occurrence of terms is sometimes difficult to understand as concepts since the choices of the terms used in the documents do matter. The improvements were developed towards better recognition of term groups as concepts for more natural human recognition. Because of the limitations of KeyGraph, another algorithmic tool, called LDAvis, was examined to see any further opportunities can be explored.

4.   LDAvis

LDA (as discussed so far) implements the concepts of probabilistic modeling of topics (Blei et al., 2003) through term distribution. However, the algorithm itself does not implement the visualization part. The network structure of the LDA results would only be stored inside the data structure of the computer memory. Something similar to topic modeling visualization (Chuang et al., 2012) would be needed. In LDAvis, which is another R package free for downloading, this gap was closed. LDAvis (Sievert & Shirley, 2014) implements the LDA algorithm and provides a web-based interactive visualization facility of topics estimated using the LDA algorithm. It provides an overall view of the available topics and shows their differences. The interactive visualization facility allows a more in-depth exploration of the terms most highly associated with each topic. The visualization facility has two panels (Figure 8.4). The left panel visualizes the topics as circles in a two-dimensional plane, whose centers are determined by computing the Jensen–Shannon divergence between the topics, and then by using multidimensional scaling to project the inter-topic distances onto a two-dimension surface for comparison. Each topic's overall prevalence is represented using the area of the circle (i.e., the topic). The right panel shows a horizontal bar chart whose bars represent the specific terms that are the most useful for interpreting the currently selected topic on the left. A pair of overlaid bars represents both the corpus-wide frequency of a given term as well as the topic-specific frequency of the term.

The λ slider ($0 \leq \lambda \leq 1$) allows ranking of the terms for each topic according to the term relevance. By default, the terms of a topic are ranked in descending order according to their topic-specific probability. Moving the slider allows adjustment of what items are to be displayed based on the rank of a term and the relevance for a specific topic. When sliding towards 1, rarer items would be included, and the constituting terms of the topic would be more abstract, while moving towards 0, fewer rare items and stronger items would be included in the topic, and the constituting terms in the topic would become more specific. The "optimal" value can be user- and situation-dependent while exploring the possibilities found there. Users are strongly advised to explore for themselves.

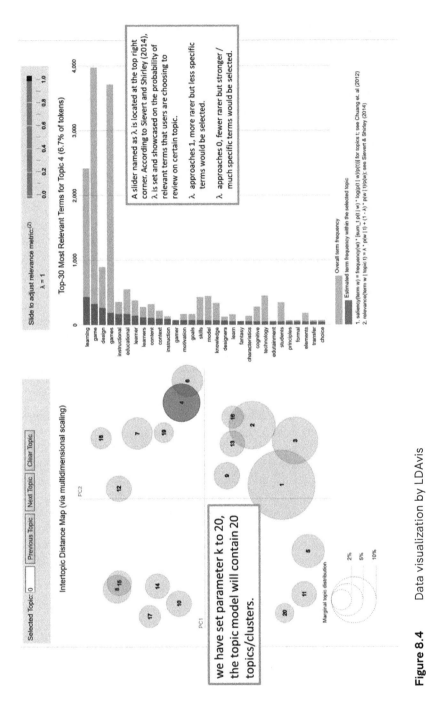

Figure 8.4   Data visualization by LDAvis

In Figure 8.5, which represents the four quadrants (i.e., Areas 1–4) from the left visualization panel of the LDAvis, the twenty topics (and the constituting terms) are classified into two principal components (PC1 and PC2). Depending on the characteristics of a topic (or bubble here), it would be located either closer to PC1 or PC2 or any possible quadrants (Areas 1–4) shown above. Their purposes in identifying norms, exceptions/outliers, etc. in a relative sense are also clarified above. Based on the above explanation, information seekers can make up their minds to locate the information from Areas 1 to 4 according to the nature of the areas. For example, if the information seekers want to locate the norm of information, the items from Area 1 may be the best candidates. However, if they want to locate exceptional information, which may be outliers or even weak signals from the corpus of the document, Area 4 can most probably provide the most exciting things for them. These fours quadrants are the most important elements in this visualization environment since some forms of classification can be done using visual means so that we can focus on the area(s) which attract us most.

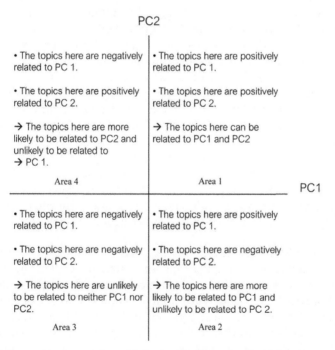

Figure 8.5   Interpretation of left visualization panel of LDAvis

LDA/LDAvis was initially designed for topic modeling and used for document classification. However, topic modeling can be applied in many different other areas according to experience. For example, if we want to know whether the corpus of documents contains the norm of information or not, we can pay attention to the numbers and the contents of the topics being modeled. If there are some new and emerging/outlier topics being found from time to time, we can believe that something new has already happened. These features can be used in educational data mining. Suppose there are some discussion forums for recording students' discussions over the study subjects, then all the forum discussion contents can be downloaded into text documents. By using LDA/LDAvis for topic modeling, the topics in the discussion content can be visualized with their constituting terms. By paying attention to the norm quadrant (Area 1) of the LDAvis left panel, we can find the mainstream discussion/information, helping to verify whether the intended learning outcomes (ILOs) can be met or not. However, if we pay attention to the outlier quadrant (Area 3), it is highly possible to find some accidental discoveries. They can be understood as unintended learning outcomes from the students' discussion content.

A high-level overview of the topics spotted from the corpus of the document would be delivered to show their similarity and differences by calculating the distances between them. Then the information seeker can browse among the topics to comprehend their meaning and prevalence visually. Moreover, the relevant terms of each spotted topic are shown for the information seekers to understand better how a latent topic can be formed. From Figure 8.6, the distance between each topic can be found in the left panel. The composition of terms inside a highlighted topic can be found in the right panel. The size of the bubble indicates the prevalence of the topic. The left and right panels are linked together for information seekers to browse all the spotted topics together with their components. These can facilitate understanding the correlations of the topics better by using visual aids. This critical feature allows viewers to interactively explore the themes of the corpus of the document and the associated terms constituting the themes with relevance figures.

In other words, the results can indicate whether any topic was in some way similar to another topic (i.e., close to positive areas of both PC1 and PC2 (i.e., Area 1) which represent the norm of the contents of the corpus of the documents) or something that deviated from the norm of the contents (i.e., Areas 2, 3 and 4). The information seekers can then further drill into the any of the k topics mined and distributed into the four quadrants to see the details to investigate further what the topics are about. This feature is handy for locating unexpected findings for evaluation of the usefulness by paying attention to areas other than Area 1. Area 3, in which negative values can be found from

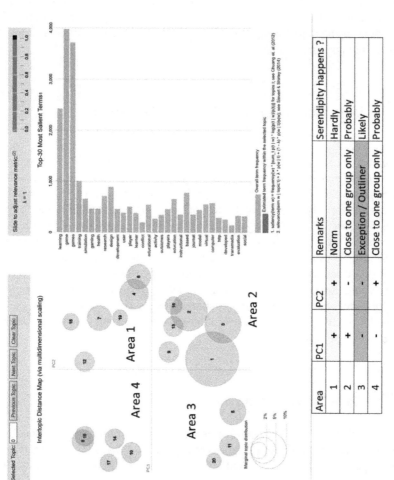

Area	PC1	PC2	Remarks	Serendipity happens ?
1	+	+	Norm	Hardly
2	+	-	Close to one group only	Probably
3	-	-	Exception / Outliner	Likely
4	-	+	Close to one group only	Probably

Figure 8.6 PC1 and PC2 of LDAvis

both PC1 and PC2, may be the place information seekers can most probably seek some surprising things, as the topics found there would not have a close connection to either of the main groups of topics. They are far from both PC1 and PC2. Therefore, this quadrant can facilitate locating serendipitous things for further evaluation of usefulness. The above situations are illustrated in the box at the bottom of Figure 8.6, which shows the four quadrants of LDAvis information with impacts on serendipity. Without analyzing the corpus of documents using these four quadrants, it is challenging to identify these unexpected findings using human means.

5.   Data Collection and Testbed Generation

After examining KeyGraph and LDAvis, we came to a stage to start data collection and generate a testbed for examining how serendipity could happen. One participant (referred to here as SPTSE1) was invited to perform a specific test of generating ideas for a research project. The participant was a research student in the Department of Education at a local university, looking to develop a game prototype for a Ph.D. study and the participant did not have any concrete ideas beforehand. The participant collected 50+ academic articles on electronic games and education from Google to create research topics. Based on this collection of articles, topic modeling was started by using both LDAvis and KeyGraph. The visualized analysis results were created from a study of research of game development for an educational faculty by the participant. Creative ideas were needed to think about the development directions of a research project.

6.   Data Visualization

Data visualization concerns the orientation and presentation of data for humans to perceive; it is important that key and/or interesting information, trends, patterns, associations, and so on revealed by the data analyses are explicitly or even vividly shown to human eyes to support, among other things, understanding and decision making, and to further stimulate creativity or innovation. It is a very important stage of the analysis, and use of proven frameworks can often ensure consistency and comprehensiveness. Based on Tufte's six principles (Tufte, 1983) of designing data visualization, a comparison table was produced (Table 8.1) to evaluate both KeyGraph and LDAvis for the visualization of important insights that can be serendipitously generated.

Table 8.1   Evaluation of visualization support by KeyGraph and LDAvis

Tufte's principles	KeyGraph	LDAvis
1. Showing comparisons	It is necessary to produce more than one KeyGraph for comparison	The topics and their corresponding constituting terms shown on the same panel of the display can be compared from one topic to another upon using mouse-over activities. Showing comparisons is very easy to discover some interesting findings. The size of the bubbles representing the topics indicates their prevalence. Moreover, the locations of the topics placed on the left panel with the four quadrants of principal components can show very important strategic signals to users because the norms or outliers can be easily identified.
2. Showing causality	The terms displayed on a KeyGraph are extracted from the corpus of documents based on their co-occurrences (rather than cause–effect relationship) discovered from the corpus	LDAvis is similar to KeyGraph in this aspect. But LDAvis implements the Monte Carlo Markov Chain algorithm (MCMC) inside. The topics and their terms are all latent/probabilistic, producing very dynamically connected networks of terms. This is a great and dynamic feature for nurturing serendipity when viewing different layers of information
3. Combining multivariate data	All co-occurring pairs of terms were shown in a KeyGraph	The topics and their corresponding constituting terms are shown after selecting the topics. The relevance of the terms to a specific topic can also be adjusted to include the weakest terms. Different layers of information are well organized by relevance selected and adjusted by users. Another important feature is the display of the percentage distribution of the terms over the entire collection of terms across different topics
4. Integrating text, images & numbers	The shape of a network of terms is shown clearly with dots and lines of different colors and patterns, respectively. However, the scope of imagination is somewhat restricted.	An excellent web-based user interface is provided as a part of the results, which integrates multiple topics and their terms. However, the visualization of the networking patterns of the terms is not shown, allowing room for imagination.

Table 8.1   Evaluation of visualization support by KeyGraph and LDAvis
(continued)

Tufte's principles	KeyGraph	LDAvis
5. Establishing credibility with documentation	Only a static diagram with limited interaction can be produced. No processed metadata about sources of data can be easily extracted	Behind the web-based interface the users can locate a JSON file which contains the processed data with metadata of probability derived from inputted sources of data. The JSON file outputted from the LDAvis would serve as the source for visualization. Users can access the JSON file for further processing or loading into other computer programs for other analytical purposes
6. Focusing on content	KeyGraph can be a bit difficult to understand based on the comments of its creators, since the connection patterns of the terms selected may be abstract	The selection of topics and the terms by the users is significant. The terms will be refreshed upon changing the selected topics to show different results based on different situations (contexts). Therefore, users can develop a feeling of controlling the contexts to display the relevant terms under some selected topics

Source: based on Tufte's (1983) six principles.

Based on the analysis in Table 8.1, LDAvis can produce a more dynamic and exciting view and has potential to reveal serendipitous findings. The subsequent scenario planning would be mainly based on using LDAvis plus KeyGraph to facilitate serendipitous findings.

7.   Scenario Planning Based on Data Visualization

Two computational tools, LDAvis and KeyGraph, were used for identifying and extracting the terms from a collection of the game-related research articles. These two tools were selected as they mimic the behaviors of connecting the "dots" by humans. The terms from the results produced by the two tools were selected to form different scenarios (A to D) in a predefined template (Figure 8.7) which was prepared for scenario planning.

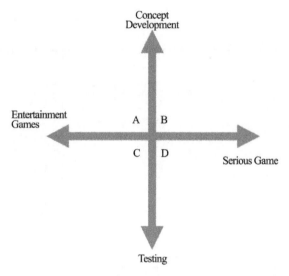

Figure 8.7   A simple framework for scenario planning

There are two perspectives in the template. The vertical axis represents the stages of development of the game, ranging from course development to testing concepts. The horizontal axis represents the nature of the games to be developed, ranging from very serious educational games to purely entertainment games. By crossing over these two perspectives, four quadrants were formed in Figure 8.7, representing the possibilities of planning directions for research and development. Stories for scenarios A to D can be developed by using some of the selected terms from KeyGraph & LDAvis related to the different quadrants, whereas in LDAvis only, keywords were identified by exploring the bubbles and changing the parameters (Figures 8.8, 8.9 and 8.10).

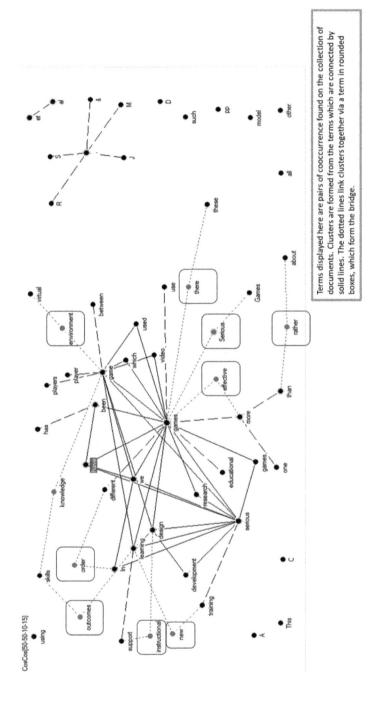

Terms displayed here are pairs of cooccurrence found on the collection of documents. Clusters are formed from the terms which are connected by solid lines. The dotted lines link clusters together via a term in rounded boxes, which form the bridge.

Figure 8.8   The KeyGraph used by SPSTE1 for scenario planning

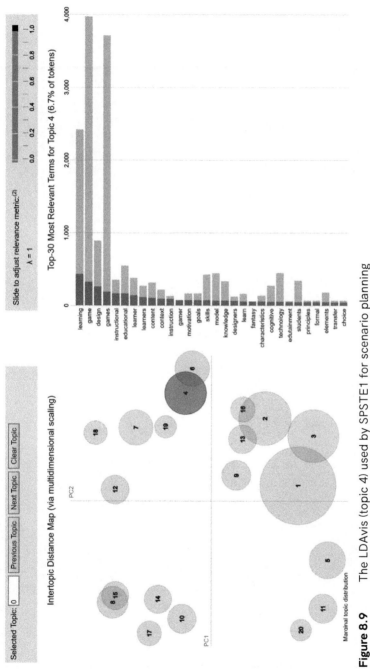

Figure 8.9 The LDAvis (topic 4) used by SPSTE1 for scenario planning

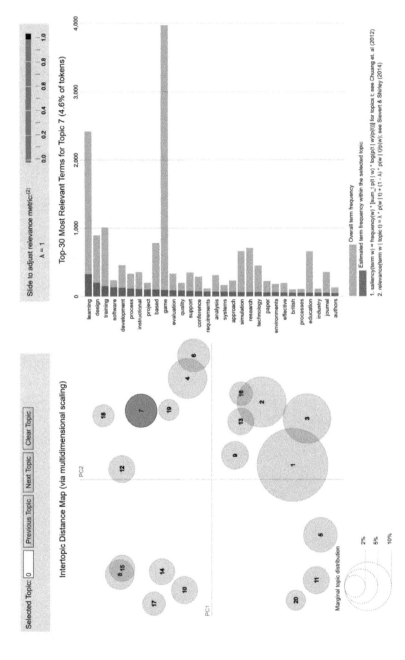

Figure 8.10   The LDAvis (topic 7) used by SPSTE1 for scenario planning

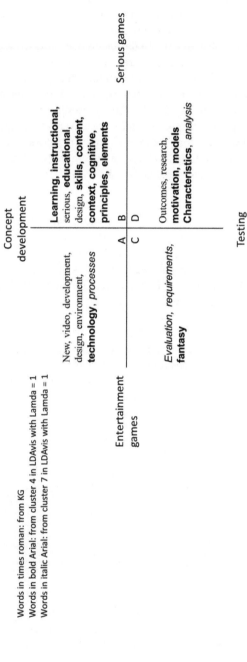

Figure 8.11 Triggers from KeyGraph & LDAvis used by SPTSE1 to create the scenarios

In quadrant A, terms like "technology," "processes," "design" and "environment" would become inspiring as this is an area for entertainment games with concept development as the key. Therefore, the concept development of any new element is needed to make the game become much more entertaining. In quadrant B, terms like "learning," "instructional," "skills," cognitive," "principles," "content" and "context" become relevant as it is an area for developing much more serious games. The players would become more serious for walking through the game to "learn" or to fulfill more cognitive satisfaction. In quadrant C, terms like "evaluation," "requirements" and "fantasy" become interesting as this is an area for designing fascinating games to entertain hardcore players as they are usually the most demanding ones asking for much more powerful features from a game. In quadrant D, testing of a serious educational game is indicated (Figure 8.11). The details are explained in the following paragraphs.

In Figure 8.11, the terms labeled in Times Roman font were taken from KeyGraph (Figure 8.8); the terms labeled in bold Arial were taken from the cluster (topic) 4 of LDAvis (Figure 8.9); and the terms labeled in italic Arial were taken from the topic (cluster) 7 of LDAvis (Figure 8.10). After extraction of the terms, the participant reorganized them into some research topics to be put into quadrants A to D based on their nature. The transition from the terms to the research topics is illustrated in Figure 8.12.

In Figure 8.12, the topics of the four quadrants were extended into scenarios (A to D), which were also related to the terms chosen in those quadrants. For example, in Figure 8.13, scenario A was developed and shown with the linkages between the terms used in the scenario and the terms selected in the quadrants. Some of the terms used in the scenario were derived terms (underlined terms) inspired

Topics Developed (brief)

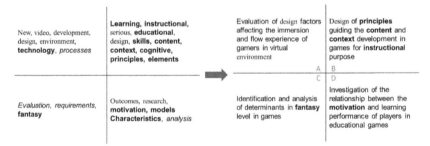

Figure 8.12   Research topics/stories developed by SPTSE1

by seeing the terms in the corresponding quadrant. Prior knowledge would play a significant role here to "link" different "dots" together. For example, the terms "video" and "technology" in that situation inspired "entertainment game" as this was a general idea to correlate "video," "technology" and "game" for ordinary people. The other parts of scenario A were also created based on the prior knowledge of SPTSE1 and the triggering effects of those terms (in Times Roman and italic Arial fonts) so that some meaningful sentences were also created to connect different parts of the sentences/terms as a narrative.

Scenario A

- This scenario involves the concept development of an entertainment game. At the beginning of the development process, the new elements that are not present in other games available in the market are the important design factors to be considered to increase the fun value and immersive experience of gamers and to ensure the market potential of the game concept.

Derived words underlined

Figure 8.13   Scenario A developed by SPTSE1

Scenario B

- This scenario is about the development of initial ideas for games for serious purposes like learning and teaching etc. As there should be a balance between the fun and educational value in the game to be designed, it would be best to arrive at a set of design principles before embarking the content and context development of the game.

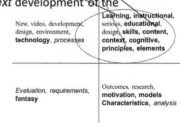

Derived words underlined

Figure 8.14   Scenario B developed by SPTSE1

Similarly, in Figure 8.14, the term "design" here would inspire "development of initial ideas" in this game-based educational research of SPTSE1. As learning and teaching are correlated, these terms would provide inspiration for each other. The terms "cognitive" and "design principles" were triggered, which were the objectives of the research of SPTSE1 in investigating the cognitive aspects of game-based educational effects in learning. In this way, the different terms were connected to form a meaningful scenario, just like a narrative. In other words, a small-scale story was created, which was triggered by the terms.

Scenario C

- The scenario relates to the <u>prototype testing</u> of entertainment games. For this type of game, the **fantasy** element is essential. It would be valuable for game developers to *evaluate* the level of **fantasy** the game developed provides to the gamers and to <u>collect feedback</u> from gamers about their *requirement* for an engaging game.

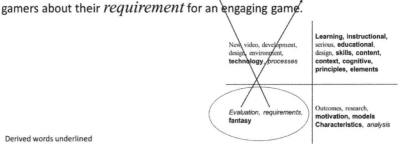

Derived words underlined

Figure 8.15   Scenario C developed by SPTSE1

Scenario D

- The scenario is related to the <u>testing of a serious game</u> developed for <u>educational purpose. In the testing, different variables in the game prototype can be varied to formulate various conditions for conducting experiments.</u> Using the experimental data, a **model** depicting the relationship between the **motivation** and learning performance of players might be constructed. <u>The "best" combination of variables to achieve the optimal learning performance can then be identified.</u>

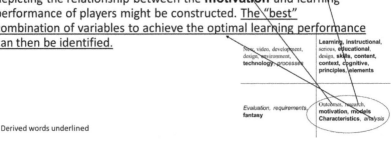

Derived words underlined

Figure 8.16   Scenario D developed by SPTSE1

In Figure 8.15, the term "evaluation" in this case inspired "collect feedback," and "requirement" inspired "prototype testing" when collecting ideas for system development. "Fantasy" is the essential element in game development to achieve successful implementation and acceptance of the game product. Therefore, the fantasy element would become the most critical area for collecting requirements and prototype testing to make the game successful. From this example, the ways to reveal the relationship between different elements based on prior knowledge could be seen.

In Figure 8.16, the last scenario is presented. The term "outcomes" inspired "testing," since this was one of essential purposes of the research of SPTSE1. The term "research" triggered the ideas of varying different variables in the game prototype to formulate various conditions for conducting experiments, which provided the essential success factors in the research of SPTSE1. The term "analysis" inspired some combinations of variables so that the best results could be obtained. From this case, the connections between the terms and the objectives and strategies of the research of SPTSE1 could be better illustrated.

8.   Conclusion

A model of innovation shown in Figure 8.17 concludes this research project. Based on the input of a corpus of documents, using some text-mining processes such as LDAvis or KeyGraph, a lot of "dots" can be produced, which can serve as triggers of serendipity. Based on the prior knowledge owned by the information seekers, the environment in which the information seekers reside, and the triggers just mentioned, some kinds of mental activities (or cognitive processes) would happen to "stir" everything involved together to form newer (re)connections of the "dots." These are the essences of serendipity. Serendipity is, therefore, to paint the future by actively creating more and more possibilities, in which unexpected but useful things can be found and articulated like connecting "dots," which also makes sense and creates values in many situations. In this research project, the test participant experienced the above through the combination of both computational and human models. Therefore, based on the above observation and hypothesis, LDA/LDAvis can be used to trigger information seekers to experience serendipity in finding something accidentally relevant and useful.

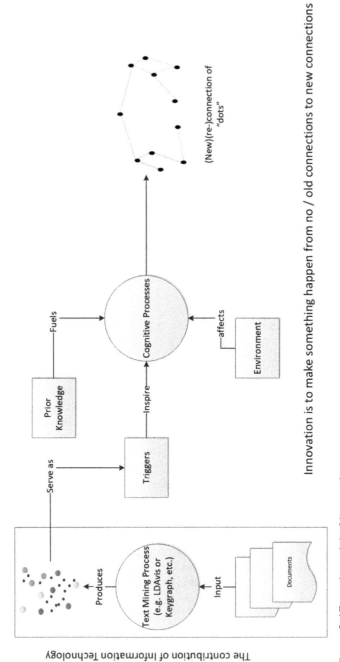

Figure 8.17   A model of innovation

9.   Future Directions

From the above results by the the participant SPTSE1 on scenario planning with KeyGraph and LDAvis as triggers, it is shown to be feasible that these computational tools can be used together to assist scenario planning. Alternatively, in the reverse direction, scenario planning, and its techniques when working through a human model, can help information seekers experience serendipitous information seeking and comprehension in generating research topics or meaningful narratives.

Although only preliminary tests for the above ideas were evaluated, this revealed scenario planning could be regarded as a human model for serendipitously connecting the "dots," and scenario planning could also be facilitated by using the computational tools used in this chapter. In a highly digitized and connected society, much of future Knowledge Management efforts need to expand and operate on "external networks" as knowledge increasingly resides in the network. Such operations may include expertise discovery, capabilities building, network learning, harnessing collective wisdom, collective problem solving and more. Hence, further development opportunities are therefore identified from the above trial runs. In other words, scenario planning can be serendipitous, especially in identifying the driving forces, scenarios and uncertainties, and their relationships to the future. That could be an exciting and rewarding project since the potentials of scenario planning could be much more widely revealed to strategic planners (Bezold, 2010).

Serendipity is the art of connecting unrelated things to produce something meaningful to the individual who had the encounter. That is why modeling serendipity can become so complicated, and it can be highly contextual and personalized. Serendipity can be closely associated with change as changes provide opportunities (triggers) to an individual, who may experience a focus shift. Therefore, anything that can help to spot changes effectively, and the conditions to allow free access to an extensive collection of information sources (e.g., documents) would become very desirable.

One of the crucial functions facilitating scenario planning is horizon scanning (Rowe et al., 2017) for detecting the environmental factors that may have significant impacts. One of the environmental factors that can easily be neglected or overlooked would be weak signals. That is usually an area which requires personal attention. When paying attention to the characteristics of the computational tools we used above, it was accidentally found that those tools can facilitate in the detection of weak signals.

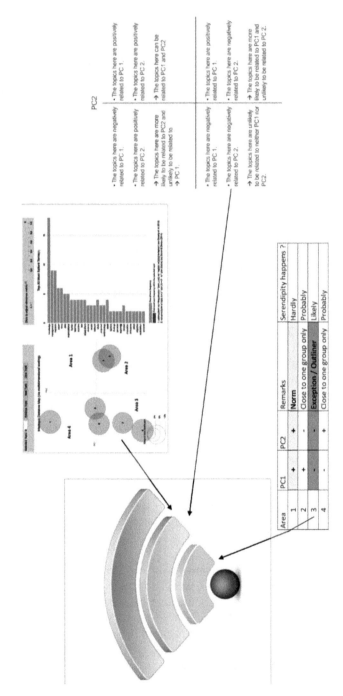

Figure 8.18 Weak signal and scenario planning

For example, the Area 3 quadrant of the left panel of the LDAvis visualization output screen (Figure 8.18) can reveal outliers or exceptional findings which generally stray away from the data norm. At least, those outliers can trigger information seekers to look elsewhere, away from the normal area, and pay attention to the weak signals. Therefore, it can help to detect weak signals from the corpus of the document. Of course, the signals need to exist in the corpus of the documents. From the observations of scenario planning undertaken for this research, it was found that using LDAvis could amplify the outcomes of imagination to increase the opportunities of having unexpected findings for experienced and deep learner(s).

Acknowledgement

The work presented in this chapter forms part of Simon Li's Doctor of Engineering dissertation project at the Hong Kong Polytechnic University. Support from the university is gratefully acknowledged.

References

Bezold, C. (2010). Lessons from using scenarios for strategic foresight. *Technological Forecasting and Social Change*, 77(9), 1513–18.

Blei, D., Edu, B., Ng, A., Edu, A., Jordan, M. & Edu, J. (2003). Latent Dirichlet allocation. *Journal of Machine Learning Research*, 3, 993–1022.

Chuang, J., Manning, C. & Heer, J. (2012). Termite: visualization techniques for assessing textual topic models. *Proceedings of the International Working Conference on Advanced Visual Interfaces – AVI '12*, 74.

de Rond, M. (2014). The structure of serendipity. *Culture and Organization*, 20(5), 342–58.

Foster, A. (2004). A nonlinear model of information-seeking behavior. *Journal of the American Society for Information Science & Technology*, 55(3), 228–37.

Foster, A. & Ford, N. (2003). Serendipity and information seeking: an empirical study. *Journal of Documentation*, 59(3), 321–40.

Han, J., Pei, J. & Kamber, M. (2011). *Data Mining: Concepts and Techniques*. Amsterdam: Elsevier.

Hoffman, M., Blei, D. & Bach, F. (2010). Online learning for Latent Dirichlet Aallocation. *Advances in Neural Information Processing Systems*, 23, 1–9.

Maeno, Y. & Ohsawa, Y. (2007). Human-computer interactive annealing for discovering invisible dark events. *IEEE Transactions on Industrial Electronics*, 54(2), 1184–92.

Merton, R. & Barber, E. (2011). *The Travels and Adventures of Serendipity: A Study in Sociological Semantics and the Sociology of Science*. Princeton, NJ: Princeton University Press.

Ohsawa, Y. (2005). Data crystallization: a project beyond chance discovery for discovering unobservable events. 2005 IEEE International Conference on Granular Computing, Beijing, Vol. 1, 51–6.

Ohsawa, Y., Benson, N. & Yachida, M. (1998). KeyGraph: automatic indexing by co-occurrence graph based on building construction metaphor. *Proceedings of the IEEE International Forum on Research and Technology Advances in Digital Libraries ADL98*, 12–18.

Ohsawa, Y. & Fukuda, H. (2002). Chance discovery by stimulated groups of people: application to understanding consumption of rare food. *Journal of Contingencies and Crisis Management*, 10(3), 129–38.

Ponweiser, M. (2012). Latent Dirichlet allocation in R. Thesis, Vienna University of Economics and Business.

Rowe, E., Wright, G. & Derbyshire, J. (2017). Enhancing horizon scanning by utilizing pre-developed scenarios: analysis of current practice and specification of a process improvement to aid the identification of important 'weak signals.' *Technological Forecasting and Social Change*, 125, 224–35.

Sievert, C. & Shirley, K. (2014). LDAvis: a method for visualizing and interpreting topics. *Proceedings of the Workshop on Interactive Language Learning, Visualization, and Interfaces*, 63–70.

Tufte, E.R. (1983). *The Visual Display of Quantitative Information*. Cheshire, CT: Graphics Press.

Wang, H. & Ohsawa, Y. (2011). iChance: a web-based innovation support system for business intelligence. *International Journal of Organizational and Collective Intelligence*, 2(4), 48–61.

Wang, H., Ohsawa, Y. & Nishihara, Y. (2011). A system method to elicit innovative knowledge based on chance discovery for innovative product design. *International Journal of Knowledge and Systems Science*, 2(3), 1–13.

Wang, H., Xu, F., Hu, X. & Ohsawa, Y. (2013). IdeaGraph: a graph-based algorithm of mining latent information for human cognition. *Proceedings of the 2013 IEEE International Conference on Systems, Man, and Cybernetics, SMC 2013*, 952–7.

Yaqub, O. (2018). Serendipity: towards a taxonomy and a theory. *Research Policy*, 47(1), 169–79.

Zhang, C., Wang, H., Xu, F. & Hu, X. (2013). IdeaGraph plus: a topic-based algorithm for perceiving unnoticed events. *Proceedings of the IEEE 13th International Conference on Data Mining Workshops, ICDMW 2013*, 735–41.

9. Decisions, advice and explanation: an overview and research agenda

Jan Vanthienen

1.   Introduction

Operational decisions are made on a daily basis, but they require a lot of knowledge (Vanthienen, 2015). Such decisions are taken frequently and are repetitive in nature (e.g., determining which insurance rate applies to a specific customer, deciding on eligibility, configuring a product to meet a customer's demands). While the impact of a single decision is typically small for the organization, their volume means that there is a significant impact on the business. Operational decisions, therefore, have to be efficient, maintainable, consistent, reproducible, compliant, reliable and explainable.

The Decision Model and Notation (DMN) standard has emerged as a way to represent the knowledge of day-to-day operational decisions in business operations. Decision modeling is already heavily used in banking, insurance, social security and standard procedures, and numerous tools incorporate DMN modeling, making the standard available for industry. Also, the research community is increasingly working on decision modeling (Aa et al., 2016; Calvanese et al., 2018; Dangarska et al., 2016; Figl et al., 2018).

2.   Decision Modeling and Management

2.1   The Decision Management Knowledge Cycle

Managing decision knowledge encompasses a number of stages, as illustrated in Figure 9.1. Decision knowledge is acquired from data, text or human expertise, and then represented and modeled in a common notation. Knowledge quality is obtained through verification and validation. Based on the body of knowledge, decisions are then embodied in executables or services, and knowledge-driven applications are built to support decision making. Finally, the execution trail will allow acquiring and refining new knowledge about the decisions in the application domain.

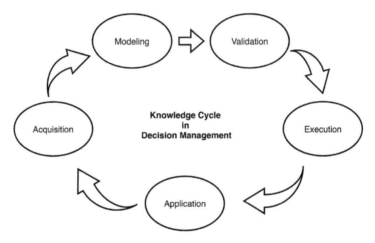

Figure 9.1   The knowledge cycle in decision management

2.2   Decision Model and Notation (DMN)

To address the need of a decision modeling standard, DMN was introduced by the Object Management Group (OMG, 2019). The primary goal of DMN is to provide a common notation for all business users (from business analysts, to technical developers, and finally to business people), and to bridge the gap between business decision design and implementation. By explicitly identifying decisions and dependencies and by describing the decision logic, the decision can be managed separately from the process itself, thereby increasing the business agility of an organization.

DMN provides distinct, but related, constructs for decision modeling: the decision requirements diagram, the decision logic and the corresponding expression language, Friendly Enough Expression Language (FEEL). A brief overview of the most important elements is provided in Figure 9.2. DMN is designed to model decisions inside or outside the context of a business process model.

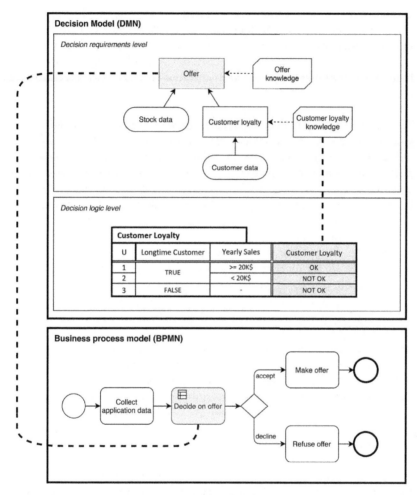

Figure 9.2   Important modeling concepts in DMN

2.2.1   The Decision Requirements Level

A Decision Requirements Diagram (DRD) is used to portray the domain of decision making at a high level of abstraction, the decision requirements level, with only a few types of constructs: the decisions, input data, knowledge models and knowledge sources, together with the interdependencies, called requirements.

Rectangles are used to depict decisions, corner-cut rectangles for business knowledge models, and ovals to represent input data. In Figure 9.2, Offer and

Customer Loyalty are decisions. They determine a value, based on input data and decision logic. Offer is the top decision. Its outcome is used in the business process model. Input data for the decisions are Stock data and Customer data. The Offer and Customer Loyalty decisions are made using knowledge, as indicated by the Offer knowledge and Customer Loyalty knowledge corner-cut rectangles.

The arrows represent requirements: solid arrows for information requirements and dashed arrows for knowledge requirements. An information requirement indicates that a decision needs the value of input data or the outcome of another decision. The Offer decision is dependent on Stock data and on the outcome of the Customer Loyalty decision, which in its turn is dependent on Customer data. A knowledge requirement indicates that a decision needs knowledge (e.g., in the form of rules) in order to determine an outcome. The Customer Loyalty decision requires Customer Loyalty knowledge to decide about the outcome. A third requirement (authority requirement) is not shown in Figure 9.2. An authority requirement indicates who or what is the source of the decision knowledge.

2.2.2 *The Decision Logic Level*

The decision logic level specifies the underlying decision logic for each decision, very often in the form of decision tables (Figure 9.2). Decision logic indicates what the decision outcome should be for specific combinations of the values of input information items. Decision tables traditionally visualize these rules with input–outcome combinations in a tabular format that is easy to use for business, guarantees completeness and consistency and offers straightforward automation (Huysmans et al., 2011).

The decision logic level also provides an expression language (called FEEL) for specifying detailed decision logic, by defining complex expressions, composed from simpler expressions. Moreover, this level offers a notation (boxed expressions) which allows these expressions to be associated with elements in the decision requirements level.

The two levels together specify a complete decision model, understandable by the business and detailed enough for automation.

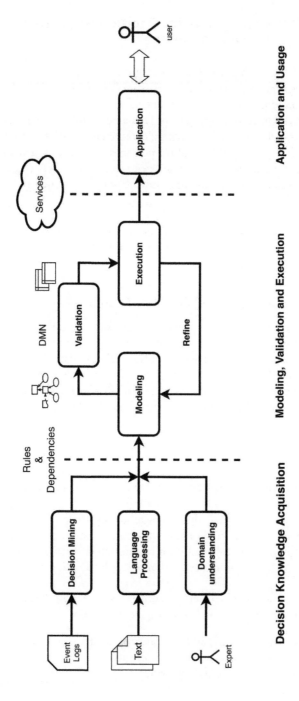

Figure 9.3 From decision knowledge to application

3. A Research Agenda for Decision Knowledge Acquisition and Modeling

Decision modeling with DMN finds its origin in decision tables, where rules for decision logic are represented in a structure of related tables. Each decision table maps combinations of input values to outcomes. Decision tables and the accompanying methodology have proven a powerful vehicle for acquiring the decision knowledge and for checking completeness, correctness and consistency (Codasyl, 1982). DMN builds upon these concepts and standardizes decision table formats in use, standardizes the relations between decisions in a decision requirements diagram, and introduces a standard expression language (FEEL).

Based on earlier research and new developments, this chapter provides a set of guidelines and research topics applicable to the full trajectory of decision modeling and management (Figure 9.3).

3.1 Single Decision Table Modeling Approaches

Operational decisions can be modeled according to different strategies, depending on what is the starting point of the modeling process: text (often augmented with expert knowledge), or historical case data. When historical case data are available, input information items and decision rules may be derived automatically from patterns in the log. Otherwise, relevant information items and rules will have to be extracted from the text, or from discussions with the domain expert.

3.1.1 Manual Modeling

Usually, the modeling process starts from an available description in the form of a text, procedure, law, and so on. A domain expert is often within reach to deal with questions that turn up during the modeling process. If not all relevant information items or rules are available up front, the modeler and the domain expert gradually discover relevant criteria and outcomes in a dialogue mode and refine the table until a full description of the decision logic is obtained.

The following basic modeling steps in constructing decision tables are distinguished, as already described in Vanthienen et al. (1998):

1. Define inputs (conditions) and outcomes of the decision situation.
2. Specify the problem in terms of decision rules.
3. Fill the decision table based on the rules.

4. If necessary, check the table for completeness, correctness, and contradictions.
5. Simplify the decision table and display it.

Note that some of these steps, including verification, can be automated, as illustrated by the Prologa tool (Vanthienen & Dries, 1994) (for an overview of verification and validation research, relevant for step 4, see Antoniou et al. 1998). Since the introduction of DMN, a lot of this research has been rediscovered in the form of verification tools for DMN models and tables (see, e.g., Calvanese et al., 2018).

Table simplification (step 5) can occur in multiple ways: reducing the number of rules by rule merging or by reordering, and splitting a table. Rule merging (table contraction) implies that rules with equal outcomes and complementary values for only one input item are joined together (Laurson & Maggi, 2017; Vanthienen & Dries, 1994). The number of rules can also be reduced by reordering the input information items (in combination with table contraction), which can be used to determine the order with the minimum number of rules. Finally, one decision table can (or should) be split into smaller tables if the table contains hidden dependencies. This is called factoring or normalization (Vanthienen & Snoeck, 1993), similar to database normalization.

3.1.2 Decision Mining from Case Data

When historical data about case attributes and their outcome are available, the decision rules can be discovered from the case data and transformed into a decision table (Baesens et al., 2003; Wets et al., 1998). This is the area of data mining or business analytics. Predictive models, based on past data, are widely used in both research and business (Baesens et al., 2009; Gopal et al., 2011; Liebowitz, 2013).

Most research, however, focuses on improving the accuracy or precision of these models and less research has been undertaken to increase their comprehensibility to the analyst or end user. Even if comprehensibility is of a subjective nature, some representation formats are generally considered to be more easily interpretable than others, and decision tables score extremely well here in terms of comprehensibility, ease of use and confidence (Huysmans et al., 2011; Martens et al., 2007).

One interesting form of analytics is business process mining, the discovery, monitoring and improvement of business process knowledge from event logs that are readily available in modern information systems, e.g., audit trails, electronic patient records, or the transaction logs of an enterprise resource planning system (van der Aalst, 2011). Process mining can be used to discover models describing processes, to monitor deviations, and to check and improve the performance of business processes.

As decisions are an important aspect of process models, it is clear that mining decisions is closely related to process mining. Mining decisions is not only about discovering the decision logic at a certain decision point in a process model. A decision is more than decision logic; it can be an entire decision model (see Section 3.2.2). Moreover, because DMN allows the separation of processes and decisions, according to the separation of concerns principle, the integrated mining of decisions and processes offers very promising research topics (see Section 5.2).

3.1.3   *Decision Mining from Text*

In many business cases, decision modeling starts from a law, text, manual, policy document or procedure. If a domain expert is not immediately available to support the modeling process, the text may be the only available source. Automatic extraction of models from text has been researched in many other modeling standards, such as process models, data models and rule models (see, e.g., Friedrich et al., 2011 for the extraction of process models from text). Mining decision rules from text, using text mining, and transforming these rules into a decision table is a promising research direction.

3.2   Full Decision Modeling Approaches

A full decision model consists of the two levels: the decision requirements level and the decision logic level. Approaches towards building decision models, therefore, will have to construct elements at both levels, showing both the dependencies between decisions and the logic of each decision.

3.2.1   *Manual Decision Modeling Strategies*

When a business analyst or a domain expert builds a decision model from a problem specification (usually a text), multiple starting points are possible: one can start from the general structure (and build the DRD first), or one can start from the detailed decision logic of each decision and work upwards towards a top decision. Mixed forms are, of course, also possible and very common. And while building the requirements diagram, it is always an option to immediately specify the corresponding logic for a decision, or postpone the detailed logic until the dependencies are completely specified. In reality, a mixture of all these approaches will be used. These strategies are similar to well-established modeling approaches in the business process management (BPM) community, i.e., bottom-up, top-down, and combined modeling approaches, adapted to suit DMN modeling.

3.2.2 Full Decision Mining from Case Data

Case data can be a wealthy source for discovering decision rules. This can be in the form of a DMN decision table, but a more complex challenge is the mining of an entire decision model from (event and) data logs, including dependencies between decisions, based on the data relations between them (Bazhenova & Weske, 2015; Smedt, Broucke et al., 2017). Usually, however, this is in combination with process discovery from event logs (see Section 5.2.2).

3.2.3 Full Decision Extraction from Process Flows

When a business process model is available, a decision model can also be extracted from the process model, based on split gateways.

In these approaches, the decision points in a process model are identified and the decision logic containing the data dependencies is derived from the process model (see Aa et al., 2016; Batoulis et al., 2015; Bazhenova & Weske, 2015). The result is a decision model including the decision requirements diagram and decision logic. The process model is adapted accordingly, where the decision logic is now in the decision model, and not hidden in the process model.

3.2.4 Full Decision Model Mining from Text

Mining decision rules from text, using text mining, and transforming these rules into a decision table is one thing. It is even more challenging to mine dependencies between decisions, and other elements of the requirements level. This is a promising research direction that is just being explored.

3.3 Additional Guidelines for DMN Decision Models

Although DMN is mainly about notation, and is not meant to include a design methodology, there is a long history of decision modeling guidelines, offering guidance to structure decisions into separate tables, in order to build sound decision tables using a stepwise methodology and to avoid table anomalies. These guidelines deal with the form as well as with the contents of the decision tables.

Structure and content:

1. Basic structure: Decision tables represent rules about related input information items and outcomes. All input information items in one rule are implicitly connected with AND.
2. Completeness, consistency: Completeness and consistency within one decision and over multiple decisions are important properties for maintainability, comprehensibility and correctness. The question of overlapping rules is a key issue in dealing with consistency and correctness.
3. Multiple outcome items: Decision tables can have multiple outcomes. If the purpose of the table is to assign an outcome to a (sub)decision, the main action will assign that outcome, e.g., true/false, classification results, values. There may also be additional outcomes, depending on the purpose of the table.

Form, conciseness and readability:

4. Table contraction: Proper rule minimization enhances readability (still avoiding overlapping rules).
5. Input order optimization: A different overall input order may produce a smaller table because of contraction.

Normalization:

6. Normalization: Decision tables can (or should) be split up if the outcomes are not dependent on all the input information items.

4.   Research Issues in Decision Model Verification

4.1   Validation and Verification of Decision Models

Verification and validation of knowledge-based systems (including decision tables) has been a major area of research, e.g., in the EUROVAV series of conferences (European Conference on Verification & Validation of knowledge-based systems) (Antoniou et al., 1998; Coenen et al., 2000). This research deals with typical rule anomalies, such as redundancy (including duplicates and subsumption), ambivalence, circularity, and deficiency (missing rules) (Preece & Shinghal, 1994; Vanthienen et al., 1998). Numerous algorithms and tools are available for checking and eliminating rule anomalies for all possible values of the input variables.

4.1.1 Verification of Single Decision Tables

Verification of decision tables mainly deals with completeness and consistency of the rules in a decision table:

- Consistency of the rules: The problem of consistency (including redundant, duplicate or subsumed rules), is closely related to the presence of overlapping rules. If the rules of a decision table are not mutually exclusive, there is at least one combination of input values that matches two rules. The outcome of the two rules can be compatible (called a multiple hit table), contradictory or equal. When the outcome is contradictory, a solution for the inconsistency has to be provided (in DMN this is called the hit policy). Even when the rules produce the same outcome, the table is more difficult to maintain and validate manually. Because decision tables are relations, this is simply the requirement of normalization (Vanthienen & Snoeck, 1993).
- Consistency can be obtained in three ways: either by (i) design, (ii) signaling and repairing inconsistent rules, or (iii) providing a policy that resolves overlapping and inconsistent combinations for the entire table (e.g., the first hit convention that gives priority to the first rule that matches the input data). Although all these approaches may finally produce a consistent table, especially the latter is known to be extremely complex and error prone.
- Completeness: Completeness implies that no combinations of input values are missing. It can be obtained in three ways: either by (i) design, (ii) looking for missing combinations after the table is constructed, or (iii) providing a remainder column which catches all missing rules. The latter solution, although complete by definition and even compact, is less elegant and much more difficult to understand, validate and maintain.

Decision table methodology has shown that completeness and consistency is very important for comprehensibility and correctness of the decision model. Overlapping rules, therefore, are considered harmful and reduce the power of the decision model (Vanthienen et al., 1998).

4.1.2 Verification of Single DMN Decision Tables

As DMN has included the decision table concept as one of the major decision logic components, all decision table research directly translates to DMN decision table research.

Actually, a lot of verification and validation research on DMN decision tables has inadvertently rediscovered decision table validation and verification research (see, e.g., Batoulis & Weske, 2018; Calvanese et al., 2018; Corea et al., 2019; Hinkelmann, 2016; Laurson & Maggi, 2017; Montali & Teinemaa, 2016; Ochoa & González-Rojas, 2017).

4.1.3 Verification of Decision Table Networks or DMN Requirements Diagrams

DMN consists of the requirements level and the decision logic level. Inputs of the decision tables at the decision logic level are represented at the requirements level as information requirements. Outcomes of the decision table constitute information requirements to higher level decisions or form outcomes to the top decision. So the requirements level shows a visual representation of the relations between decision tables, and could be derived from them.

Whenever an information item in a decision table A is the outcome of another decision table B, obviously every possible value of the information item should be a possible outcome of table B, and every possible value of the information item in A should be the outcome of a rule in B. The opposite is not necessarily true: B can produce more outcomes than what is used in A if table B is reused somewhere else.

This type of verification refers to inter-tabular anomalies, anomalies that could arise due to the interaction between different tables. They are basically similar to the possible anomalies that could occur with one table: unfirable rules, missing rules, unusable outcomes, etc., but now between tables (see Vanthienen et al., 1997 for an overview of inter-tabular verification and a toolset dealing with these anomalies).

4.1.3.1 Syntactic verification

Because the requirements level corresponds to the relations between decision tables, it basically contains no more information than what is present in the decision tables, if only tables are used. But it is still useful to only model the information requirements if not all rules in the decision tables are fully specified yet. Obviously, when information requirements are modeled manually (not derived from the tables), there should be a full match between an information requirement in the DRD and an information item in the table. Most tools will ensure this automatically.

4.1.3.2 Verification over rule chains

While the previous verification of missing rules, missing information items or unusable outcomes is rather straightforward, because it is only based on the static description of the tables, things become more complicated when dependencies between information items are present.

When an input information item in one table is repeated in another table, e.g., some part of the decision logic in a certain decision may become unreachable or inconsistent for specific input values. Checking this consistency and completeness between interconnected decision tables, i.e., over rule chains, is a much more challenging problem than static verification or verification of single tables (see Vanthienen et al., 1997 for a solution for inter-tabular verification).

5.   Research on Decision and Process Integration

Business process management (BPM) and decision management (DM) improve the efficiency and effectiveness of organizations. While business processes are modeled in a structured and executable way, little attention is given, however, to the decision and knowledge aspect in business processes. Moreover, complex decisions are often modeled as processes, e.g., using cascaded gateways.

Decision management introduced an approach for modeling decisions independently (Batoulis et al., 2015, 2017; Biard et al., 2015; Mertens et al., 2017; Song et al., 2019a, 2019b; Taylor et al., 2013; Vanthienen & Caron, 2013) and aims at the separation of decision knowledge from business processes, thereby simplifying process modeling. This separation of concerns is crucial for the modeling and maintainability of both processes and decisions, but it raises the question how both approaches can be combined, both in modeling and mining (Janssens et al., 2016).

5.1   Integrated Modeling of Decisions and Processes

Decisions could be considered as local, not related to other elements of the process. A decision model is then a further refinement of a decision activity in a process model and multiple decisions in a process lead to isolated decision models.

But that is not the full intent of DMN. Decision models can contain multiple related decisions and top decisions in a single decision model. Related decisions have elements in common (e.g., decision logic, input data), and therefore belong in the same model, but are still different decisions at different places in the process model. These decisions, however, may extend over process modeling elements, produce intermediate events or data, or require a specific ordering in the process model, so the decision model is not completely isolated.

It is, therefore, important to apply an integrated approach for decision and process modeling and to ensure consistent integration between both models (Janssens et al., 2016). Potential inconsistencies are, e.g., unused decision outcomes, missing intermediate process actions, unnecessary decision activities, unsound ordering of decision activities or missing input data. Consistent integration ensures the correct separation between decision and process models according to integration principles (Hasić et al., 2018).

5.2   Integrated Mining of Decisions and Processes

Decision mining in processes (as introduced in Rozinat & van der Aalst, 2006) is able to build predictive models that explain why certain paths are followed at fixed decision points in a process. This approach is control flow-driven and can be called decision point analysis. Additionally, and since the introduction of DMN, interesting new approaches have introduced the discovery of DMN models from process data (Batoulis et al., 2015; Bazhenova et al., 2016). The emphasis, however, is still on explaining the control flow, or how the techniques at least incorporate control flow constructs in the models.

In accordance with the separation of concerns principle, control-flow agnostic techniques have been proposed for the integrated mining of both a process and a decision model based on extensive decision-process logs (Smedt, Broucke et al., 2017; Smedt et al., 2019; Smedt, Hasić et al., 2017). In this approach, mining decisions is independent from, but consistent with, the control flow, which produces an integrated, but separated view of the decisions and process.

6.   A Research Agenda for Decision Model Execution and Usage

When properly specified, and now that appropriate tooling is available, decision models are executable. This means that, if the values for input information items can all be obtained, a straightforward execution will determine the outcome of the decision, inside or even outside a business process. This is the major application of decision modeling and DMN nowadays. Numerous business applications can be found in insurance, finance, healthcare, rules, laws and regulations, etc. (see, e.g., Hasić & Vanthienen, 2020) for an income taxation case). But there is more than straightforward input to output execution.

6.1 Incomplete Data

A decision model captures relevant decision knowledge, and current tools use this knowledge in one way: Given all relevant input, what is the outcome of the decision?

In real-world applications, other functionalities are interesting and should be possible: Reasoning with missing data, e.g., could already provide useful consequences based on the data that is available. This would allow answering questions like: Are certain decision outcomes still possible, given incomplete information? Or, which missing input information would be relevant in order to determine the outcome of a decision? The decision knowledge is already present in the model, but more powerful reasoning engines will be necessary. Current research in this area shows some very promising directions (Dasseville et al., 2016).

6.2 Optimal Execution

In a number of cases, attention could be paid to execution efficiency or more flexible forms of code generation. By generating least-cost execution trees dealing with condition test times and case frequencies, the average execution time of a decision can be minimized, by transforming decision tables into optimal test sequences (see, e.g., Codasyl, 1982 for an overview of optimization algorithms).

6.3 Explanation

Explainability is becoming a hot topic in AI. When decisions are made by intelligent systems and algorithms, trust is of utmost importance. One of the major reasons to trust a model or system is the ability to understand and explain in detail the underlying knowledge. The ability to explain is not only desirable; it is often required by regulators for accountability reasons. Black box decisions will not offer this advantage. Explainability is also important because it allows for evaluation and improvement of the decisions, correction of unwanted effects and inclusion of missing decision logic.

When it comes to explainability of the decisions taken, DMN offers a number of advantages: separation of concerns, modular structure and a comprehensible representation of the decision logic. Decision tables have a proven record in ease of use, completeness and consistency (Huysmans et al., 2011).

6.4   Decision Analysis, Simulation, Advice and Optimization

DMN offers a business-friendly, but still limited representation of business decision knowledge. The advantage is that it can be directly built and maintained by business experts, but for more sophisticated applications, the expressive power and reasoning mechanisms will have to be extended. The challenge here is to preserve the ease-of-use for domain experts, and extend the functionality by linking it to knowledge representation and reasoning achievements, optimization techniques, constraint satisfaction methods, etc. (interesting developments in this area can be found in Dasseville et al., 2016; Deryck et al., 2018; Feldman, 2016; Paschke & Könnecke, 2016).

Consider, for instance, the application domain of eligibility for loans in a bank. That is the decision knowledge. Ideally, this knowledge should be comprehensible to the business experts, well-organized, explainable (e.g., for legal reasons) and multi-purpose for different types of applications or questions. Typical questions might be:

- Decision: Is this person, given all relevant data, eligible for a loan?
- Explanation: Why can this person not get a loan?
- Incomplete inputs: Given what we know already, what is the maximum loan amount this person might get?
- Simulation: What would be the result if the values of a few information items change?
- Advice: What are important information items to get a loan?
- Goal seeking: What would have to change for this person to be eligible for a loan?
- Optimization: What are the parameter values for this person that maximize the loanable amount?

The knowledge remains the same, but the questions are different. Answering these questions requires powerful knowledge representation and reasoning techniques (see, e.g., De Cat et al., 2018). On the other hand, it is important that business domain experts are still able to formulate, understand and validate the relevant knowledge.

When decision knowledge is represented in a standard and comprehensible way, other advantages appear. It now becomes possible to analyze the knowledge using advanced, but generic business intelligence techniques, answering questions such as:

- Fairness: Does the knowledge correspond to what one would expect in terms of changes in information item values?
- Compliance: Is the decision knowledge compliant with existing rules and regulations?
- Decision monitoring: How many cases actually obtained a certain decision outcome?
- Policy evaluation: Given the number of historical cases, do we have to change the decision rules?
- Simulation and prediction: What would be the aggregated outcome of a policy change?
- Policy optimization: What can we do to increase certain decision outcomes?

7.   Conclusion

The introduction of the Decision Model and Notation (DMN) standard triggered decision management and modeling as important research subjects. There is a wealth of research topics to be discovered for the management, modeling and exploitation of decision knowledge. DMN offers a business-friendly representation of business decision knowledge. The advantage is that it can be directly built and maintained by business experts, but for more sophisticated applications, the expressive power and reasoning mechanisms can still be extended. The challenge here is to preserve the ease-of-use for domain experts, and extend the functionality by linking it to knowledge representation and reasoning achievements.

References

Aa, H. van der, Leopold, H., Batoulis, K., Weske, M. & Reijers, H. A. (2016). Integrated process and decision modeling for data-driven processes. In M. Reichert & H. A. Reijers (eds.), *Business Process Management Workshops 2015* (Vol. 256, pp. 405–17). Springer.

Antoniou, G., van Harmelen, F., Plant, R. & Vanthienen, J. (1998). Verification and validation of knowledge-based systems: report on two 1997 events. *AI Magazine*, 19(3), 123–6.

Baesens, B., Mues, C., Martens, D. & Vanthienen, J. (2009). 50 years of data mining and OR: upcoming trends and challenges. *JORS*, 60(S1). https://doi.org/10.1057/jors .2008.171.

Baesens, B., Setiono, R., Mues, C. & Vanthienen, J. (2003). Using neural network rule extraction and decision tables for credit-risk evaluation. *Management Science*, 49(3), 312–29. https://doi.org/10.1287/mnsc.49.3.312.12739.

Batoulis, K., Haarmann, S. & Weske, M. (2017). Various notions of soundness for decision-aware business processes. *International Conference on Conceptual Modeling*, 403–18.

Batoulis, K., Meyer, A., Bazhenova, E., Decker, G. & Weske, M. (2015). Extracting decision logic from process models. *International Conference on Advanced Information Systems Engineering*, 349–66.

Batoulis, K. & Weske, M. (2018). Disambiguation of DMN decision tables. In W. Abramowicz & A. Paschke (eds.), *Business Information Systems* (pp. 236–49). Springer International Publishing.

Bazhenova, E., Buelow, S. & Weske, M. (2016). Discovering decision models from event logs. *International Conference on Business Information Systems*, 237–51.

Bazhenova, E. & Weske, M. (2015). Deriving decision models from process models by enhanced decision mining. *Business Process Management Workshops*, 256, 444–57.

Biard, T., Le Mauff, A., Bigand, M. & Bourey, J.-P. (2015). Separation of decision modeling from business process modeling using new "Decision Model and Notation" (DMN) for automating operational decision-making. *Working Conference on Virtual Enterprises*, 489–96.

Calvanese, D., Dumas, M., Laurson, Ü., Maggi, F. M., Montali, M. & Teinemaa, I. (2018). Semantics, analysis and simplification of DMN decision tables. *Information Systems*, 78, 112–25.

Codasyl (1982). A modern appraisal of decision tables. *Report of the Decision Table Task Group*. Association for Computing Machinery.

Coenen, F., Bench-Capon, T. J. M., Boswell, R., Dibie-Barthélemy, J., Eaglestone, B., Gerrits, R., Grégoire, E., Ligeza, A., Laita, L. M., Owoc, M. L., Sellini, F., Spreeuwenberg, S., Vanthienen, J., Vermesan, A. I. & Wiratunga, N. (2000). Validation and verification of knowledge-based systems: Report on EUROVAV99. *Knowledge Eng. Review*, 15(2), 187–96.

Corea, C., Blatt, J. & Delfmann, P. (2019). A tool for decision logic verification in DMN decision tables. *Proceedings of the Dissertation Award, Doctoral Consortium, and Demonstration Track at the 17th International Conference on Business Process Management, BPM 2019, 2420*, 169–73. http://ceur-ws.org/Vol-2420/papeDT11.pdf.

Dangarska, Z., Figl, K. & Mendling, J. (2016). an explorative analysis of the notational characteristics of the decision model and notation (DMN). *Enterprise Distributed Object Computing Workshop (EDOCW), 2016 IEEE 20th International*, 1–9.

Dasseville, I., Janssens, L., Janssens, G., Vanthienen, J. & Denecker, M. (2016). Combining DMN and the knowledge base paradigm for flexible decision enactment. *CEUR Workshop Proceedings, 1620.*

De Cat, B., Bogaerts, B., Bruynooghe, M., Janssens, G. & Denecker, M. (2018). Predicate logic as a modeling language: the IDP system. In *Declarative Logic Programming: Theory, Systems, and Applications* (pp. 279–323).

Deryck, M., Hasić, F., Vanthienen, J. & Vennekens, J. (2018). A case-based inquiry into the decision model and notation (DMN) and the knowledge base (KB) paradigm. *International Joint Conference on Rules and Reasoning, 248–63.*

Feldman, J. (2016). What-if analyzer for DMN-based decision models. *RuleML (Supplement).* https://www.semanticscholar.org/paper/What-If-Analyzer-for-DMN-based-Decision-Models-Feldman/5c2fec3b05eeaef974464f22cc68692b6fa4de2c.

Figl, K., Mendling, J., Tokdemir, G. & Vanthienen, J. (2018). What we know and what we do not know about DMN. *Enterprise Modelling and Information Systems Architectures (EMISAJ),* 13. https://emisa-journal.org/emisa/article/view/163.

Friedrich, F., Mendling, J. & Puhlmann, F. (2011). Process model generation from natural language text. *International Conference on Advanced Information Systems Engineering,* 482–96.

Gopal, R. D., Marsden, J. R. & Vanthienen, J. (2011). Information mining—reflections on recent advancements and the road ahead in data, text, and media mining. *Decision Support Systems,* 51(4), 727–31. https://doi.org/10.1016/j.dss.2011.01.008.

Hasić, F., De Smedt, J. & Vanthienen, J. (2018). Augmenting processes with decision intelligence: principles for integrated modelling. *Decision Support Systems,* 107, 1–12.

Hasić, F. & Vanthienen, J. (2020). From decision knowledge to e-government expert systems: the case of income taxation for foreign artists in Belgium. *Knowl. Inf. Syst.,* 62(5), 2011–28. https://doi.org/10.1007/s10115-019-01416-4.

Hinkelmann, K. (2016). Business process flexibility and decision-aware modeling—the knowledge work designer. In D. Karagiannis, H. C. Mayr & J. Mylopoulos (eds.), *Domain-Specific Conceptual Modeling, Concepts, Methods and Tools* (pp. 397–414). Springer. https://doi.org/10.1007/978-3-319-39417-6.

Huysmans, J., Dejaeger, K., Mues, C., Vanthienen, J. & Baesens, B. (2011). An empirical evaluation of the comprehensibility of decision table, tree and rule based predictive models. *Decision Support Systems,* 51(1), 141–54.

Janssens, L., Bazhenova, E., Smedt, J. D., Vanthienen, J. & Denecker, M. (2016). Consistent integration of decision (DMN) and process (BPMN) models. In S. España, M. Ivanovic & M. Savic (eds.), *Proceedings of the CAiSE'16 Forum, at the 28th International Conference on Advanced Information Systems Engineering (CAiSE 2016), Ljubljana, Slovenia, June 13–17, 2016* (Vol. 1612, pp. 121–8). CEUR-WS.org. http://ceur-ws.org/Vol-1612/paper16.pdf.

Laurson, Ü. & Maggi, F. M. (2017). A tool for the analysis of DMN decision tables. In L. Azevedo & C. Cabanillas (eds.). *Proceedings of the BPM Demo Track 2016 Co-located with the 14th International Conference on Business Process Management (BPM 2016), Rio de Janeiro, Brazil, September 21, 2016.* (Vol. 1789, pp. 56–60). CEUR-WS.org. http://ceur-ws.org/Vol-1789.

Liebowitz, J. (2013). *Big Data and Business Analytics.* CRC Press.

Martens, D., Baesens, B., Gestel, T. V. & Vanthienen, J. (2007). Comprehensible credit scoring models using rule extraction from support vector machines. *European Journal of Operational Research,* 183(3), 1466–76. https://doi.org/10.1016/j.ejor.2006.04.051.

Mertens, S., Gailly, F. & Poels, G. (2017). Towards a decision-aware declarative process modeling language for knowledge-intensive processes. *Expert Systems with Applications*, 87, 316–34.

Montali, M. & Teinemaa, I. (2016). Semantics and analysis of DMN decision tables. *Business Process Management: 14th International Conference, BPM 2016, Rio de Janeiro, Brazil, September 18–22, 2016. Proceedings*, 9850, 217.

Ochoa, L. & González-Rojas, O. (2017). Analysis and Re-configuration of decision logic in adaptive and data-intensive processes (short paper). *OTM Confederated International Conferences "On the Move to Meaningful Internet Systems,"* 306–13.

OMG [Object Management Group] (2019). Decision model and notation, version 1.3. https://www.omg.org/spec/DMN/1.3/PDF.

Paschke, A. & Könnecke, S. (2016). RuleML-DMN translator. *RuleML (Supplement)*.

Preece, A. D. & Shinghal, R. (1994). Foundation and application of knowledge base verification. *International Journal of Intelligent Systems*, 9(8), 683–701.

Rozinat, A. & van der Aalst, W. M. (2006). Decision mining in ProM. *International Conference on Business Process Management*, 420–25.

Smedt, J. D., Broucke, S. K. L. M. vanden, Obregon, J., Kim, A., Jung, J.-Y. & Vanthienen, J. (2017). Decision mining in a broader context: an overview of the current landscape and future directions. In M. Dumas & M. Fantinato (eds.), *Business Process Management Workshops—BPM 2016 International Workshops, Rio de Janeiro, Brazil, September 19, 2016, Revised Papers* (Vol. 281, pp. 197–207). https://doi.org/10.1007/978-3-319-58457-7.

Smedt, J. D., Hasić, F., Broucke, S. K. L. M. vanden & Vanthienen, J. (2017). Towards a holistic discovery of decisions in process-aware information systems. In J. Carmona, G. Engels & A. Kumar (eds.), *Business Process Management—15th International Conference, BPM 2017, Barcelona, Spain, September 10–15, 2017, Proceedings* (Vol. 10445, pp. 183–99). Springer. https://doi.org/10.1007/978-3-319-65000-5.

Smedt, J. D., Hasić, F., Broucke, S. K. L. M. vanden & Vanthienen, J. (2019). Holistic discovery of decision models from process execution data. *Knowl. Based Syst., 183*. https://doi.org/10.1016/j.knosys.2019.104866.

Song, R., Vanthienen, J., Cui, W., Wang, Y. & Huang, L. (2019a). A DMN-based method for context-aware business process modeling towards process variability. *Business Information Systems—22nd International Conference, BIS 2019, Seville, Spain, June 26–28, 2019, Proceedings, Part I, 353*, 176–88. https://doi.org/10.1007/978-3-030-20485-3_14.

Song, R., Vanthienen, J., Cui, W., Wang, Y. & Huang, L. (2019b). Context-aware BPM using IoT-integrated context ontologies and IoT-enhanced decision models. In J. Becker & D. Novikov (eds.), *21st IEEE Conference on Business Informatics, CBI 2019, Moscow, Russia, July 15–17, 2019, Volume 1—Research Papers* (pp. 541–50). IEEE. https://doi.org/10.1109/CBI.2019.00069.

Taylor, J., Fish, A., Vanthienen, J. & Vincent, P. (2013). Emerging standards in decision modeling. https://core.ac.uk/download/pdf/34582447.pdf.

van der Aalst, W. (2011). *Process Mining: Discovery, Conformance and Enhancement of Business Processes* (Vol. 2). Springer.

Vanthienen, J. (2015). On smart data, decisions and processes. In A. L. N. Fred, J. L. G. Dietz, D. Aveiro, K. Liu & J. Filipe (eds.), *KDIR 2015—Proceedings of the International Conference on Knowledge Discovery and Information Retrieval, part of the 7th International Joint Conference on Knowledge Discovery, Knowledge Engineering and Knowledge Management (IC3K 2015), Volume 1, Lisbon, Portugal, November 12–14, 2015* (p. 5). SciTePress. http://ieeexplore.ieee.org/document/7526887/.

Vanthienen, J. & Caron, F. (2013). Modeling business decisions and processes—which comes first? *KDIR/KMIS 2013—Proceedings of the International Conference on Knowledge Discovery and Information Retrieval and the International Conference on Knowledge Management and Information Sharing, Vilamoura, Algarve, Portugal, 19–22 September, 2013*, 451–6. https://doi.org/10.5220/0004623904510456.

Vanthienen, J. & Dries, E. (1994). Illustration of a decision table tool for specifying and implementing knowledge based systems. *International Journal on Artificial Intelligence Tools*, 3(2), 267–88. https://doi.org/10.1142/S0218213094000133.

Vanthienen, J., Mues, C. & Aerts, A. (1998). An illustration of verification and validation in the modelling phase of KBS development. *Data Knowl. Eng.*, 27(3), 337–52. https://doi.org/10.1016/S0169-023X(98)80003-7.

Vanthienen, J., Mues, C. & Wets, G. (1997). Inter-tabular verification in an interactive environment. In J. Vanthienen & F. van Harmelen (eds.), *Proceedings of the Fourth European Symposium on the Validation and Verification of Knowledge-Based Systems, EUROVAV'97, June 26–28, 1997, Katholieke Universiteit Leuven, Leuven, Belgium* (pp. 155–65). Katholieke Universiteit Leuven, Belgium.

Vanthienen, J. & Snoeck, M. (1993). Knowledge factoring using normalisation theory. *International Symposium on the Management of Industrial and Corporate Knowledge (ISMICK'93), October*, 27–8.

Wets, G., Vanthienen, J. & Timmermans, H. J. P. (1998). Modelling decision tables from data. *Research and Development in Knowledge Discovery and Data Mining, Second Pacific-Asia Conference, PAKDD-98, Melbourne, Australia, April 15–17, 1998, Proceedings*, 412–13. https://doi.org/10.1007/3-540-64383-4_48.

10. KM, analytics, and AI: a winning combination to survive the post-truth world

Kimiz Dalkir

Introduction

Fake news, alternative facts and misinformation have been around for a very long time. Burkhardt (2017) notes that any tool that can help produce an impact on what people believe is a valuable tool. The newest addition to this toolkit is the Internet and social media that allow user-generated content to be quickly and widely shared with others. In a recent survey, Delellis and Rubin (2020) found that 87% of Canadian internet users agreed that fake news on social media is a problem, 75% said they had encountered fake news, and 57% had been taken in by a fake news item.

Recent studies (e.g., Andrei et al., 2019) indicate misinformation is a global problem and the number of people believing fake stories and conspiracy theories – such as those related to climate change, and vaccine conspiracies – continue to increase and to generate serious consequences in the real world. The consequences of misinformation are particularly serious when there is an intent to defraud and even more dire when it concerns health information such as the anti-vaccine movement and the 2020 COVID-19 pandemic. While there were a few attempts to reduce the online spreading of fake news by big technology companies (e.g., Google, Facebook, Twitter) and some non-profit organizations (e.g., fact-checking website FactCheck), these did little to halt the tsunami of fake news which continues to grow.

Information management and knowledge management (IM/KM), big data and analytics, and artificial intelligence (AI) solutions can all play a role in helping to combat misinformation (Ingram et al., 2011). IM/KM looks at how

171

content is created, shared and then accessed, understood and acted upon. Big data has made possible a wide range of predictive analytics to identify patterns and predict what can happen next. Finally, AI researchers have been working on detection of such content such as gossip and rumors. These approaches and tools can be integrated in order to better detect and, ideally, prevent, the creation, spread and consumption of fake news.

How IM and KM Can Help

The conceptual foundations of IM/KM explain how people seek out, find and then decide which information (and which sources of information) to use (Figure 10.1). Health information and knowledge management examines how people look for, find, and use information about their health. Wilson (1997) identifies source credibility, features of the content and characteristics of the information consumer as key elements in information and knowledge management. The IM/KM cycle applies to people actively looking for information as well as those who passively receive content through browsing internet and social media sites (Edwards et al., 2009).

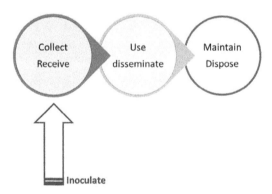

Figure 10.1   High-level information and knowledge processing cycle

The first step is to assess whether or not content is true or fake. Information literacy is a term that refers to how capable users are in making this distinction. Bartlett (2020) refers to these literacy skills as the ability to evaluate the credibility of online information. This is particularly important for health-related content. These skills are needed by anyone venturing on to the Internet and social media sites. Froehlich (2020) stresses that it is essential to develop pedagogical techniques to teach these skills. He advocates a multifaceted approach that addresses common features of fake news, the different types that exist, the difference between facts and second-hand information, the different purposes of fake news (e.g., to deceive, to defraud), the major psychological biases that come into play, and how to recognize cognitive authorities, among others. Other studies have focused on designing information as easily "digested" chunks such as using infographics to increase literacy levels. For example, the International Federation of Library Associations and Institutions developed an infographic that summarizes the recommendation to look at the source, read beyond a headline, or ensure that the content is not meant to be humorous or satirical (Asr and Taboada, 2019).

To use a medical analogy, information literacy skills can be acquired or improved by "inoculating" users so that they do not consume misinformation. Interventions are used to increase the level of awareness and comprehension of information consumers so that they pay attention to key factors (e.g., is the source credible? Do other (credible) sources also report the same content? Is the language professional or does it use emotional terms?). One early prevention technique is to inoculate people against fake news by increasing their level of resistance to appealing and persuasive fake content.

One example of inoculation is a fake news game called Bad News (https://www.getbadnews.com) that can be embedded directly into social media sites (Roozenbeek and Van Der Linden, 2019). This game has been used by schools and governments to expose people to small doses of misinformation techniques (including scenarios about COVID-19) in order to decrease their susceptibility to fake news. Another preventative approach involves subtle prompts that nudge people to consider accuracy; for example, periodically asking users to rate the accuracy of randomly selected posts. The crowdsourced accuracy ratings generated by this process may also be useful for identifying misinformation, as has been found for crowd ratings of source trustworthiness.

Fact-checking services can complement information literacy. Users send content to fact-checking websites, which typically employ humans to do the verification, or to automatic systems. Both approaches look for clues in the type of language, specific words or styles such as exaggerations or very emotional words (Asr and Taboada, 2019). Fact-checking services were originally intended to help journalists check out the veracity of content before publication. Today, publicly available sites are used to report and consult the latest information about the credibility and validity of information providers such as emails and websites. However, the general public needs to be aware that these services exist, take the time to visit them, and know how to use them (Çömlekçi, 2020). Most people still prefer to find information by using a search engine such as Google and how this information is assessed and verified is really just left up to the content consumer (Külcü, 2020). Fact-checking activities can also be carried out through crowdsourcing. Haigh et al (2018) describe a good example of crowdsourced fact checking by volunteer Ukrainian activist journalists who used literacy skills to screen out fake news and stop its spread. They serve as intermediaries between users and fact-checking services. Seen through a KM lens, these volunteers are acting as knowledge brokers.

Bolisani et al. (2019) point out that "the proliferation of fake news by means of social media can contribute to the production of counter-knowledge" (p. 161). Fake knowledge can be studied in the same way as "true" knowledge: the content, how it is shared and how it is used; however, the KM literature and research on fake news is scarce and fragmented. KM literature typically focuses on the bright side of KM; it barely mentions the dark side where knowledge is distorted, suppressed or misappropriated due to personal or organizational motives. KM models can prove just as useful in addressing misinformation at the individual/personal, group and organizational/societal levels as they are in addressing truthful content (Alter, 2006). One of the more relevant models is that of McElroy and McElroy (2003) which integrates the notion of knowledge claims (Figure 10.2).

Content need not be binary – some parts can be true and others not, e.g., truth, intentional lies, unverified knowledge, official information, gossip or objective information. The decision to share or not as well as the decision to trust, believe and act upon this content can be studied at the traditional three KM levels of individual (cognition), group (social behavior) and organizational/societal (policies, legislation). Fake content competes with valid content for the same audience in a context where people face information overload combined with less time to sort through it all. Personal knowledge management (PKM) obviously plays a large role in what a given person accesses, believes, understands and accepts with respect to content. Groups or networks can share content they believe to be valuable and this then becomes embedded in organizational/societal knowledge bases.

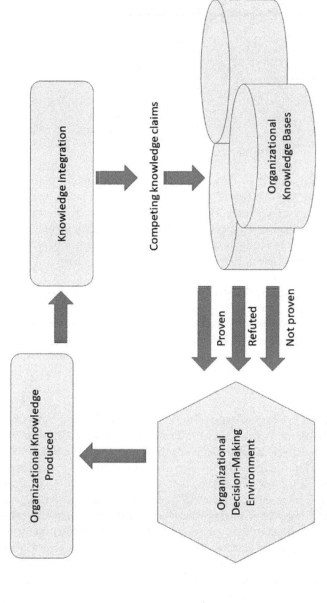

Figure 10.2 McElroy knowledge management model

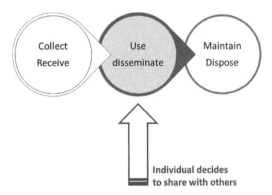

Figure 10.3   Sharing and dissemination

The whole raison d'être of social media is to share content that participants create (Figure 10.3). When fake news concerns health issues, the risk is even higher. The recent example of the COVID-19 pandemic showed a number of false claims that were quickly shared and which led to people at least contemplating actively engaging in dangerous behavior or not believing credible recommendations to safeguard their health and that of others.

Communities or networks of like-minded members tend to have very effective knowledge sharing habits. This is largely due to the fact that a great deal of trust exists between members. This trust is in turn built up over time and repeated gestures of reciprocity between members. On the other hand, very little trust has been built up regarding more official channels of communication. These elements make online knowledge sharing communities the "perfect storm" for the spreading of fake news.

Filter bubbles are formed when people start to obtain their news exclusively from their online networks and information avoidance behavior begins to form as they actively block out other sources. Filter bubbles, or echo chambers, are forms of knowledge networks where both valid but also biased information is often amplified and reinforced (Jamieson and Cappella, 2008). Social networks are effective means of knowledge sharing but they tend to also increase the negative impacts of misinformation. Fake news is often more attractive and it can then be shared very quickly and extensively to other members of the network. The speed of sharing leaves very little time for any critical assessment of the veracity of the shared content. Ideally, everyone should make use of cognitive authorities, which can be a person or a document. Wilson (1983) suggests that "those we think credible constitute the potential pool of cognitive authorities on which we might draw" (p. 16), where credibility stems from "competence" and "trustworthiness." Unfortunately, few take the time when it is just so much easier to share with and receive content from your trusted likeminded circle of peers and friends.

Tandoc et al. (2018) provide another example from their study which found that individuals first rely on their own judgment to authenticate information and if they are still not certain, they will next turn to external resources. In most cases, however, these are not external authorities such as the World Health Organization or Centers for Disease Control, but their own online networks. Külcü (2020) found that online resources were more popular than contacting family and friends (e.g., face-to-face or phoning). More than 82% of the participants follow the current developments in social media and the mass media that has similar views with them. Participants are in a state of uncertainty about their confidence in the information they access and use on the Internet. However, the use of multiple sources to verify information is low. They tend to confirm the relative suspicious information from different news channels. Verification rate from public authority sources is below 50%.

While those who are well-versed in the scientific or analytical method tend to have a head start in tackling fake news, they are nevertheless not completely immune. The tried and true methods of assessing resources, looking for triangulation or multiple sources to corroborate content and critical thinking skills in general, are valuable but not sufficient. Researchers are accustomed to all results being subject to close scrutiny and continued cycles of validation/falsification by others who replicate the research studies. For the general public, however, the notion of knowledge validation and internalization (as described by Nonaka and Takeuchi's 1995 SECI model) are not intuitive on their part. Internalization refers to not only accessing and understanding content but concluding that the content is sound and valuable, and that they will make use of it.

Scientific knowledge tends to be complex and, especially in times of health crises, the general public will always find it easier to consume and believe easy content that is simple, presented in bite-sized chunks and sent to us by people we know and trust personally. The notion that knowledge is not a series of absolute facts but actually something that is continuously constructed is an often difficult concept to grasp. While healthy debate is an integral part of the scientific process, the general public sees this as a failing and turns more readily to fake news that "prescribes" exactly what to do and what not to do. Finally, it is more difficult and time-consuming for the average information consumer to crosscheck facts, find fact-checking websites to consult, assess the credibility of the source and so on. When there is no single generally accepted authority, people tend to construct their own mental models of the world in order to reduce uncertainty and the anxiety that goes along with it. These mental models are often "faulty" in the sense that they do not reflect scientific reality but they are made of beliefs that help individuals make sense of a chaotic world (Figure 10.4).

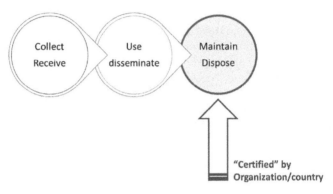

Figure 10.4   Knowledge evaluation

KM can help manage the complexity of knowledge, including health knowledge. Scientists and policymakers can benefit from adding the IM/KM information cycle to their toolkits when it comes to sharing health knowledge. Public decision makers and health professionals should be more aware that the average person makes decisions based on a mix of knowledge (rational facts) but also emotions, beliefs and personal biases. A traditional top-down approach to communicating information officially will often be seen as patriarchial or condescending at best, and deliberately manipulative and a conspiracy, at worst. Last but not least, all information and knowledge creation, sharing and validation channels, including social media, need to be part of the health information ecosystem.

Kim et al. (2018) describe an example of crowdsourcing to reduce the spread of misinformation, which also serves as a powerful emergent form of validation. The power of the network of users can be brought to bear and stood in place of any hierarchical authority and all users need to be active members the information ecosystem. What is needed is more than just the Facebook feature that was added to allow users to report non-factual content by clicking on a link. Ideally, users who suspect an online newsfeed story may fake flag it. If enough users flag it to exceed the pre-set threshold, then the story is sent to a third-party fact-checking service. Kim et al. (2018) developed an algorithm

(Curb) that was effective in quickly selecting stories from Twitter and Weibo to send to fact checking, which is very promising. Whenever someone is exposed to a story they find suspicious, they can flag it as misinformation. This content is then sent to a third-party fact checker. It is then "certified" as true or fake. Manual fact checking is of course very labor intensive and therefore expensive. AI that can provide algorithms to do this type of validation would be great but the state of the art is not there yet. The authors developed the Curb algorithm that is capable of selecting which stories should be sent for fact checking, which will help slow down the speed of spreading misinformation.

Pennycook et al. (2018) address another aspect of fake news that is very disturbing: persistent belief even in the face of evidence to the contrary. There is a well-known psychological phenomenon that is responsible for this type of behaviour called Repetition Theory (Hasher et al., 1977). The more people are exposed to content, the more they are likely to believe it. Studies also show that people tend to remember facts and events that have been repeatedly mentioned, even if that repetition was a debunking. It is therefore best to stop fake news as early as possible before too many people consume it. The instant sharing online through social media contributes to this and lends content a false sense of validity. Studies show that even a single one-time exposure increases how people perceive the accuracy of the content even after a week has elapsed. People continue to believe the misinformation is valid even when it is labeled as fake by fact-checking services. The scope and impact of repetition on beliefs is greater than has been previously assumed. This means the inoculation phase is the best one to target before fake news begins to be shared widely.

In KM studies, this is a "force for good" in that knowledge sharing is highly effective amongst knowledge networks as peer-to-peer sharing of content is perceived as sharing of valuable and vetted content. The number of times the same content is shared (and is therefore seen) is greatly increased. Unfortunately, if the content is not valid then it, too, is frequently shared and believed very strongly. Information literacy, education and fact-checking services are necessary but they are not sufficient to combat fake news. There are also a number of intelligent algorithms that can be used to detect and hopefully to prevent the propagation of fake news.

Analytics and AI to Create and Detect/Prevent Fake News

Analytics and AI techniques can detect fake news in four major ways: by analyzing the content, the writing style, the spread pattern and the credibility of content creators and sharers. Content can be verified using fact-checking services, both expert-based or crowdsourced, as previously discussed. However, in addition to manual fact checking, there are automated systems that make use of information retrieval (IR) and Natural Language Processing (NLP) approaches (Zhou and Zafarani, 2018).

Fake content tends to differ from valid content in the greater use of exaggerations and highly emotional words and these can be detected in online texts. For example, many studies look at how well the headline matches the content of the article. Most fake headlines are very provocative but share little in the way of commonly occurring words with the actual text. The way in which fake news is disseminated also exhibits unique patterns that can be detected. The two major methods are to either look at only the fake news spread pattern or to compare fake news propagation with that of valid content. In general, fake news spreads much faster and further than valid news. Fake news tends to provoke more emotional responses such as shock or anger, and is written in more opinionated or provocative styles. However, these approaches rely upon manually created dataset-specific databases of textual features. Finally, the last approach looks at who created and who shared the content, typically by identifying a website that has been flagged as being not credible, analyzing the headlines, the comments on the content and who shared this content. This is referred to as a form of cognitive authority.

Detecting fake news based on content and style is a form of sentiment mining, which is used to detect emotions and opinions for such applications as election polling. Ajao et al. (2019) looked at messages posted to online social networks to analyze the characteristics of fake news based on sentiments. The hypothesis is that there exists a relation between fake messages or rumors and sentiments of the texts posted on Twitter. The authors note that previous research studies have detected fake content based on writing style, author personality or even features such as the finding that liars tend to tell more complex stories, tend not to use the first person (e.g., "we" instead of "I") and use more negative than positive emotional words. Sentiment analysis can be done using linguistic word counting, which identifies the ratio of negative emotional words in a tweet to the number of positive emotional words. The higher the ratio, the more likely it is to be fake content. Fake content also had a higher incidence of use of all capital letters, exclamation points and quotations, as well as embedded images, videos or GIFs.

Natural language processing can be used to build a system to automatically detect misinformation in news. The main challenge in this line of research is collecting quality data, i.e., instances of fake and real news articles on a balanced distribution of topics. An example is Asr and Taboada's (2019) MisInfoText repository which provides full text news articles and a manual assessment of their truth content. This dataset is balanced across classes, and split into training, validation and test sets. In order to perform automatic classification of news texts, modern NLP and machine learning methods require large amounts of training data. There are very few such datasets, because individual labeling is a time-consuming task. However, one good source is the set of fact-checking websites. Unfortunately, there are not enough of them and we still don't have the large volume of data needed to make effective use of them.

Another approach is to identify fake news based on the speed and dissemination pattern. For example, Wu and Liu's (2018) TraceMiner application models the propagation of messages in a social network, which tends to be faster and ranges much further. They focus on spreaders, people who share fake news within their filter bubbles. Fake content tends to have similar diffusion patterns. They are also more likely to be spread from similar sources, by similar people and in similar sequences. The message can be a piece of news, a story or a meme that has been posted and forwarded in social networks by the spreaders. Traces or information on who posted and who spread the content can then form a corpus of data that can be mined and analyzed.

Bondielli and Marcelloni (2019) note that both fake news and rumors are very popular forms of misinformation that need to be detected as early as possible in order to contain possible consequences. Rumors are excellent examples of knowledge claims discussed earlier in the context of the McElroy model of knowledge management: They may be true, they may be false or they may remain unproven. A number of machine learning approaches have been developed to detect fake rumors. Most are based on supervised learning which requires a large dataset in order to both develop (train) and implement automatic detection systems. The authors note that more recent approaches using deep learning have proven very effective in analytics including text mining and NLP analytic applications. The major advantage of deep learning approaches is that they learn from simpler inputs. The authors believe the trend in favor of supervised deep learning will continue in many areas, including the detection of rumors and fake news.

Ruchansky et al. (2017) argue that automatically detecting fake news using NLP is limited by the fact that we do not have an exhaustive understanding of all linguistic characteristics. They further argue that relying only on propagation patterns is equally limited by manually generated social graphs that are highly dependent on media such as Facebook (e.g., FB likes). Checking the credibility of sources and authors is also labor-intensive and often ambiguous. Detecting fake news thus remains a "challenging problem that is not yet well understood" (p. 797). As each method has different limitations, the authors incorporated data on from all three approaches: features of the content, the way it spreads and characteristics of those who produced and shared this content: text, response and source. They developed a Recurrent Neural Network to automatically extract critical data to detect whether the content was fake or valid.

This notion of integrating vs. competing approaches is probably the best method to adopt in tackling such an interdisciplinary challenge as that posed by fake news. The elements of big data, analytics, AI, KM and IM all have a role to play in evolving solutions.

Future Trends and Research

Five key research priorities are discussed for the next three to five years: increasing literacy, developing more tools to detect and prevent the spread of fake news, creating hybrid or semi-automated approaches that leverage the strengths of people and technology, developing new types of research methods, and establishing a more comprehensive, interdisciplinary approach.

1.   Increased Literacy

Further research is needed on information literacy and education about misinformation, and manual and automated tools to help detect fake news as well as prevent their rapid and widespread dissemination. Montgomery and Gray (2017) note that information will always have value and power. Being able to assess the veracity of information is therefore an essential skill for informed citizens. For the information professional, delivering this veracity is a basic expectation, as well as providing a competitive advantage in productivity, knowledge management, furthering business development and risk management. However, everyone, not just information professionals, will need to develop and practice as the Internet has created an ever-expanding volume of information. The level of user interaction with misleading content remains very high in social media (e.g., Andrei et al., 2019). This is despite efforts by such sites as Facebook collaborating with fact-checking websites and allowing users to report fake news with a one-click option. In fact, this option backfired as users actually shared flagged stories more. Part of the problem resides in echo chambers or filter bubbles, which means that some people will be exposed to only one point of view, and will find it easier to believe stories that reaffirm that point of view (Constine, 2018).

Çömlekçi (2020) discusses the idea of "establishing a fact-checking school" in the future in conjunction with the ultimate goal of spreading fact-checking practices throughout society and creating an ecosystem to combat fake news. However, traditional journalists do not want or are not ready to join this ecosystem. It is difficult to reach all parts of society and fake news spreads faster than fact-check analyses. These all stand out as important problems and limitations of fact-checking services.

2.   Tools

Continued efforts are needed to develop widely accepted benchmark datasets that not only can be used by manual fact-checkers but also train and develop automated fake news detectors (Bondielli and Marcelloni, 2019). This is fundamental as we need to be able to evaluate the effectiveness of each approach and compare the approaches among them. Feature engineering is also a priority area to help us better understand the importance of certain features for classification, as well as their ability to generalize on the problem and possibly manage concept drift in a real-world scenario. The use of visual features has not received much attention in the literature. However, as photo and video manipulation tools become available to wider audiences, visual features to distinguish between true and fake content are increasingly important and could be seen as enabling users with tools that can automatically validate the information as reliable may result in a drastic reduction in the sharing of fake claims.

3.   Hybrid Approaches

Automated approaches are almost always more effective when they are combined with human agents. Both Bondielli and Marcelloni (2019) and Çömlekçi (2020) highlight the importance of user feedback to help spot false knowledge claims. Van Bavel et al. (2020) advocate the use of fact checking on sources to detect fake news, together with automated AI or analytics-based applications to keep up with the vast amount of content to be analyzed. This is particularly true in cases such as the 2020 COVID-19 pandemic where the "infodemic" was almost as destructive as the new corona virus. Ruchansky et al. (2017) advocate building models that incorporate concepts from reinforcement learning and crowdsourcing. Including humans in the learning process could lead to more accurate and, in particular, more timely predictions.

4.   Complementary Research Methods

A diverse range of research methods needs to be employed in order to study the problem of fake news. In particular, more experimental research is needed in order to empirically validate ways of detecting and preventing fake news. This is particularly important in order to better understand the causality behind human behaviors such as why we are drawn to fake news, why we believe in it and why it is so hard for us to make use of critical thinking skills when faced with emotionally laden content.

Greater research scope is needed as many studies focus on a given type of fake content (e.g., news), a specific website, a specific social media site, specific types of users and even a specific language (e.g., English). The sociocultural factors are as important as individual cognitive biases when it comes to fake news. Zhou and Zafarani (2018) point out that analyzing fake news across domains, topics, websites and languages allows one to gain a deeper understanding of fake news and identify its unique and varying characteristics, which can further assist in fake news' early detection. Another example is to identify generic propagation patterns of fake news in order to better predict how fake news is going to further spread.

Increasing research focus should be on the need for fake news detection at an early stage before it becomes widespread, so that one can take early action for fake news mitigation and intervention. Early detection is especially important for fake news as the more fake news spreads, the more likely people will trust it, and it is difficult to correct users' perceptions after fake news has gained their trust (Zhou and Zhafarani, 2018).

> Fighting back fake news proliferation and spreading is a difficult problem. It is safe to say that our aim should be to minimize their impact, since it is impossible to eliminate the fake news altogether. (Campan et al., 2017, p. 4456)

Finally, the KM and analytics research agenda for the next three to five years should include more longitudinal research in general to better understand knowledge sharing behaviors over time in order to ascertain how such elements as trust, knowledge sharing, validation and internalization take place (Bolisani et al., 2019).

5.   Interdisciplinary Approach

More research is needed on improved recommendation and/or personalization algorithms, better detection of misinformation, and more stringent regulation policies for search engine and social media providers (Bartlett, 2020).

> Detecting and mitigating falsified information is a challenging yet important research domain that includes the areas of information propagation, information retrieval, social network mining, text mining, machine learning and social sciences. Interdisciplinary problems require an interdisciplinary solution ... (Fung, 2020, p. xv)

The solution lies in an interdisciplinary approach, one that involves public and private entities such as the online industry, academia, media and society (Andrei et al., 2019). Creating and maintaining a context of trust depends on both institutions and citizens. Knowledge management, particularly elements such as social capital and knowledge sharing, have a pivotal role to play and more research is needed on how KM can help tackle fake news. IM can contribute a great deal from the literacy and education perspectives. Analytics, big data and AI have much to provide in the form of tools that can help us detect and, ideally, prevent the creation and spread of misinformation.

Mele et al. (2017) identify the short-term research priority to establish multidisciplinary community-wide shared resources for conducting academic research on the presence and dissemination of misinformation on social media platforms:

> Moving forward, we must expand the study of social and cognitive interventions that minimize the effects of misinformation on individuals and communities, as well as of how socio-technical systems such as Google, YouTube, Facebook, and Twitter currently facilitate the spread of misinformation and what internal policies might reduce those effects. More broadly, we must investigate what the necessary ingredients are for information systems that encourage a culture of truth. (p. 3)

In a similar vein, Bolisani et al. (2019) recommend looking at a holistic ecosystem of health information and knowledge, one that includes all relevant components such as experts, policymakers, the general population, official news/media channels, and social media channels.

The challenge is to provide not only a truly integrated approach but also a truly seamless one. This means that users should have everything within the same online environment that they are using to access content. A good example of research in this direction is Auberry (2018) who addresses how colleges and universities can judge what content is reliable and valid. The author discusses a pilot program that librarians at Indian River State College developed to incorporate news literacy into the learning management system used for all courses.

Conclusion

Hage et al. (2020) discuss the underlying assumption that users are rational beings and are therefore expected to act as objective critical thinkers. Numerous studies have shown that we are instead prone to a number of cognitive biases that we prefer to receive content from our trusted like-minded networks and even in the face of irrefutable evidence, we often choose to deliberately ignore facts ("information avoidance"). The authors strongly support a socio-technical approach to addressing attempts to deceive online users.

Delilles and Rubin (2020) note that one barrier to increasing the level of information literacy among citizens is determining who is responsible for teaching them. K-12 teachers? College and university professors? Is there, in fact, one ideal teacher or source? Better information literacy skills can definitely help users detect fake news better and, hopefully, then decide not to share it with others. The authors note that more research needs to be done to teach all the psychological, social and political elements involved in literacy, not to mention how best to evaluate how well people are applying these critical thinking skills when consuming news. The path to the truth has never been more treacherous, and neither news creators nor news media are neutral. In fact, instead of improving universal access, social media continues to deepen the digital divide as "alternative" facts co-exist with the truth, albeit in different filter bubbles (Külcü, 2020).

Organizations and nations are still in the very early stages of thinking about how to address the growing impact of fake news. Some promising examples include the European Union research initiative called the Social Truth project, which is working towards this vision of a future in which netizens are well equipped to detect online misinformation:

> The extreme growth and adoption of Social Media, in combination with their poor governance and the lack of quality control over the digital content being published and shared, has led information veracity to a continuous deterioration. Current approaches entrust content verification to a single centralised authority, lack resilience towards attempts to successfully "game" verification checks, and make content verification difficult to access and use. In response, our ambition is to create an open, democratic, pluralistic and distributed ecosystem that allows easy access

to various verification services (both internal and third-party), ensuring scalability and establishing trust in a completely decentralized environment. (Choraś et al., 2019, p. 1)

This approach involves journalists, news editors, search engines, online users and literacy-teaching material providers. The European Union's High Level Group on Fake News and Online Disinformation (de Cock Burning, 2018, pp. 5–6) outlines their recommended multidimensional approach "based on five pillars designed to:

1. Enhance transparency of online news, involving an adequate and privacy-compliant sharing of data about the systems that enable their circulation online;
2. Promote media and information literacy to counter disinformation and help users navigate the digital media environment;
3. Develop tools for empowering users and journalists to tackle disinformation and foster a positive engagement with fast-evolving information technologies;
4. Safeguard the diversity and sustainability of the European news media ecosystem, and
5. Promote continued research on the impact of disinformation in Europe to evaluate the measures taken by different actors and constantly adjust the necessary responses."

The American "fairness doctrine," introduced in the 20th century to guarantee fair, honest and balanced broadcasting, was abandoned in 2011. Some countries, such as Germany and Italy, have implemented misinformation legislation but these countries are in the minority (Hesketh, 2020). Health misinformation leads to the most serious consequence possible as it may involve literal life and death decisions about one's health. As Van Bavel et al. (2020) put it:

> To effectively counter fake news about COVID-19 around the world, governments and social media companies must rigorously develop and test interventions. This includes identifying treatments that effectively reduce belief in misinformation, while not undermining belief in accurate information. (p. 5)

While a number of technologies and tools exist to help us fight health misinformation, technology alone will not be enough. A comprehensive integrated solution will ideally involve:

1. Ways in which people can learn to be more aware of and better protect themselves from fake news (e.g., Pattison 2018 uses the catchy phrase: "skeptics not cynics" to describe the ideal, informed online citizen).

2. A hybrid system of users and automated intelligent tools that can analyze patterns in big data and use these analytics to detect and, even better, prevent, the spread of fake news;

3. Organizations with effective policies, and countries with effective legislation, that results in serious, real-world consequences of intentionally creating and disseminating fake news (Dalkir and Katz, 2020).

References

Ajao, O., Bhowmik, D. & Zargari, S. (2019, May). Sentiment aware fake news detection on online social networks. In *ICASSP 2019 IEEE International Conference on Acoustics, Speech and Signal Processing (ICASSP)* (pp. 2507–11). IEEE.

Alter, S. (2006, January). Goals and tactics on the dark side of knowledge management. In *Proceedings of the 39th Annual Hawaii International Conference on System Sciences (HICSS'06)*, Vol. 7, pp. 144a–144a. IEEE.

Andrei, A. G., Zait, A. & Alexandru, V. A. (2019). On the spread of misinformation through online media: a knowledge management approach. BORDERS WITHOUT BORDERS: systemic frameworks and their applications. In *Proceedings, 6th Business Systems Laboratory International*, Pavia University, Italy, January 21–3.

Asr, F. & Taboada, M. (2019). Big data and quality data for fake news and misinformation detection. *Big Data & Society*, 6(1), 1–14.

Auberry, K. (2018). Increasing students' ability to identify fake news through information literacy education and content management systems. *The Reference Librarian*, 59(4), 179–87.

Bartlett, J. (2020). Information literacy and science misinformation. In K. Dalkir & R. Katz (eds.), *Navigating Fake News, Alternative Facts, and Misinformation in a Post-Truth World*, pp. 1–17. IGI Global.

Bolisani, E., Cegarra-Sánchez, J., Cegarra-Navarro, J. G. & Martínez, E. (2019). Imperfect knowledge, fake knowledge, counter knowledge: case studies and institutional countermeasures. In *Proceedings ECKM 2019 20th European Conference on Knowledge Management*, p. 160. Academic Conferences and Publishing Limited.

Bondielli, A. & Marcelloni, F. (2019). A survey on fake news and rumour detection techniques. *Information Sciences*, 497, 38–55.

Burkhardt, J. M. (2017). History of fake news. *Combating Fake News in the Digital Age*, 53(8), 5–9.

Campan, A., Cuzzocrea, A. & Truta, T. M. (2017). Fighting fake news spread in online social networks: actual trends and future research directions. In *Proceedings 2017 IEEE International Conference on Big Data*, pp. 4453–7. IEEE.

Çömlekçi, M. F. (2020). Combating fake news online: Turkish fact-checking services. In K. Dalkir & R. Katz (eds.), *Navigating Fake News, Alternative Facts, and Misinformation in a Post-Truth World*, pp. 273–89. IGI Global.

Choraś, M., Pawlicki, M., Kozik, R., Demestichas, K., Kosmides, P. & Gupta, M. (2019). Social truth project approach to online disinformation (fake news) detection and mitigation. In *Proceedings of the 14th International Conference on Availability, Reliability and Security*, pp. 1–10.

Constine, J. (2018). Facebook shrinks fake news after warnings backfire. *Tech Crunch*, April 28. Available at https://tcrn.ch/2jb7gcp (accessed May 4, 2020).

Dalkir, K. & Katz, R. (eds.) (2020). *Navigating Fake News, Alternative Facts, and Misinformation in a Post-Truth World*. IGI Global.

de Cock Buning, M. (2018). A multi-dimensional approach to disinformation. *Report of the independent High Level Group on fake news and online disinformation*. Publications Office of the European Union. Available at: http://dspace.library.uu.nl/handle/1874/386085 (accessed May 4, 2020).

Delellis, N. S. & Rubin, V. L. (2020). 'Fake news' in the context of information literacy: a Canadian case study. In K. Dalkir & R. Katz (eds.), *Navigating Fake News, Alternative Facts, and Misinformation in a Post-Truth World*, pp. 89–115. IGI Global.

Edwards, M., Davies, M., & Edwards, A. (2009). What are the external influences on information exchange and shared decision-making in healthcare consultations? A meta-synthesis of the literature. *Patient Educ Couns*, 75(1), 37–52.

Froehlich, T. J. (2020). Ten lessons for the age of disinformation. In K. Dalkir & R. Katz (eds.), *Navigating Fake News, Alternative Facts, and Misinformation in a Post-Truth World*, pp. 36–88. IGI Global.

Fung, B. (2020). Foreword in K. Dalkir & R. Katz (eds.), *Navigating Fake News, Alternative Facts, and Misinformation in a Post-Truth World*. IGI Global.

Hage, H., Aïmeur, E. & Guedidi, A. (2020). Understanding the landscape of online deception. In K. Dalkir & R. Katz (eds.), *Navigating Fake News, Alternative Facts, and Misinformation in a Post-Truth World*, pp. 290–317. IGI Global.

Haigh, M., Haigh, T. & Kozak, N. I. (2018). Stopping fake news: the work practices of peer-to-peer counter propaganda. *Journalism Studies*, 19(14), 2062–87.

Hasher, L., Goldstein, D. & Toppino, T. (1977). Frequency and the conference of referential validity. *Journal of Verbal Learning and Verbal Behavior*, 16(1), 107–12.

Hesketh, K. (2020). Spiritualism and the resurgence of fake news. In K. Dalkir & R. Katz (eds.), *Navigating Fake News, Alternative Facts, and Misinformation in a Post-Truth World*, pp. 222–37. IGI Global.

Ingram, A., Kett, M. & Rushton, S. (2011). *Spies, Vaccines and Violence: Fake Health Campaigns and the Neutrality of Health*. Taylor & Francis.

Jamieson, K. & Cappella, J. (2008). *Echo Chamber: Rush Limbaugh and the Conservative Media Establishment*. Oxford University Press.

Kim, J., Tabibian, B., Oh, A., Schölkopf, B. & Gomez-Rodriguez, M. (2018). Leveraging the crowd to detect and reduce the spread of fake news and misinformation. In *Proceedings of the Eleventh ACM International Conference on Web Search and Data Mining*, pp. 324–32.

Külcü, Ö. (2020). Verification of information and evaluation of approaches of information professionals in accessing accurate information. In K. Dalkir & R. Katz (eds.), *Navigating Fake News, Alternative Facts, and Misinformation in a Post-Truth World*, pp. 162–83. IGI Global.

McElroy, M. W. & McElroy, L. (2003). *The New Knowledge Management: Complexity, Learning, and Sustainable Innovation*. Routledge.

Mele, N., Lazer, D., Baum, M., Grinberg, N., Friedland, L., Joseph, K., ... & Mattsson, C. (2017). Combating fake news: an agenda for research and action. Available at https://www.sipotra.it/old/wp-content/uploads/2017/06/Combating-Fake-News.pdf (accessed May 4, 2020).

Montgomery, L. and Gray, B. (2017). Information veracity and the threat of fake news. *The Emerald Handbook of Modern Information Management*, 409–35. Emerald Publishing.

Nonaka, I. & Takeuchi, H. (1995). *The Knowledge-Creating Company: How Japanese Companies Create the Dynamics of Innovation*. Oxford University Press.

Pattison, D. (2018). Fake news: teaching skeptics, not cynics. *Knowledge Quest*, 47(1), 62–4.

Pennycook, G., Cannon, T. D. & Rand, D. G. (2018). Prior exposure increases perceived accuracy of fake news. *Journal of Experimental Psychology: General*, 147(12), 1865–80.

Roozenbeek, J. & Van Der Linden, S. (2019). The fake news game: actively inoculating against the risk of misinformation. *Journal of Risk Research*, 22(5), 570–80.

Ruchansky, N., Seo, S. & Liu, Y. (2017, November). CSI: A hybrid deep model for fake news detection. In *Proceedings of the 2017 ACM on Conference on Information and Knowledge Management*, pp. 797–806.

Tandoc, Jr., E. C., Ling, R., Westlund, O., Duffy, A., Goh, D. & Zheng Wei, L. (2018). Audiences' acts of authentication in the age of fake news: a conceptual framework. *New Media & Society*, 20(8), 2745–63.

Van Bavel, J. J., Baicker, K., Boggio, P. S., Capraro, V., Cichocka, A., Cikara, M., ... & Drury, J. (2020). Using social and behavioural science to support COVID-19 pandemic response. *Nature Human Behaviour*, 4, 460–71.

Wilson, P. (1983). *Second-Hand Knowledge: An Inquiry into Cognitive Authority*. Greenwood.

Wilson, T.D. (1997). Information behaviour: an interdisciplinary perspective. *Information Process Management*, 33(4), 551–72.

Wu, L. & Liu, H. (2018, February). Tracing fake-news footprints: characterizing social media messages by how they propagate. In *Proceedings of the Eleventh ACM International conference on Web Search and Data Mining*, pp. 637–45.

Zhou, X. & Zafarani, R. (2018). Fake news: a survey of research, detection methods, and opportunities. *ACM Computing Survey*, 1, 1–40. Available at https://arxiv.org/pdf/1812.00315.pdf (accessed May 4, 2020).

11. Privacy and data: some research venues

Kenneth Carling and Johan Håkansson

The issue of data privacy is often reduced to secure data transactions by cryptographic techniques. However, in a liberal democracy the issue of privacy connects to fundamental questions about the co-existence and collaboration between its citizens. One is the conflict between self-interest and the interest of the commons, whereby research on privacy topics is found in distant and disparate research streams. Sharing of data perceived as private may drastically increase collective welfare, while reducing it for single citizens. In this chapter, we present a metaphor to highlight the fundamentals of privacy and explain how the access to new data-processing technologies provokes new questions to be addressed. Furthermore, we illustrate how various research streams differ in presumptions and privacy topics of interest, and we stress the potential knowledge-producing value of bridging these streams. We end by pointing out some particularly interesting research venues for privacy and data.

1. A Game of Poker

A running definition of privacy can be thought of as the ability of an individual or group to conceal information about themselves, thereby expressing themselves selectively. In the era of the Internet, any digital expression can travel fast and broadly, and can cause persistent general concern amongst private individuals regarding protection of their privacy. However, the privacy paradox phenomenon has been recognized in the literature suggesting an inconsistency between attitudes to privacy and actual behavior (Kokolakis, 2017). In short, it has been reported that individuals value privacy highly, while at the same time disclosing private data liberally in various digital forms. Another phenomenon observed is the argument supporting privacy data disclosure, "I have nothing to hide" (Solove, 2007).

To get at the core of the reason why a private person might and perhaps ought to conceal her privacy data, we provide an illustrative metaphor. The metaphor begins with a very simple zero-sum game and illustrates the re-distributive effects on rendering some private data public. The metaphor will then increase in complexity and considerations of non-zero-sum situations are offered. At each instance, a business opportunity arises and the metaphor could therefore be read as an illustration of how a market develops.

Consider four private individuals seated around a table to play poker (Figure 11.1). For ease of computation, these players are equally skilled in the game and try to maximize their wins, and the standard card deck is shuffled and dealt properly. Five cards are dealt to each player, face down. In each game each player decides whether to fold or place a fixed bet amounting to X, revealed to the others after the betting round. Depending on the players' bet, the pot may vary between 0 and 4X. The player with the best poker hand collects the pot. There is no privacy intrusion, which means, in this game, that the expected win for each player equals zero.

Figure 11.1   Poker game

Source: Photograph by Mark Douet.

Consider now a situation where there is a mirror placed behind Player A so the other three players can see her poker hand; that is, her private data are in the public domain. If she is dealt the best hand, the others will fold and she re-collects her own bet from the pot. Otherwise, the three other players will, in expectation, share her X bet in each game in which she is betting. Consequently, Player A's expected loss due to privacy intrusion amounts to nX, whereas the expected win, thanks to the data sharing, for the other three players is $nX/3$, where n is the number of games on which she is betting. There are some important points to note from this construct. The first point is that the privacy intrusion lowers the welfare of Player A, while it increases it for the others. The second point is that the intrusion re-distributes welfare in a zero-sum game like the construct, whereas in a non-zero-sum game all the players could attain a higher level of welfare although the increase is not equally large. The third point is that sometimes a monetary value could be assigned to the private data. In the illustration, the three players ought to be willing to pay up to $nX/3$ for having Player A's private card data revealed by a mirror. Hence, one can envision a market for data (see Laudon, 1996). The fourth point is that most persons would find the construct immoral and require regulations, such as forbidding a mirror, which hinders disclosing her privacy card data. And the fifth point is that "forbidding a mirror" requires a body to decide on forbidding it. In a liberal democracy, the mechanism for the decision is usually stipulated in the constitution or equivalent where the decision ought to reckon with the fact that punishments or regulations themselves induce costs.

Suppose, now, that the mirror is cracked, such that her poker hand looks blurry to the others and they are hardly able to identify her cards. Should the mirror necessarily be removed? Yes, you might say, as she would still expect a loss, albeit less than if the mirror was uncracked. The odds are, however, in favor of your subscribing to the privacy paradox as you, at the same time, swipe your credit card for payments and keep your phone's position software activated, allowing your surrounding players to see your poker hand in a cracked mirror.

The cracked mirror implies that the other players' expected win is in the range $0 - nX/3$, where the expectation will depend on how much the cracks will blur the mirror vision for the other players. Would you still find it immoral if the mirror is badly cracked and the other players only get a hunch of her poker hand? At what point of vision blurriness would your moral indignation dissolve? If you insist that the mirror should be removed, no matter how cracked it is, then let us replace the mirror in the metaphor with a door of reflective metal – should that also be removed? Your stand on these questions is important because what has been outlined above as a silly thought experiment is happening in our everyday lives. In a poker game, players are trying to read each other's reactions and count cards. In the devised game, card counting is a pointless exercise, however, as the deck is reshuffled each round and no dealt card is exposed during betting. Now, take the metaphor one step further: the mirror is removed, but each of the three other players (apart from Player A), has brought a machine to the poker table – the three machines are identical in terms of technical sophistication.

Without the machines, the four equally skilled players apply (unknown to the others) a betting strategy; that is, to bet if the dealt poker hand is amongst the top 50% of hands. There are $52 * 51 * 50 * 49 * 48 \approx 3 \cdot 10^8$ possible hands that can be ordered in terms of poker value, so the betting strategy implies betting if the hand is amongst the $1.5 \cdot 10^8$ best hands. In this case, all four players have the same expected, equaling zero, win. The introduction of the machines changes the situation. Suppose the machine uses a supervised k nearest neighbor (k-NN) algorithm to predict the betting strategy of Player A in the following way: Player A's digital footprint retrieves data on her educational and financial status and her way of reasoning from social media and blog posts, and so on, in combination with data on her facial expressions during the game. The machine uses these data to look up k persons who provide a very good match to her and, based on what is known about their betting strategies, it predicts that Player A adopts the strategy to bet if the poker hand is amongst the top 50% of hands, and notes further that a Player A-type is persistent in the strategy during the course of a poker game. As a consequence, the machine recommends its patron to adjust his betting threshold to, say, those amongst the top 25% of hands. As in the case of a somewhat cracked mirror, the expected win is in the range $0 - nX/3$ for the other players, with a greater expectation due to the greater predictive accuracy of the machine.

Referring to the five points made above in relation to the mirror construct, are the three other players immoral? Remember that the machine is only using data on Player A that she has freely shared elsewhere in no relation to the poker game. Would it be in the self-interest of the three other players to buy a machine (and the data and the data acquisition features that come with it)? Should the machine be forbidden? If yes, exactly what part of the machine should be forbidden – after all, you do want to have a calculator when you are filling in your tax forms!

The value of data extends beyond the metaphor. Data has always been valuable. A sailor carrying goods to trade benefited from data on prevailing wind directions. Data on family heritage was useful for the corresponding partners in arranging marriages. What is new is the escalating amount of business services that data and machines can provide. And these services exploit the technologically induced drop in resource usage for data acquisition, storage and processing.

2.   Current Research Streams under Zero-Sum Game Situations

The jurisprudential research literature puts focus on the moral aspect of privacy. Daniel J. Solove is an influential scholar and his perspective on privacy emerges clearly in his paper, "I've nothing to hide" (Solove, 2007). Surely, most of us when bringing up the issue of privacy and data intrusion have received this response where the respondent signals no concerns with potential data intrusion, as he or she is a righteous person and therefore would fare well in any game situation as a consequence. From the mirror metaphor above, it should be clear that such a belief is naïve, if not foolish. Solove (2007, p. 772) concludes:

> The nothing to hide argument speaks to some problems, but not to others. It represents a singular and narrow way of conceiving of privacy, and it wins by excluding consideration of the other problems often raised in government surveillance and data mining programs. When engaged with directly, the nothing to hide argument can ensnare, for it forces the debate to focus on its narrow understanding of privacy. But when confronted with the plurality of privacy problems implicated by government data collection and use beyond surveillance and disclosure, the nothing to hide argument, in the end, has nothing to say.

Arguably, Solove and other legal scholars tend to envision state-sanctioned data intrusion of individual privacy. However, the relevance of his point applies to any relation between a collective, be that in the form of a corporate company, or other organization and the private self. In this perspective it is customary, for good reasons we may add, to view the private as the weak, naïve, and poorly articulated part. For instance, Solove (2005, p. 480) writes:

> Often, privacy problems are merely stated in knee-jerk form: "That violates my privacy!" When we contemplate an invasion of privacy – such as having our personal information gathered by companies in databases – we instinctively recoil. Many discussions of privacy appeal to people's fears and anxieties. What commentators often fail to do, however, is translate those instincts into a reasoned, well-articulated account of why privacy problems are harmful. When people claim that privacy should be protected, it is unclear precisely what they mean. This lack of clarity creates a difficulty when making policy or resolving a case because lawmakers and judges cannot easily articulate the privacy harm. The interests on the other side – free speech, efficient consumer transactions, and security – are often much more readily articulated. Courts and policymakers frequently struggle in recognizing privacy interests, and when this occurs, cases are dismissed or laws are not passed. The result is that privacy is not balanced against countervailing interests.

We shall shortly return to the intriguing term "balance" in the last sentence of Solove's text. As a generic remedy for improper data intrusion, data acquisition of the private is frequently accompanied with a request of "informed consent": in research involving humans, for instance, it has long been customary to inform participants in drug trials about new products and seek their voluntary consent (see, e.g., Resnik, 2019). The rationale is that voluntary engagement in an activity of which the private self is fully informed cannot be regarded as an intrusion. In fact, this argument is a pillar in the law on General Data Protection Regulation (GDPR) issued by the European Union in 2016, and later subsequently adopted by several non-European states and generally respected by the corporate world. However, Solove (2013) refers to this informed consent as "privacy self-management" and casts serious doubts as to whether it would effectively put the four players in the poker game metaphor on an equal and fair footing. One reason to doubt, he argues, is the empirical and behavioral science research that indicates severe cognitive problems that undermine privacy self-management. Another equally compelling argument is the insurmountable difficulty for the private person to monitor and ensure that her digital data in the hands of others are used for the purpose for which she gave her consent.

The perspective that the private self needs protection due to being the weak part extends beyond legal scholarly writing. Culnan and Williams (2009) assume the same perspective in the field of management science. However, they reason as if the corporates have a self-interest in balancing private individuals' data privacy in their exploitation of the machine. While we certainly acknowledge the existence of business ethics and altruistic behavior in general, we note that Culnan and Williams (2009) do not back up their theoretical arguments empirically. Do we really believe that the three players in the poker room would deliberately avoid glancing at the slightly cracked mirror?

So does someone try to address the "balance" question arising in Solove's (2007) quotation above? The answer is yes; the economist! Acquisti et al. (2016) carry out an extensive review of the "the economics of privacy." If the three players in the mirror metaphor are willing to pay for the machine to improve their outcome of the poker game, why should Player A not consider trading her privacy data? After all, for the uncracked mirror we know that her loss will amount to nX, and thus this might be the price she should ask to accept the presence of the mirror in the poker room. As is evident in the metaphor, and pointed out much earlier by Posner (1981), privacy, and the lack of it, is redistributive in the sense that the sharing or not of privacy changes the relative welfare of the concerned actors.

To get a sense of what questions intrigue economists, it would first be wise to recognize that privacy is multifaceted, as Solove (2005; 2007) has noted. He dissected privacy into seclusion, secrecy, solitude, anonymity, autonomy and freedom. Economists tend to focus on informational privacy. Acquisti et al. (2016) summarize the core questions for economists:

1. Are there privacy "equilibria" that benefit both data holders and data subjects?
2. What is the allocation of surplus gained from the usage of individuals' personal data?
3. How should that surplus be allocated – based on market forces, treating privacy as another economic good, or based on regulation, treating privacy as a fundamental right?
4. Should an allocation favor the data subject as the owner of the data, or the data holder who invested in collecting and analyzing the information?

A fundamental point we want to put across is that the answers to these questions may be sought amongst economists, but they are profoundly important to anyone interested in regulations or technological implementation that concern privacy. We want to make two points in relation to question 1. The first is that in the absence of a yes to the question, it is hard to believe in a functioning and civilized trade market for private data. Indeed, and this is the second point, Acquisti et al. (2016) conclude that the answer is context-dependent, implying that an answer needs to be provided on a case-by-case basis. Does an "equilibrium" exist in the mirror metaphor? Let us presume that all players are aware of the value of the information shared by the mirror and that they all are risk-neutral due to the poker game running many rounds; further, Player A sensibly requires full compensation for the incurred loss in welfare due to her hand being in the public domain. Then, considering the associated costs of negotiating the price and executing the economic transaction, it seems more likely that one of the players will get up and either remove the mirror, or cover it with a blanket, for example.

As for question 2, it is straightforward to assess the surplus gained by the three players in the context of the mirror being $nX/3$ for each of them. What is the surplus with the introduction of the machine for the three players? We only have the interval of $0 - nX/3$ and where on this interval depends on the predictive accuracy of the machine in identifying Player A's betting strategy which, in turn, depends on the propensity of Player-A-alikes to share private data. An inherently difficult aspect, as stressed by Varian (1997), is that the Player-A-alikes, including Player A, will have a hard time in assessing secondary usages of their privacy data. For instance, the Player-A-alikes would never have envisioned their sharing of privacy data would affect the outcome of this metaphorical poker game!

To make things even more complex, the introduction of the machine implies that at least one additional actor has been added to the poker room (questions 3 and 4). There are a few firms that manage the data lakes or data platforms at which public and historically private data are kept, processed and commercialized (Bendrath and Mueller, 2011). That is, they are the vendors of the machine to the three players. Suppose that the predictive accuracy of the machine is such that the three players will expect to win $nX/6$. How should this surplus be distributed between the player and the machine vendor, or, in other words, at what price should the machine be sold?

In the metaphor, it is uncontroversial to discard a market solution and ask for regulations; that is, to have the mirror removed and ban the machine. Why is this? The mirror and the introduction of the machine would only redistribute the welfare between the players, keeping the collective welfare unchanged. Actually, the machine comes with a cost to be paid by someone, and therefore the collective welfare is actually decreased by its entrance to the poker room. Consequently, Player A's privacy ought to be protected. However, in other contexts privacy protection may decrease individual and collective welfare. Laudon (1996) argues that legal protection of privacy is outdated and a system based on property rights over personal information would better satisfy the interests of the private and firms. Acquisti et al. (2016, p. 480) state:

> ... market-based solutions and regulatory approaches to privacy protection are not polar opposites. They are better perceived as points on a spectrum of solutions – from regimes that rely entirely on firms' self-regulation and consumers' responsibility (even in the absence of clearly defined and assigned property rights over personal data), to regimes with strict regulatory protection of data.

They also stress that a fruitful venue of research would be to examine various regulatory features rather than contrasting regulation versus no regulation. In the next section, we take a look at new phenomena, driven by technological opportunities, arising under the presumption that sharing privacy data will drastically increase collective welfare.

3. Technology-Optimistic Research Streams Oblivious to the Game Situation

We now turn to two recent phenomena arising thanks to, and propelled by, advancement in information and communication technology, namely *Smart Cities* and the *Internet of Things*, of which the success of both hinges on digital sharing of private selves' data. Both of these phenomena promise to "drastically increase collective welfare"; i.e., they do not induce a zero-sum game, but they are silent on the re-distributive effects.

At the heart of the Smart City concept lies a theory that human interconnectivity, coupled with appropriate hard infrastructure, is decisive for urban competitiveness. And in turn, the latter promotes economic growth which translates into increased collective welfare. Information and communication technology is the enabler for human interconnectivity. This theory has been highly influential in the European Union and its strategic documents frequently point to the need for member states to implement the Smart City paradigm on national and regional levels. One reason for assigning this value to human interconnectivity is the matching of complementary skills and skill transfers. However, another reason is obviously the sharing of private data amongst (at least) peers. Caragliu et al. (2011) have examined whether the Smart City paradigm, indeed, appears to increase collective welfare. They regress per capita GDP as a function of six features of a Smart City and find that the per capita GDP is positively correlated with all six features, amongst which one finds Multimodality Accessibility and e-Government. The two features singled out are critically contingent on digital data sharing of private data. Although one might object that Caragliu et al. (2011) have only shown a correlation, rather than a causation, between economic welfare and Smart City features, their results provide some support for Smart Cities to "drastically increase the collective welfare." What is remarkable in Caragliu et al.'s (2011) work and subsequent work extending the concept to Smart sustainable cities (Bibri and Krogstie, 2017; Hashem et al., 2016) is the failure to identify the redistribution of wealth resulting from the data sharing enabling the Smart (sustainable) City. For instance, Hashem et al. (2016) write in their abstract:

> Big data offer the potential for cities to obtain valuable insights from a large amount of data collected through various sources, and the IoT allows the integration of sensors, radio-frequency identification, and Bluetooth in the real-world environment using highly networked services ... These new challenges focus primarily on problems related to business and technology that enable cities to actualize the vision, principles, and requirements of the applications of smart cities by realizing the main smart environment characteristics ... The visions of big data analytics to support smart cities are discussed by focusing on how big data can fundamentally change urban populations at different levels.

Here they recognize the importance of "privacy enhancing technologies" (Borisov et al., 2004) to mitigate security issues and data integrity, but they neglect the issue of information privacy. Considering the strong promotion of the Smart City by the state, it appears to us that economists' insights as to whether and how to mix a regulatory framework with intellectual proprietary rights of one's private data deserve scholarly attention.

The focus and the research agenda on the Internet of Things (IoT) suggest an equally naïve understanding of information privacy. The IoT, nowadays deeply integrated in Smart Cities, promises to alleviate everyday-life burdens for citizens and improve businesses operations as a result of technology and data sharing (Atzori et al., 2010). As with other influential scholars (e.g., Botta et al., 2016; Lin et al., 2017) offering research direction on IoT, Atzori et al. consistently recognize privacy as a technical problem to be overcome with improved technology, thereby overlooking the redistributive nature of data sharing. It is very hard to believe that a Smart City or IoT paradigm will be embraced by a society, on a long-term basis, regardless of how much collective benefits they may bring, unless a deeper understanding of information privacy is integrated in these research agendas.

4.   Suggested Topics for Further Investigation

The literature focusing on private data, privacy and ethical issues in a situation of more or less atomized data collection and data sharing is rather scarce. This gives us the opportunity to highlight interesting future research in the area. Using the poker game as a metaphor and some typical research agendas in separate disciplines, we have illustrated the fundamental importance of private data as well as various positive and negative consequences with regard to collecting, processing and sharing such data.

We believe that there is a need for more cross-disciplinary research where privacy and ethical questions from regulatory, economic and technological perspectives are combined in the area of internet economy (see also Weber, 2015; Aquisti et al., 2016; Eckhoff and Wagner, 2018). Clearly, various technological solutions exist that focus more or less on the consumer's need for privacy in a market situation of personal data sharing. One future research topic could be how various levels of privacy-enhancing technologies affect market and business opportunities and the need for regulation. In such an endeavor, we emphasize the value of deeply reviewing the technological feasibility.

It is not only individuals who value their personal data and have concerns about sharing it with others, but companies collecting data on human behaviors are also interested in keeping that data to themselves to protect their business models. However, in a market where data and sharing data is of major importance, but where neither individuals nor companies want to share their data, the likelihood of suboptimal solutions with less possibility for individuals to have control over their privacy is high. Research exploring a game theoretical approach in testing various privacy-enhancing technologies could be worthwhile in order to find optimal technological and regulatory set ups that enhance a market based on data sharing.

Another fruitful direction of research suggested by Acquisti et al. (2016) would be to attempt to address the question to what extent the combination of sophisticated analytics and massive amounts of data of private selves will increase collective welfare, as well as to what extent it will merely re-distribute wealth.

Yet another topic that would be interesting to explore is the forming of collisions. Organizations like companies are collisions of owners and employees. We have not come across any such initiative. Referring to the metaphorical game, it seems reasonable to expect that the three machines would form a collision to efficiently ruin Player A. The collision could share the poker hands of the three players to ensure that only the player with the best of these three hands bets, and his decision could be made based on not only knowing his own five cards, but also 15 out of the 52 cards. What kind of new reasons to forming collision does the existence of machines give rise to? What rules will such collisions apply? Will collisions formed around the machine give rise to new organizational structures operating under a new logic?

From the literature, it is also obvious that awareness among consumers of how privacy may affect the economy, where collecting and sharing data are important features, is often low and needs to be increased (see also Weber, 2015; Eckhoff and Wagner, 2018; Allam, 2019). This issue is sometimes referred to as the digital divide and it is high on the political agenda. Many European countries, for instance, have introduced digital competence in the curriculums for elementary schools. As an example, in Sweden, teaching in the compulsory school has recently introduced knowing-how programming and how to create algorithms (Skolverket, 2018). One may therefore hope that in the long-run awareness among consumers and citizens may improve. The current and short-term situation, however, is much more unclear and that is problematic, as the recent development of the Internet economy based on automatic data collection and data sharing is fast. We therefore suggest a research vein focusing on identifying current privacy awareness-raising programs for adults and the evaluation of their effects with regard to how it affects internet behavior. In doing so, the awareness gap between the naïve consumer and the educated, informed consumer can also be evaluated.

Furthermore and finally, consumers are citizens and they are also to a large extent knowledge workers. The present paradigm of Knowledge Management (KM) is that competitiveness of a company is primarily driven by knowledge and its knowledge sharing among their knowledge workers. Tzortzaki and Mihiotis (2014) state:

> Knowledge only becomes organizational when employees are motivated through company culture to share experiences and use collective knowledge [...] Knowledge workers can choose to share or not share their knowledge, depending on their perceptions of the fairness of the rewards they receive from the organization.

So, in light of trading data discussed earlier and a focus on core questions in KM, how is perception of fairness in data/knowledge sharing achieved amongst knowledge workers in an organization? And, considering the evolution towards networks of organizations, how can fairness perception be achieved and maintained? Moreover, the KM paradigm has been imperative for the development of Intellectual Capital measures for management purposes. Should it be accompanied with "data sharing capital" measures?

Acknowledgments

Several people have influenced this chapter, but we would like to mention foremost the undergraduate students at our department who studied research methods during the spring of 2020. Their suggested topics in the domain of privacy and AI taught us much about a younger generation's view on this deeply human issue of privacy. We are grateful to Irene Gilsenan Nordin for, as always, enthusiastically, reviewing and commenting on the style of writing and proof reading, and to Arend Hintze for carefully scrutinizing the metaphor employed in this work. Any errors and ambiguities remain the sole responsibility of the authors.

References

Acquisti, A., Taylor, C. & Wagman, L. (2016). The economics of privacy. *Journal of Economic Literature*, 54(2), 442–92.
Allam, Z. (2019). The emergence of anti-privacy and control at the nexus between the concepts of safe city and smart city. *Smart Cities*, 2(1), 96–105.
Atzori, L., Iera, A. & Morabito, G. (2010). The internet of things: a survey. *Computer Networks*, 54(15), 2787–805.

Bendrath, R. & Mueller, M. (2011). The end of the net as we know it? Deep packet inspection and internet governance. *New Media & Society*, 13(7), 1142–60.

Bibri, S. E. & Krogstie, J. (2017). Smart sustainable cities of the future: an extensive interdisciplinary literature review. *Sustainable Cities and Society*, 31, 183–212.

Borisov, N., Goldberg, I. & Brewer, E. (2004). Off-the-record communication, or, why not to use PGP. *In Proceedings of the 2004 ACM workshop on Privacy in the electronic society*, 77–84.

Botta, A., De Donato, W., Persico, V. & Pescapé, A. (2016). Integration of cloud computing and internet of things: a survey. *Future Generation Computer Systems*, 56, 684–700.

Caragliu, A., Del Bo, C. & Nijkamp, P. (2011). Smart cities in Europe. *Journal of Urban Technology*, 18(2), 65–82.

Culnan, M. J. & Williams, C. C. (2009). How ethics can enhance organizational privacy: lessons from the choicepoint and TJX data breaches. *MIS Quarterly: Management Information Systems*, 4, 673–87.

Eckhoff, D. & Wagner, I. (2018). Privacy in the smart city—applications, technologies, challenges, and solutions. *IEEE Communications Surveys & Tutorials*, 20(1), 489–516.

Hashem, I. A. T., Chang, V., Anuar, N. B., Adewole, K., Yaqoob, I., Gani, A., Ahmed, E. & Chiroma, H. (2016). The role of big data in the smart city. *International Journal of Information Management*, 36(5), 748–58.

Kokolakis, S. (2017). Privacy attitudes and privacy behaviour: a review of current research on the privacy paradox phenomenon. *Computers & Security*, 64, 122–34.

Laudon, K. C. (1996). Markets and privacy. *Communications of the ACM*, 39(9), 92–104.

Lin, J., Yu, W., Zhang, N., Yang, X., Zhang, H. & Zhao, W. (2017). A survey on internet of things: architecture, enabling technologies, security and privacy, and applications. *IEEE Internet of Things Journal*, 4(5), 1125–42.

Posner, R. A. (1981). The economics of privacy. *The American Economic Review*, 71(2), 405–9.

Resnik, D. B. (2019). The role of intuition in risk/benefit decision-making with research human subjects. In J. Liebowitz (ed.), *Developing Informed Intuition for Decision-Making*, 149–60. Taylor & Francis.

Skolverket. (2018). Curriculum for the compulsory school, preschool class and school-age education [revised 2018]. Nordstedts, Stockholm. https://www.skolverket .se/andra-sprak-other-languages/english-engelska.

Solove, D. J. (2005). A taxonomy of privacy. *University of Pennsylvania Law Review*, 154, 477–560.

Solove, D. J. (2007). "I've got nothing to hide" and other misunderstandings of privacy. *San Diego Law Review*, 44, 745–72.

Solove, D. J. (2013). Introduction: privacy self-management and the consent dilemma. *Harvard Law Review*, 126, 1880–903.

Tzortzaki, A. M. & Mihiotis, A. (2014). A review of knowledge management theory and future directions. *Knowledge and Process Management*, 21(1), 29–41.

Varian, H. R. (1997). Economic aspects of personal privacy, in ch. 1 of United States Department of Commerce, *Privacy and Self-Regulation in the Information Age*. https://www.ntia.doc.gov/report/1997/privacy-and-self-regulation-information -age.

Weber, R.H. (2015). Internet of things: privacy issues revisited. *Computer Law & Security Review*, 31, 618–27.

12. Lessons learned and best practices in KM: a personal perspective

Douglas Weidner

Introduction

This chapter focuses on lessons learned and best practices across four KM-related domains, but from a practitioner's viewpoint. The first domain is the major *socio-economic trends* that affect how we fundamentally think about KM. In other words, is KM just another technology-based discipline or the discipline that will enable peak performance as we go through a major episodic cultural change? The answer substantially impacts the second, more evidence-based focus: do we have a robust, proven *Methodology* to enable the requisite KM Team *Implementation Activities* that improve their likelihood of success? Third, what are some of the uncommon, but emergent, and possibly even more essential *strategic KM initiative types* (besides the original Repositories, CoPs (Communities of Practice) and Expert Locators) that should be our emphasis and how can they be effectively communicated to leadership? The latter two categories (overall KM implementation methodology and the relevant strategic initiative types) need evidence-based insights to improve the KM practitioner's likelihood of success. This means improvements in organizational performance, health and sustainability. Then, finally, we will close with a peek into emerging *maturity model* technology, which could be also much enriched by research.

Knowledge Management (KM) is yet to be accurately defined or even fully understood. At present, it is a puzzle comprised of many personal viewpoints and experiences, as proven by the diversity of eye-witness authors in this book. Each of us has our own perspectives, probably even biases.

This chapter includes my own individual perspective on the evolution of KM from 1995 to the present, with a special focus on the lessons we have learned, and the best practices that have emerged. Someday, someone will be able to view KM's entire formative stage and write the seminal work on the history of KM's startup and early progress.

But, more important at the moment, are the immediate questions that include: Where is KM now? What are present best practices? and finally, Where is KM going in the foreseeable future?

There is one more personal disclosure that strongly impacts my ability to have gained many insights. In the late 1990s, I was inspired to create a robust KM learning program for the emerging KM team members who were desperate for guidance. They were appointed as KM team leaders and told by their management to "Go buy me one!" Unfortunately, that was certainly not a prescription for KM success, though few knew why.

But, en masse, the 10,000 such KM team members who sought guidance and the certification designation: Certified Knowledge Manager (CKM), provided both the challenge and the feedback of the 'wisdom of the crowd,' so to speak. They provided the impetus to determine what was critically needed by KM practitioners and what worked, but only if one listened carefully.

Based on my personal KM experiences and continuous student evaluations, I have a perspective on where KM is now, lessons learned and present best practices, but the last question on the way forward is admittedly very speculative. Though outside the scope of this chapter, I can make a few educated guesses as extrapolations of present trends in a few narrow domains, especially maturity models. Since artificial intelligence (AI) is well covered by the other authors, certainly more expert at AI than I am, I will not discuss AI except for its impact, along with robots and drones on the episodic change that is already underway and as the ultimate driver of maturity models, such as the KM Institute's MATURE™.

Plato was right. Necessity is indeed the mother of invention. From my unique personal vantage point, the predicate for my present KM insights, conclusions and even possible biases emerged. Let me tell you the story that naturally leads to insights about lessons learned and best practices.

Consider some of the roots of necessity. In the early- to mid-1990s, I was a consultant at a U.S. Department of Defense (DoD) think tank focusing on Business Process Reengineering (BPR) and Financial Analysis. Though BPR had great potential, it was too complex to be executed in an ad hoc manner, which resulted in mediocre success compared to expectations. So, DoD commissioned a team of diverse management consultants, myself included, to uncover the reasons for mediocrity and to resolve them. Some obvious complications emerged immediately, which involved both methodology and competency.

Methodology: BPR was being implemented as if it was just another IT initiative. Think of the following: here's what we have now (As-Is) and here's what we would like to have (To-Be), but unfortunately without enough attention to the strategies to get there.

When that knowledge gap was studied more carefully, the methodology solutions were obvious to most of us. Some, like myself, were steeped in strategic planning. Others were change management experts. Fortunately, those were the two obvious missing ingredients. Both types of participating practitioners learned much from each other. I became a committed change management proponent. Others developed a better appreciation for strategic planning. A good outcome for all, especially those of us who later became involved in KM.

Competency: But, what about upskilling the practitioners, who were primarily IT experts? They were skilled in information technology – system design/architecture and coding, but not necessarily the complexities of strategic planning or change management. Hence, it was determined that we needed to flesh out these two disciplines and document them with sufficient detail so they were implementable. Which we did. It became a robust BPR methodology with the requisite strategic planning and change management embedded within its natural phases, when and where applicable.

At the end of this enrichment process, it was determined that the methodology should be published and distributed to all of DoD's BPR vendors. I was asked to publish the methodology as a representative of the non-commercial, more neutral think tank.

The initial publishing assumption was it should be a typical, hard-copy procedure manual. However, by the mid-1990s digitalization was catching on – phone books were becoming digital files, not thick binders. More on digital 'Yellow Pages' below.

So, I lobbied for an electronic procedure manual as an alternative – obvious today, but quite radical in 1994. The compelling argument was: "You can't depend on thousands of admin folks to remove/replace the many changes that would be necessary to continuously enrich the initial manual." Also, appreciate how many trees could be saved, which might have been the primary driver. And, if admin staff were converting to electronic phone books, then tech-savvy BPR folks should at least attain the present 'disruptive' technology As-Is.

Figures 12.1 and 12.2 show the original Knowledge Base Tool (KBase Tool), but with the later KM Methodology (1996) vs. the initial BPR methodology. Of course, 1995 graphics are not representative of today's look and feel (a picture is worth a thousand words). But, the functionality is essentially the same.

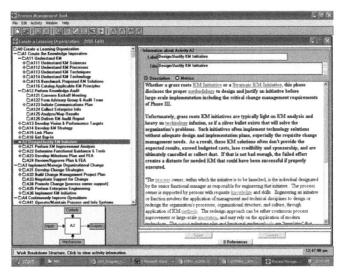

Figure 12.1 The original knowledge base tool: the WBS of DoD's KM methodology

Figure 12.1 depicts the original KBase Tool, with initial KM Methodology. This KBase design had three typical components that now seem universal, including an organizing scheme in the left-hand stub and a description in the right-hand window. For a process-oriented KBase, the categorization is typically a work breakdown structure (WBS) or roles. Each WBS activity has a corresponding description.

Obviously, the description is typically an insufficient level of knowledge for actual performance of a complex activity, so the 'References' button at the bottom of the right-hand window is typically invoked. It leads to the ultimate knowledge objects or nuggets seen in Figure 12.2.

Figure 12.2 The original knowledge base tool with resource screen: the 'books of knowledge'

Figure 12.2 depicts the critical third key feature, the actual Knowledge objects themselves, using what I thought to be a creative '*books of knowledge*' metaphor. Each book has a particular type of knowledge labeled with both a title and an icon. Icons have emerged to be the more powerful visual approach versus text labels. In 1995, I knew the emerging research, but using clip art icons didn't seem fully adequate, so text labels were added as well. The books were constant, but whether they had content varied. Grayscale books were empty.

Every variation of KBases that I have seen since 1995 (and there haven't been many, other than for call centers), have included these three critical components: an organizing scheme (e.g., WBS or roles); a description of the selected activity; and the ultimate knowledge nuggets/objects, but often such objects have links external to the KBase. Perhaps in the repository? But, they must be no more than just a click away!

In 1995, I had high hopes for such intensive, granular process knowledge, provided at the time of need, but my expectations were premature. Today, in our more complex environments, especially with high turnover, we must 'Rethink Learning.' In such environments, what used to be called performance support (the online help manual/KBase), are now repurposing the Process KBases as training tools. The concept (proficiency-based learning) posits that we don't need to teach an entire complex process just in case a practitioner needs some aspect of it at a future date. Rather, in a much shorter timeframe, teach them how to use the KBase Tool, which can be used as needed, just-in-time, so to speak. Training costs are reduced and time-to-competency can be accelerated. Note, the costs to develop a KBase were always a deterrent, but as processes get more complex and BPR is implemented, many organizations are mapping their processes to gain better understanding and to enable continuous improvement. If processes are already mapped, creating a KBase is the next, logical step. If the KBase is to supplant formal training, typical training development costs can be used to populate the KBase instead.

But, as mentioned above, consider this serendipitous epiphany vis-à-vis the phone books, made by someone – if we have invested much in digitizing phone books, how much more would it take to just open up a few more fields to store a profile, maybe a list of expertise categories? In 1995, such rudimentary *expert locators* were actually still called the *Yellow Pages*, which was destined to become one of about 15 *Strategic KM Initiatives*, but certainly not the initial, primary driver and enabler of KM.

When the BPR e-manual was completed, it satisfied the Knowledge-Age imperative to 'get the best knowledge to the right person at the right time,' which could easily be the KM mantra. But in 1995, KM was definitely and primarily about *repositories*, another emerging Strategic KM Initiative.[1]

By 1995, KM was poking itself just above the horizon, and presumably noticeable by any BPR consultant or strategic planner. That metaphor was the stimulus for our logo (Figure 12.3), which unfortunately is still a truism. I, myself, was engaged in converting the BPR methodology into a KM methodology for DoD practitioners as KM emerged.

In addition, while I definitely saw the power of repositories, I personally believed at that time that very granular, process-oriented KBases were the ultimate KM endgame. In retrospect, that insight was an overstatement, since

---

[1]   See T.H. Davenport, D.W. DeLong and M. Beers (1997), Building successful knowledge management projects. Working paper based on 31 projects in 23 companies, available at https://www.semanticscholar.org/paper/Building -Successful-Knowledge-Management-Projects-Davenport-Long/0d768994 d39d1aa5f3313ba689c0fc9520e96b16. The paper was later developed as T.H. Davenport and L. Prusak (1998), *Working Knowledge: How Organizations Manage What They Know*, Harvard Business Press.

many other strategic KM initiative types were emerging by 2000. And, it was also pre-mature as the KM emphasis was clearly on repositories, and remained that way, well into the future.

In the late 1990s, some additional *KM methodologies* started to emerge; e.g., Amrit Tiwana's *Knowledge Management Toolkit*, 2000.[2] I later dubbed it *KM (as a) System Approach* compared to KM as a Transformation.

Figure 12.3   KMI logo inspired by KM rising

Enter the Twenty-First Century: The Socio-Economic Trends of the Knowledge Age

In this section, I will focus on the first of the four categories or domains. With the above background as a precursor, let's summarize the KM status at about 2000, when many organizations started becoming very attuned to focusing on knowledge (humans) vs. just information (information technology/tools).

Socio-Economic Trends. Initially, and still today, most think of KM as an IT system – a repository, or the software to support CoPs or expert locators, etc. A few others were beginning to think something bigger, much bigger, was underway in the economy. Consider Peter Drucker's early quote: "Every few hundred years ... there occurs a sharp transformation ... a few short decades, society rearranges itself ... 50 years later ... a new world ... We are currently living through just such a transformation."[3]

---

2   Amrit Tiwana (2000), *Knowledge Management Toolkit: Practical Techniques for Building a Knowledge Management System*, Pearson.

3   Peter F. Drucker (1993), *Post-Capitalist Society*, Butterworth-Heinemann.

Consider this: If one said "Stone Age, Bronze Age, Iron Age, etc., what is their motive? No doubt, to emphasize the impact of metallurgical advancements on human history, from basic weapons and tools to structural steel for skyscrapers and bridges. But, in my considered opinion, there is a much more dramatic and relevant view of human history.

Human history has had four major episodic events with a dramatic impact on human occupations. For millennia, human history was all about muscle power – Hunter-Gatherers, Agrarian Age and Industrial Age. Most recently, it became all about computer power, hence the Information Age.

Now, an even more dramatic episodic event is happening, Knowledge is Power! Hence, the Knowledge Age.

These ages, especially recently, are examples of the effects of disruptive technologies that are changing our world. Robots, drones and AI have begun to replace humans, dramatically changing human occupations. In two to three generations, they will replace most all routine industrial and administrative-type work.

In the traditional industrial view, business is about people, process and technology. Admittedly, the people component was often shortchanged. In the Knowledge Age (Society/Economy/Era), KM is more about people than ever before. Correction – it's about our brains, which determine both aptitudes and attitudes. Aptitudes (skills and competencies) are well understood and readily impacted as needed. Attitudes are potentially more impactful, but much less understood, especially with regard to positive impacts. In my opinion, employee engagement (focus on attitude as well as aptitude) will be a key driver and differentiator in the Knowledge Age.

KM Methodology and Critical KM Team Implementation Competencies

A number of KM methodologies have emerged since the early DoD version in 1995–96. Some are published in books; some are proprietary, typically in-house at consultancies. Most are traditional, IT-oriented methodologies that can satisfy the imperative to "Go buy me one!" The strengths of most are that they are built on a long track record of successful IT implementations, especially if infused with some modern, more agile techniques. Some are even well-documented. Think a complete book of content, rather than a mere info-graph.

Unfortunately, some KM systems such as repositories require more than just key-stroke mastery, but a change in attitudes, as well, which are not typical needs of IT system implementations or upgrades. Hence, traditional change management often falls short of expectations and many repositories have had less than stellar KM performance results, as measured by employee satisfaction – can you find the information and knowledge that you need at about the time you need it?

The methodology weaknesses are primarily based on both change management orientation and lack of rigor – most are mere frameworks or roadmaps rather than the robust methodologies I envisioned being enabled by KBase Tools. There are fundamentally two change management orientations: Transformational or Transactional.

Traditional change management is transaction-oriented. Primarily, traditional change management focuses on a Communication Plan – inform every applicable person that a new system is coming, and a Training Plan – make sure each affected person is prepared before the system is delivered, not after.

The actual differences are too numerous for this chapter to serve as a primer, but suffice to say – fundamental or transformational organizational change is much more comprehensive, more complex to implement than an upgrade or the swapping out of a system. Transformation requires a much more robust and demanding Awareness Campaign, typically with a clear and compelling *Call-to-Action*; certainly top executive involvement; specific, dedicated efforts to gain buy in; and even quick wins to prove the efficacy of the new culture and associated initiatives.

So, how do we fine tune a comprehensive KM methodology to focus on the most critical needs of "students" (typically, working professionals) as they return to work to start or re-start the KM implementation? Since we have an army of such folks, let's leverage the CKM student involvement and feedback to uncover the most critical KM Strategies and competencies for which the diverse graduates need mastery to be successful, listed in Table 12.1.

Briefly, here's the back story. In the initial CKM days (2001–10), much of the CKM content was lecture – for students to gain KM awareness and understanding in order to hopefully initiate programs within their own organizations. As KM became more comprehensive and complex, including desirable transformational changes versus merely traditional change management, learn-by-doing workshops became a more relevant and effective learning modality. We winnowed the 40–50 in-class discussions and brief exercises into about ten major KM Strategy deliverables. We called the new approach the KM PRACTICUM™ to make visible this learning design shift from gaining understanding of KM to actually acquiring and practicing the ability to perform KM.

So what did we learn regarding critical KM competencies? The research methodology was far short of clinical trials. But, it seemed quite effective if we rightfully assume the students were the multitudes of the motivated boots on the ground needed to get a diverse pulse of operational KM. The learning objectives were less aligned with testing by traditional multiple choice questions than by a student's own estimate of their personal mastery of the activities they themselves thought to be critical. In brief, during 2019 and into 2020, we asked a series of graduating students what they thought about the criticality of the workshop activities just performed, and also their personal mastery – their actual abilities to deliver KM, starting the next week after the workshop.

Here are the criteria concerning the criticality of the various KM PRACTICUM™ exercises:

1. Not sure
2. Not needed
3. Possibly needed
4. Definitely needed
5. Critically important

In Likert Scale-fashion, we deemed the KM PRACTICUM™ exercises with result numbers 4 and 5 as very desirable practitioner learning objectives – either definitely needed or critically important. As a cross-check, we polled our very experienced instructors as well. In general, there was a high correlation between student and instructor rankings, with these following KM PRACTICUM™ surfacing as critical learning objectives for the KM certification program and presumably for KM implementation success.

Our own course learning objectives became two-fold. They were for students to concur on the most critical activities, whatever they might be (but certainly influenced by the instructor's emphasis and the expanded workbook content), and by graduation to be able to perform those same activities, as practitioners – reasonably confident they would be able to perform that activity, rather than just aware of and understanding it, or mastery – fully confident they would be able to successfully perform that activity. In summary, if students rated a specific KM PRACTICUM™ as critical, then we hoped they gained personal mastery as well and we provided much resource material for post-class study if necessary.

Table 12.1   Critical competencies essential for KM implementation

Typical issues that concern attendees and the criticality of competencies needed	Students	Instructor	KM PRACTICUM™ (gain mastery) and *Learn-by-Doing KM strategies*
1. Be able to motivate and create a sense of urgency in my organization to transform in face of competitive pressures, disruptive technologies and many other emerging strategic issues that KM can impact	90%	100%	KM PRACTICUM™ #1 Call-to-Action *Understand the situation – episodic change in human occupations. Create understanding in others – clear, compelling vision, overcome complacency*
2. Be able to clearly define KM for diverse audiences in my organization (aka elevator speeches and KM101-type presentations)	87%	80%	KM PRACTICUM™ #2 Define KM *Diverse audiences. Executives, K Workers, especially buy-in from KWer specialists*
3. KM Metrics: Be able to promote confidence and trust in KM, based on attaining proven, evidence-based results (precursor to 'Quick Wins' imperative)	84%	80%	KM PRACTICUM™ #3 Measure KM success *KM metrics*
4. Be able to create and gain confidence in a KM Roadmap (have a robust KM methodology customized to your organization)	85%	60%	KM PRACTICUM™ #4 Own a KM Methodology *Understand a transformational change methodology*
5. Be able to get leadership buy-in to KM as a strategic imperative	93% 95% TBD	100% 100% 60%	KM PRACTICUM™ #5 KM Awareness Campaign KM PRACTICUM™ #6 Quick Wins KM PRACTICUM™ #7 Transformational Change
6. Be able to get leadership to invest in relevant KM Initiatives? Be able to lead discussions among senior operating execs (potential sponsors), that align their operating characteristics with proven strategic KM initiatives	89% 79%	80% 60%	KM PRACTICUM™ #8a KM Solutions Matrix™ KM PRACTICUM™ #8b Knowledge Transfer Process

Table 12.1   Critical competencies essential for KM implementation **(continued)**

Typical issues that concern attendees and the criticality of competencies needed	Students	Instructor	KM PRACTICUM™ (gain mastery) and *Learn-by-Doing KM strategies*
7. Understand internal governance and KM requirements, and be able to create an accepted KM Team Charter	TBD	80%	KM PRACTICUM™ #8c Governance/KM Team Charter
8. Understand and be able to overcome the proven barriers to KM success	95%	100%	KM PRACTICUM™ #9 Overcome Barriers to Success
9. Understand, and be able to get KM started, or re-started if it has been lagging, or to make substantive improvements based on what has been learned	85%	80%	KM PRACTICUM™ #10 Way Forward *Create your own plan*

Note: (1) The KM PRACTICUM™ are arranged by the sequential order of in-class coverage, not highest criticality; e.g., some exercises are natural pre-requisites to others or require more advanced understanding that comes later in the course. (2) Some students had no pre-class knowledge of KM, but learned quickly. Others had little post-class responsibility for KM implementation, which was the biggest impact on scores below 100%. In other words, if the results were screened for actual post-class responsibility, they would have differed – probably even higher percentages would have resulted, but this methodology did seem to screen out issues of lesser concern by practitioners.

Strategic KM Initiative Types

If the students were mostly or fully able to do the PRACTICUM KM™ implementation activities, then the question was, which strategic KM initiative types were essential in their own organization and were therefore potential investment opportunities? In the early days, KM was often a tool looking for a place to implement it, a hammer thinking everything was a nail. That may have been a suitable strategy for a repository, because almost everyone thought they needed one, but there was only a shortlist of other strategic KM tools, e.g., CoPs, Expert Locators, known to most practitioners.

So, we changed the customary implementation process, especially early startup. We created an alternative startup tool – a KM Solutions Matrix™, rather than the traditional Knowledge Audit (see below for KM Solutions Matrix discussion and Figure 12.4).

A thorough knowledge audit was a relatively expensive activity and could have a negative influence on moving forward in a poorly funded KM startup. Our limited in-class research of those who had actually done a knowledge audit indicated average costs of about USD250,000, and a three- to six-month timeframe. Besides, an audit is primarily just an assessment or diagnostic, not a prescription, and such an assessment was not trivial, typically well beyond anyone without some formal training and experience doing them. In addition, a diagnostic without a prescription possibly falls short of usual expectations.

What we envisioned was a tool that could get the top management of each functional area within any organization to talk about their own unique, perceived needs. To enable that, we created a list of major strategic issues. The issues were expressed in terms of operational characteristics and associated business goals that all leadership would understand, especially the specific functional leaders to which any specific issue would apply (Table 12.2).

What the leadership does not know at the outset is that each described organizational characteristic is a proxy for a proven strategic KM initiative type, such as a repository, CoPs, Expert Locator and many others, now numbering about 15 distinct KM initiative types.

If an operational characteristic/business goal is applicable, then a discussion can follow which is based on the KM team having a proven, well-documented solution/strategy/application quite relevant to that specific functional area within an organization. It is intuitive that organizational leaders who know what issues their functional areas face would be motivated by such information.

Below is a sample output of a recent class. Attendees studied all the column one characteristics and scored their response according to five categories per below. We tallied the percentages of both applicable levels 4 and 5, which are shown in the last column.

1. Not applicable to us at all
2. Unlikely applicable to us
3. Possibly some applicability
4. Definitely some applicability
5. Directly/very applicable to us

Table 12.2 shows typical operating characteristics and applicable strategic initiatives, along with recent class results (% of students who indicated their organization had that specific characteristic).

Table 12.2   Strategic KM initiatives for traditional operational
characteristics/business goals

Traditional operational characteristics/ business goals	Strategic KM initiatives (solutions)	Results
1. *Complex projects* with enough simi- larities that you could learn from one project to the next. Improve strategic project outcomes (less time/cost, better project results, etc.). Avoid repeating past project management mistakes. Improve the project body of knowledge	Lessons Learned Management. Process/ Methodology (LLMP). Learn before, during and after each project	75%
2. *Multiple, essentially identical operations* (assembly plants, marketing, admin., retailing, product dev., etc.), where you need to transfer best practices from one location to another. Reduce dramatic performance differentials between operating units by replicating best prac- tices. Reduce duplication of effort	Best Practices Management. Process/ Methodology (BPMP). Transfer best practices, where the best is often twice as good as the worst	67%
3. *Innovation*. Competitive pressures, disruptive technologies and many other issues that might threaten performance, health and long-term sustainability. Meet growing competitive pressures. Continuously improve operations, prod- ucts and services. Create new products/ services	Create Useful New Knowledge to continuously improve performance	92%
4. Much ongoing *training* needed to upskill the workforce, especially in complex or rapidly changing environments, or if experiencing high turnover (continuous learning)	Rethink Learning. Transition from 'just-in-case' training to 'just-in-time,' performance support, and proficiency-based learning	100%
5. Improve *onboarding* to meet the chal- lenges of organizational expansion and/ or high employee turnover	Personal Knowledge Mgmt. (PKM)™, especially onboarding	83%
6. *Expert Locator*. Need quick access to *expertise* to help solve specific complex issues, and/or need for experts for project staffing. Need more knowledge-sharing for better and faster decision making. Need to locate experts faster for improved win ratio. Often can't staff key positions, due to gap between proposal and award	Expert/Expertise Locator and/or Communities of Practice (CoPs). Possibly use Social Network Analysis (SNA)	83%

Traditional operational characteristics/ business goals	Strategic KM initiatives (solutions)	Results
7. *Knowledge Flight*. Retain expert knowledge being lost due to *retirement*. Retain expert knowledge being lost due to turnover, role changes or downsizing	Knowledge Capture, Transfer & Retention. Continuity	83%
8. *Customer Satisfaction*. Essential to growth, sustainability. Improve evidence-based customer satisfaction, and analytics. Leverage Net Promoter Score (NPS)	Customer Satisfaction & Analytics. Implement NPS process	83%
9. *Organizational Performance*. Need to monitor, measure, share operational insights. Better understand performance for decision making and improvement. Need dashboard (or data capture/presentation tools). Possibly, ISO compliance.	KM Metrics, Performance Evaluation for Effectiveness. Predictive analytics for improved operational understanding and customer and competitor environment	75%
10. *Content/Document/Records Management*. Eliminate knowledge silos. Promote knowledge sharing. Improve 'findability' and 'discoverability'	Repositories. Taxonomy Search Engine Optimization (SEO) , etc.	83%
11. *Employee Engagement*. Increase and sustain employee well-being, motivation, personal development (engagement)	Personal Knowledge Management (PKM)™	75%

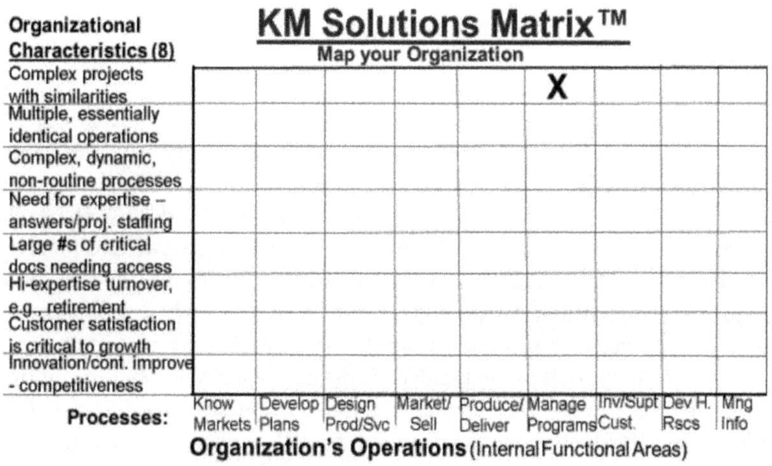

Figure 12.4   KM Solutions Matrix™

Figure 12.4 is a graphic of the KM Solution Matrix™. The bottom row represents all the attending executives in a typical organization. Each would recognize which column they own. Once the left-hand stub was explained, each would simply check the cell (X) or cells that are the intersection of their Functional Area/Operation (column) with an applicable organizational characteristic (row). As an example, the Vice President of Program Management should recognize the Organizational Characteristics of Row #1.

But only if, in this organization, program management is about complex projects with enough similarities that each project can learn from others (see Organizational Characteristics #1 – Complex Projects in Table 12.2).

If the VP of Production had multiple assembly plants, he/she might check Row #2, and so on.

Consider, if the CEO scheduled this workshop, and you as a VP placed an X in one or more cells, don't you think it would behoove you to schedule a meeting with the KM Team to discuss what strategic KM Initiative they have that has been well-documented to improve operations just like yours?

Maturity Models

Robust KM methodologies and Artificial Intelligence (AI) will enable us to move from traditional maturity models to informative, evidence-based predictive models. Such models are not just typical assessment tools (diagnostics), but will likely be powerful, prescriptive tools as well.

Here's a quick background primer: Maturity models were popularized in the late 1990s by the Software Engineering Institute's Capability Maturity Model (CMM)˙. Because of the CMM˙, there was a burst of efforts in 1999 to develop a similar Maturity Model for KM (e.g., KM Maturity Model (KMMM)˙ by Siemens AG, KM Landscape by Microsoft, and my own Knowledge Maturity Model (KMM)™. Quite frankly, most of the early maturity models were weak examples of what might be possible if the basis for each assessment was evidence-based versus just ad hoc, if models are enriched by proven prescriptions, and, if the models are expanded from merely a KM thread to multiple threads that include all factors that are truly essential to success. In other words, should KM be the only focus of our maturity analysis and attention, or should our attention be on the performance, health and sustainability (maturity) of the entire organization, enabled by KM, analytics, AI, and anything else that has potential to accelerate attainment of such objectives?

The answer is more than obvious, and hence maturity model development is a KM imperative in the Knowledge Age, but a much more sophisticated approach is needed.

So, by 2010, I believed we needed a tool that wasn't just an assessment (diagnostic), but could be enriched by the KM methodology to provide the requisite prescriptions as well, eventually supported by AI. It is appropriately called MATURE™, the acronym based on the six progressive levels shown in Figure 12.5.

Figure 12.5   The KM maturity model, MATURE™

It may not be obvious from the spiral, maturity roadmap, but here is how it functions. There are a number of simultaneous actionable threads being evaluated. For each thread at each level, one or more questions are asked to determine key maturity factors at that level for that specific thread. The answers are on a five-point Likert scale. Typically, 4–5 indicates maturity for that level. Scores below 4 indicate a less than mature situation, prescriptions warranted, but always evaluated with traditional return-on-investment (ROI) criteria.

The multiple threads are determined by deciding on the most critical strategic concerns of the organization under study. Barring such specific knowledge, the most important concerns for all organizations are in the generic model, which includes: human capital, customer satisfaction, innovation, analytics, KM and transformational change management.

Conclusions

Where KM is going will, of course, be based somewhat on where it's been (its roots), and what technology disruptions are going to shape its ultimate future, e.g., robots, drones and artificial intelligence. This chapter has addressed some of the key advances that have taken place over the last 25 years, which include:

1. *Socio-economic trends.* Many now think KM is more than just a set of IT tools, especially just a repository, but rather that KM is the discipline that will enable outstanding performance (a learning organization) in the Knowledge Age. If true, we need more than traditional change management in favor of transformational change.
2. *KM methodology and critical KM team implementation competencies.* Early on, KM practitioners were often in over their heads – asked to do many complex activities for which most were ill-prepared. Now we know a set of implementation competencies that can substantially increase the likelihood of implementation success.
3. *Strategic KM initiative types.* Also, early on, KM was focused on just a few strategic initiatives, mostly repositories and a few ad hoc knowledge sharing techniques (Expert Locators, CoPs). Now we have uncovered and documented 15 proven strategic KM initiatives. These include, as examples:
   i.   Generic knowledge sharing, but also how to transfer expert knowledge from retirees.
   ii.   Ad hoc CoPs, but proven (evidence-based) techniques to increase the likelihood of success.
   iii. Not only KM101s to introduce KM to employees (awareness), but techniques to make knowledge managers (PKMers) into high-performing, engaged personal knowledge workers in the Knowledge Age.
   iv.   Traditional training, but a rethinking of learning including new virtual/hybrid modes and even the implementation of some earlier, detailed/granular knowledge bases and micro-learning to overcome process complexity and high turnover.

4. *Maturity models*. There will emerge disruptive technologies, such as maturity models, that will substantially improve our organizational performance evaluation abilities, resulting in AI-inspired prescriptions for continuous improvement. Whether sustaining or disruptive, continuous innovation will be a characteristic of a Learning Organization, and a predictor of Knowledge Age excellence and sustainability.

In conclusion, this is my considered opinion. KM is definitely not just another system or tool. It is a evidence-based transformational discipline that focuses on human optimization in the Knowledge Age to create learning organizations that substantially and reliably improve organizational performance, health and sustainability.

Index